NINETEENTH-CENTURY
PIANO MUSIC

NINETEENTH-CENTURY PIANO MUSIC

NINETEENTH-CENTURY PIANO MUSIC

A Handbook for Pianists

by

KATHLEEN DALE

With a Preface by
DAME MYRA HESS

GEOFFREY CUMBERLEGE
OXFORD UNIVERSITY PRESS
LONDON NEW YORK TORONTO
1954

Oxford University Press, Amen House, London E.C.4

GLASGOW NEW YORK TORONTO MELBOURNE WELLINGTON
BOMBAY CALCUTTA MADRAS KARACHI CAPE TOWN IBADAN

Geoffrey Cumberlege, Publisher to the University

Printed in Great Britain by
Latimer, Trend & Co. Ltd. Plymouth

PREFACE

One of the questions that beset the enthusiastic amateur pianist, student, or potential concert performer is the choice of repertoire. He may not possess an extensive library of his own, and public libraries are not always within reach; how great a help it is, therefore, to have a bird's-eye view of the whole of a particular period.

Kathleen Dale has supplied just this in her book on Nineteenth-Century Piano Music. Not only does she provide a fully comprehensive survey of a most important field of piano literature, embracing as it does the principal classical and romantic masterpieces, but she gives a very clear picture of the structure and forms used in them.

The importance of structure in music is too often overlooked: the pianist is apt to wallow in the sheer sensuous beauty of the sound of his instrument. This may be fascinating for the player and please the listener momentarily, but it can never give a just or true interpretation of the music.

In addition to the acknowledged masterpieces, Kathleen Dale examines many lesser works, which adds greatly to the interest and usefulness of her book. Nor has she omitted the sadly neglected category of piano duets. Too few people realize that composers such as Schubert produced some of their very finest works for this medium, which can be enormously enjoyed by any pair of enterprising enthusiasts.

Apart from the pleasure this book will give to readers, it will surely prove a most useful guide to anyone wanting to enlarge their musical experience. In warmly recommending it, may I wish its readers many hours of happy discovery?

MYRA HESS

December 1953

CONTENTS

CONTENTS

PROLOGUE

The Scope of the Book

THIS book is designed primarily for pianists who make music for their own delight. It is not intended as a contribution to musicology or as a manual for students preparing for examinations in musical form and history, but simply as a companion to the intensive study of the best-known and most representative piano music of the nineteenth century.

For this reason it deals very largely, though not quite exclusively, with standard works; that is to say, with such generally accepted compositions as may already form the basis of the pianist's own library or may easily be purchased, or borrowed from public libraries. As most of the musical material referred to should thus be readily accessible, music-type illustrations are used only sparingly.

The most important of the works surveyed are presented in historical perspective, with some account of the origins and ancestry of the classes to which they belong, and with such brief discussion of the form, the content, and the musical and pianistic styles of the individual compositions as it is hoped may enhance the player's own interest and enjoyment in performing them. None of the works are submitted to minute analysis, but a small number are described in detail wherever treatment of this kind may possibly help the reader to gain a clearer understanding, either of the general principles of musical construction, or of the technical devices used in composition.

The piano music written during the nineteenth century is as enormous in quantity as it is varied in style. The momentous changes in artistic ideals which occurred during the course of the century resulted in the emergence of new types of composition, while many of the well-established types continued to be cultivated with unabated zeal. At times, classical and romantic music flourished side by side.

In view of the heterogeneity of the works composed through-out this long period it has been found more practical to survey them in conformity with their nature rather than according to the date-order in which they were composed. They are arranged into categories determined either by their structure: sonatas, variations, rondos, fantasies, contrapuntal forms and textures; their type: studies, miniatures, dances, transcriptions, piano duets; or their style: abstract, impressionistic, or descriptive. Nevertheless, chronological order has been maintained as far as possible within each category.

Some of the larger categories have had to be sub-divided. For instance, the sonata occupies four chapters: the first sketching its history and structural principles and its treatment by Beeth-oven as a musical form; the second considering the Beethoven sonatas from the aspects of style and expression; the third examining the sonatas of Beethoven's younger contemporaries, Weber and Schubert, and the fourth surveying the post-classical sonata from Mendelssohn to Grieg. The chapter on variations is divided between intellectual, romantic, and virtuosic types; that on studies, between *études* or concert-studies, technical studies, and pieces for beginners.

The plan of sorting the musical material into well-defined classes has been adopted with the intention of preserving some kind of order in the treatment of so many different varieties of composition. The chapters are to a large extent self-contained. They can be studied as separate units by readers desiring in-formation on specific subjects. At the same time, opportunities have been taken of drawing attention to the connexions that exist between the several categories, as well as to the relation-ship of piano compositions by individual composers to their works of other kinds: orchestral, chamber, vocal, etc.

Sometimes it has been difficult to decide which of two or three chapters would be the more appropriate place for the discussion of compositions which either fall between two periods or which are equally representative of two or more categories. To determine, for instance, whether John Field's sonatas should be treated as classical (in date) or as post-classical (in style) or whether they should be examined side by side with his more important nocturnes; whether Grieg's Ballade should be considered as a set of variations or as a piece of romantic music; whether Chopin's Polonaise-Fantasy should be included among fantasies or among music in dance forms; or whether Schumann's *Carnaval* should be appraised as programme music, dance music or as a set of miniatures. In equivocal cases such as these, cross-references have been made wherever possible between the chapters in which the works are respectively mentioned.

These various methods of treating the subject-matter have been devised with the aim of deepening the interest of pianists in the music they play, and of helping them to acquire closer acquaintance with its artistic essentials so that they may derive increasing satisfaction from interpreting it.

* * * *

Acknowledgements are due to Hinrichsen Edition Ltd., the proprietors of Peters Edition, for permission to quote from Edvard Grieg's *Slåtter*, op. 72, and from Johan Halvorsen's arrangement of a *slåt* for violin solo.

I

The Piano before Beethoven

Origin of the piano; early piano music; definition of the terms Classical and Romantic as applied to music, poetry

THE nineteenth century was the golden age of pianoforte music. It witnessed the final displacement of the harpsichord and the establishment of the piano, at first as the favourite, and then as the only recognized keyboard instrument for concert and domestic purposes. It saw the production of a vast quantity of music, the finest of which has become indispensable to every grade of performer, professional and amateur. During the nineteenth century some of the greatest composers of all time enriched the literature of the piano with enduring masterpieces. Other composers, now equally well known, though lesser in stature, also endowed the instrument with works which are loved and enjoyed, wherever it is played. Beethoven, Schubert, Weber, Mendelssohn, Liszt, Chopin, Schumann, César Franck, Brahms, Tchaikovsky, Dvořák, and Grieg are the names that immediately spring to mind when nineteenth-century piano music is under discussion. These are the composers whose works occupy the principal position in the present survey, although many others are considered throughout its pages. As for the works themselves, their number is legion and their diversity bewildering. Sonatas, ballades, fugues, nocturnes, rondos, études, variations, polonaises, and lyric pieces are only a few of the many types of composition which flourished during the hundred years in question.

When the year 1800 dawned, the piano was by no means a new, a rare or a seldom-played instrument. Indeed, it had

— 1 —

The Piano before Beethoven

Origin of the piano; early piano music; definition of the terms
Classical and Romantic as applied to music.

THE nineteenth century was the golden age of piano music. It
witnessed the final displacement of the harpsichord and the
establishment of the piano, at first as the favourite, and then as
the only recognized keyboard instrument for concert and domestic purposes. It saw the production of a vast quantity of
music, the finest of which has become indispensable to every
grade of performer, professional and amateur. During the nineteenth century some of the greatest composers of all time enriched the literature of the piano with enduring masterpieces.
Other composers, now equally well known though lesser in
stature, also endowed the instrument with works which are
loved and enjoyed, wherever it is played. Beethoven, Schubert,
Weber, Mendelssohn, Liszt, Chopin, Schumann, César Franck,
Brahms, Tchaikovsky, Dvořák, and Grieg are the names that
immediately spring to mind when nineteenth-century piano
music is under discussion. These are the composers whose works
occupy the principal position in the present survey, although
many others are considered throughout its pages. As for the
works themselves, their number is legion and their diversity
bewildering. Sonatas, ballades, fugues, nocturnes, rondos, *études*,
variations, polonaises, and lyric pieces are only a few of the
many types of composition which flourished during the hundred
years in question.

When the year 1800 dawned, the piano was by no means a
new, a rare or a seldom-played instrument. Indeed, it had

been in use during the latter half of the previous century; it had been growing in the public favour and had already inspired a not inconsiderable number of compositions. At last it had gained almost total supremacy over the long-established harpsichord, which from thenceforth disappeared rapidly from the scene.

Let us consider for a moment the fundamental difference between the piano and the harpsichord so that we may see how it was that the former came to supersede the latter.

In the early days of keyboard instruments, dissatisfaction with the limitations in their powers of expression, as compared with those of stringed instruments, was increasingly felt by musicians. The player's touch on the keys of the harpsichord, whether it was heavy or light, made no appreciable difference to the amount or the quality of the sound produced. Neither had it any control over accentuation or gradation of tone, nor any power to give prominence to a single melodic strand in the musical texture. Contrast and variety in tone-colour could be secured only by the use of different manuals, pedals or stops. The keys of the much smaller clavichord were to some extent responsive to the player's fingers, but the subdued tone of the instrument itself was ineffective in comparison with the greater resonance and brilliance of the harpsichord. Moreover, on neither of these instruments was it possible to produce the exquisitely expressive crescendo and diminuendo which are the natural prerogative of the human voice and of stringed and wind instruments.

Experiments with a mechanical device to impart to the harpsichord a quality approximating to the sustained sounds of bowed instruments were undertaken towards 1600. It was not until a century later that this vital problem of the rise and fall in tone was solved in quite another manner by the Italian harpsichord-maker, Bartolommeo Cristofori, who invented the first historically authenticated piano: the 'Gravicembalo col piano e forte' at Florence in 1709. By devising the simple but ingenious expedient of using hammers to strike the strings instead of metal jacks or quills to pluck them, Cristofori took the first step towards undermining the harpsichord's pre-eminence among keyboard instruments. Incidentally, he provided a stimulus to the creation of an entirely new style of writing for the keyboard. He improved upon his invention in 1720 and perfected it in 1726, but his work seems to have found little favour in his own country. It did, however, apparently inspire one Ludovico di Giustini to the composition of a set of *Twelve Sonatas for the Cimbalo di piano e forte*, which was published at Florence in 1732. As the Sonatas, which are in the form of suites in several short movements, bear written indications of grading in dynamics, this isolated volume is considered to comprise the first printed music written specifically for the piano.

Cristofori died in 1731, and thereafter the making of pianos languished in Italy. Fortunately he was not the only pioneer in this particular field; others had simultaneously been at work in France, Germany, and England, in which countries progress was maintained in the production of different types of the same instrument. During the 1730s the first German pianos made by Gottfried Silbermann were submitted to J. S. Bach. He accorded them some small measure of approval but retained his lifelong preference for the clavichord. His sons, Wilhelm Friedemann, Carl Philipp Emanuel, and Johann Christian greeted the new instrument with enthusiasm, especially the last-named, who settled in England and who was the first to perform publicly upon the piano as a solo instrument in London in 1768. Mozart, too, warmly welcomed the piano and made it increasingly known to the musical public on the continent by the brilliant performances he gave upon it of his own concertos.

Strangely enough, it was an Italian, Muzio Clementi, who was destined to make the first really important contribution to the literature of the solo piano with a set of three Sonatas, op. 2, published in London in 1773. The Roman-born Clementi, who was Mozart's senior by four years and who was a prolific composer as well as a magnificent performer, had been brought to England as a boy of fourteen in 1766 to study music. It was almost certainly the growing vogue for the piano in this country which determined him when he reached manhood to make his headquarters in London rather than in his native Italy, where the piano had aroused so little general interest. He wrote the sonatas just mentioned, which he designated 'for the piano or harpsichord', during 1770, the very year which saw the birth of the greatest of all composers who have ever written for the piano, Ludwig van Beethoven.

One year later, Haydn, then in his fortieth year, wrote his first sonata 'for the pianoforte or harpsichord', the well-known and expressive Sonata in C minor, which was also the first of his keyboard compositions to bear dynamic indications and his first sonata in the minor mode. This sonata, which was his twentieth for the keyboard, remained for several years unpublished, and in the meantime, Haydn had reverted to composing for the harpsichord. It was not until later that he wrote more consistently for the piano and with increasing understanding of its possibilities. The last and greatest of his works in this medium —the essentially pianistic Sonata in E flat major, printed as No. 1 in most performing editions—was composed in 1798.

Even Beethoven wrote his earliest keyboard works, including the first eight of his sonatas, 'for the harpsichord or pianoforte'. Only in 1795 did he produce his First Concerto and in 1799 the two Sonatas of op. 14 definitely for the piano.

As Clementi continued to compose until within a few years of his death in 1832, some of his works may justifiably be considered as nineteenth-century music. His large and interesting output of sonatas, many of which are still easily available, is not cultivated by pianists to-day. His reputation as a composer of serious music has been obscured both by his greater fame as a performer and as a writer of studies and by the overwhelming genius of Beethoven.

Almost the same fate has overtaken the compositions of his younger contemporary, J. L. Dussek, and for almost the same reasons. Like Clementi, Dussek has for so long been thought of as a writer of 'educational' sonatinas that his pianistically fascinating large-scale compositions which were written between 1782 and 1810 have fallen into oblivion as far as public performance is concerned. They are now almost exclusively the preserve of the historian. Beethoven's works consequently form the natural and inevitable starting-point of this survey. But although our study is scheduled to begin at the year 1800 we shall often need to look back to preceding periods to trace origins or to make comparisons with earlier music. In so doing, we may hope to gain a clearer understanding and a greater appreciation of the works which were written during the period to be reviewed.

*　　*　　*　　*

Beethoven is commonly spoken of as a 'classical' composer, yet when it comes to a more exact definition of the term, he cannot be described as being exclusively 'classical' in his musical outlook. He cannot be placed in the same category as the most typical classical composers, Haydn and Mozart, the main body of whose production also falls within the same so-called Classical period. Beethoven's classicism was strongly permeated by romantic elements. In his works we may watch the development of the tendency which was later to exert a powerful influence upon the whole musical output of the nineteenth century.

The Romantic period begins officially in 1830, but many compositions written earlier in the century are almost as romantic in conception as any dating from the height of the period, while others written much later retain all the distinctive attributes of classicism. Before we can arrive at any satisfactory appreciation of the diverse styles of nineteenth-century piano music we must attempt to disentangle and define the classical and romantic elements which are blended in widely varying degrees in the compositions of our prescribed period. They are, indeed, to some extent, in those of almost every age, earlier or later.

*　　*　　*　　*

'Classicism' in music is the outcome of the composer's objective attitude of mind towards his art; of his intention to lay emphasis on perfection of form rather than on intimacy of expression, and of his paramount feeling for symmetry and balance. During the Classical period some of the best-known and still most frequently used musical forms, those of the sym-

B

phony, the sonata, and the solo concerto, became stabilized. The types then perfected have ever since constituted the standards by which subsequent works in their respective categories are criticized, however far their composers may have deviated from them. The conception of fugue was brought to its highest point of development much earlier, by J. S. Bach during the late Baroque period (1675-1750). It bears the stamp of classicism by reason of its objective, intellectual character.

Romanticism is a comprehensive term which resists exact definition, even when it is confined to one single branch of the creative arts. It is exemplified in music by the insistence laid upon the expression of personal feelings and emotions or upon abstract ideas which have universal significance. It is also characterized by impatience with the restraints imposed by conventional forms, by the introduction of the picturesque and the exotic, and by the attempt to translate other arts into music or to combine the phenomena of other arts with music itself. In a few words: romantic music relies to a large extent upon assistance from philosophic concepts, literary or pictorial sources. Classical music makes its effect by musical means alone.

In this survey we shall often find compositions which display an equal admixture of classical and romantic elements. For instance, when studying sonatas we shall see that Beethoven transformed a classical structure into a framework for romantic descriptive music in his 'Lebewohl' Sonata (Les Adieux), a composition in which he avowedly set out to portray the emotions inspired by parting, absence, and reunion. Later, when examining contrapuntal forms and textures, we shall note that Grieg composed a romantically expressive *Lyric Piece* (Op. 38, no. 8) in strict canon at the octave throughout both its contrasting sections.

2

The Sonata

(1)

The classical sonata; history up to Beethoven; definition of the types of form of individual movements; Beethoven's sonatas as whole works discussed from the aspects of architecture and design.

THE sonata is the most comprehensive in structure and the most varied in type of all large-scale music written for the keyboard. Its origins date far back in musical history, but it is an ever-expanding, ever-changing organism, susceptible of infinite modification. It has fascinated composers during the span of well over two centuries and still shows little sign of losing its hold upon creative musical minds. Throughout its long history it has borrowed features from almost every other type of musical form and texture, retaining or rejecting them in accordance with its own capacity for assimilation. In design it has varied from comprising a series of short movements akin to those of the suite to being composed in one long unbroken movement resembling a fantasy. In tonality it has expanded from one key to two or more nearly related or strikingly contrasted keys. During its evolution it has incorporated the rondo, the air with variations, the canon, the fugue and several types of dance within its ample scope. Its most characteristic movement, which owes its formal outline to the *da capo* aria, is based upon the same structural principles as that of symphonies and of large-scale chamber works (quintets, quartets, trios, etc.). With these great cyclic art-forms the piano sonata as a whole is thus closely allied.

During certain phases of its history the sonata has been

regarded by composers as the most important part of their production for the keyboard. Not until the end of the Classical period did they begin to neglect it in favour of less exacting kinds of piano composition and to submit it to transformation so fundamental as to make it almost unrecognizable when compared with examples of its rudimentary state. Yet despite the strange vicissitudes it experienced throughout the nineteenth century, especially during the Romantic period (1830-1900), the piano sonata has emerged triumphant into the twentieth century to be cultivated by composers mutually so different in outlook as Scriabin, Bartók, Hindemith, Prokofiev, Bax, and Tippett.

The piano sonata as we know it to-day is generally considered to date from the time of Carl Philipp Emanuel Bach (1714-88). He was by no means the first composer of keyboard sonatas, but it was he who systematized the work of his predecessors in this sphere and who determined the constitution of the sonata for many years to come. His own most typical variety of sonata is in three separate movements. One or more of these is in first-movement or sonata form; the form that he himself was largely responsible for establishing on a firm basis and for transmitting to his successors for expansion undreamed of in the earlier eighteenth century. Other types of movement that he often included in his sonatas were the rondo and the 'tempo di minuetto', both of which, like first-movement form, were also to undergo remarkable developments in structure and style before many years had elapsed.

Between 1740 and 1786 Emanuel Bach wrote about 150 sonatas, of which unprecedented number only the merest fraction is known to practising pianists. These compositions, which are alternately severely intellectual and over-florid in style, are well suited for performance on the harpsichord and the clavichord. They do not lend themselves so readily to effective interpretation on the piano, nor do they appeal to the modern player as strongly as they do to the historian. Yet pianists owe Emanuel Bach a debt of gratitude. His pioneer work in the sphere of the sonata exerted a powerful influence upon Haydn,

Mozart, and Beethoven, all of whom acknowledged him as their master, and each of whom in turn established new traditions in sonata-writing.

It is not within our present purpose to examine the sonatas of the later eighteenth-century composers except in so far as they throw light upon those written during the nineteenth century. Nevertheless, as we cannot fully recognize and enjoy the distinctive qualities of the last-named compositions before knowing something of their immediate ancestry, we must glance at the principal characteristics of the sonata-production of Beethoven's most notable predecessors: Haydn (1732–1809), Mozart (1756–91), Clementi (1752–1832), and Dussek (1760–1812).

Haydn wrote about fifty sonatas over a long period of more than thirty years, during which time the form grew in his hands from diminutive to impressive proportions. He made a beginning with simple compositions in three short movements which he wrote for his harpsichord pupils and entitled 'divertimento' or 'partita' (alternative names for suites). Thereafter he gradually broadened his conception of the sonata as a whole form, modifying its structure by varying the number of the movements and arranging them in diverse order. He introduced new kinds of movement; in particular, interesting species of variations and rondos. One of his innovations was the inclusion of the minuet-and-trio in the scheme; not in all the sonatas but in a sufficiently large number to ensure this type of movement's becoming naturalized in the sonata-structure of his own time and later.

Haydn's sonatas are distinguished by characteristics which are far to seek in those by Emanuel Bach: namely, in melodic charm, rhythmic lilt, and in a certain lightness of touch which lends them great fascination. They are rich, too, in expressive power. The piano writing in the later sonatas is highly imaginative and effective with its bold harmonies and animated contrapuntal style. It is full of interest for the player, not only in itself but inasmuch as it points forward to that of Beethoven and Schubert.

Haydn lived long enough to become much more intimately acquainted with the special qualities of the piano than did

Mozart, who wrote the whole of his keyboard sonatas within fifteen years and the majority of them in early manhood. The older master excelled the younger in writing sympathetically for the solo instrument. The younger, who was incomparably more brilliant as an executant, was stimulated to his finest efforts when collaborating with another instrumentalist or with the orchestra. His sonatas for violin and piano and his concertos contain much the most interesting and effective part of his writing for the keyboard. His eighteen piano sonatas, on the other hand, possess unique charm in their clarity of texture and in the subtlety of their structural planning. All are in three movements. In this respect they differ as a series from Haydn's, among which two sonatas are written in four movements, and nine in only two movements.

A distinctive feature of Mozart's sonatas is his treatment of first-movement form, into which he breathed new life by re-arranging its smaller component parts into a multitude of different patterns, thereby introducing a strong element of surprise. Mozart admitted the minuet-and-trio and the air with variations only twice each into his sonatas, but he made comparatively greater use of the rondo than did Haydn.

From these two masters and from Emanuel Bach, Beethoven inherited the tradition of the classical piano sonata as an established art-form which, though variable in the number and types of its individual movements, was sufficiently well-defined in structure to constitute a sure foundation for further development.

*   *   *   *

Beethoven's indebtedness to Clementi and Dussek was of another kind. Both these composers were outstanding performers and both confined their creative activities very largely to writing piano music. They were familiar with every known pianistic device current in their day and were deeply interested in experimenting in the production of novel effects. It is only natural that in focusing so much of their attention upon the layout of their compositions and upon the writing of brilliant passages they should have surpassed Haydn and Mozart in these respects while not equalling them in structural mastery. They exercised a profoundly stimulating effect upon the piano style of the rising Beethoven. Through him, the influence of these now neglected pianist-composers made itself felt far down the nineteenth century.

*　　*　　*　　*

Beethoven saluted the year 1800 with his Sonata in B flat major, op. 22, a work of fine proportions in four movements, contemporary with his First Symphony. The types of structure that he used for each movement are clearly derived from those established by his predecessors, but the entire composition reveals a new and more dramatic conception of the sonata as an organic whole.

By what stages had he arrived at this easy mastery of structural design and effective piano style?

Beethoven was a born composer of sonatas. At the age of thirteen he wrote three, which show at a glance that from a tender age he had not the slightest compunction in reshaping the contours of conventional structures in accordance with the pressing needs of his own musical invention. Each of these youthful essays follows a different plan in the arrangement of its three movements and even the same types of movement vary greatly in outline. All three sonatas are remarkable for the assurance and fluency of their workmanship. One of them makes an unforgettable impression by the unusual design of the first movement and by its sustained expressive power.

This is no. 2 in F minor, which anticipates the 'Appassionata' Sonata both in key and in intensity of mood, and the 'Pathétique', with which it shares the distinctive characteristic of a slow introduction that recurs later during the movement. A marked similarity exists, too, between the opening themes of the Allegro and that of its renowned successors. The exquisitely tranquil slow movement of this early Sonata in F minor reveals an amazing depth of feeling, to which the exuberance and vigour of the Finale present a striking contrast. In addition to being an unmistakable forerunner of the two great works just mentioned, as well as an extremely effective piece for the player, the whole composition possesses interest for the student of the Beethoven sonatas in showing that some of the characteristics of the master's mature style were already present in the boy's prentice works. They include sudden contrasts in dynamics, relentless rhythmical drive and the repetition of short figures or phrases for the purposes of emphasis and expression.

These sonatas, known as the 'Bonn' Sonatas, were written in 1783. The series of the Thirty-two, one of the most vital sections in the whole of Beethoven's production and the greatest collection of piano sonatas by any composer, was inaugurated in 1795–6 with the Sonatas in F minor, A major, and C major, op. 2, nos. 1–3. They were dedicated to Joseph Haydn, from whom Beethoven had received some instruction and whom he admired as a composer even if he held a poor opinion of his methods of teaching. Although the sonatas of op. 2 and their successors up to and including op. 14, no. 2, were composed before 1800, they must of necessity be included in our survey. No one who is interested in Beethoven's piano works could be satisfied to omit this momentous opening section of a series which it is equally rewarding to study as a whole entity and as a collection of single items.

*   *   *   *

In the earlier part of this chapter reference was made to various types of sonata movement, but no details were given of their structural characteristics. Now that we are to consider the individual sonatas among a collection which includes an increasing number of different kinds of movement we must turn our attention to the few technicalities in the way of definition and description which are indispensable to the endlessly fascinating study of the formal and architectural aspects of music. For this preliminary purpose the sonatas of Beethoven's op. 2 provide an eminently satisfactory basis. Their twelve movements (four to each sonata) exemplify several of the types of form which occur most frequently in the sonatas written during the late eighteenth century and throughout the whole of the nineteenth century.

*   *   *   *

The majority of pieces of instrumental music belong to one of two principal types of structure: *binary* (twofold) or *ternary* (threefold). The former type comprises pieces in which the first complete section comes to a close in a new key and the second section, which opens in a new key and is based upon material used in the first, ultimately returns to the original key. The two sections are often very unequal in length. *Simple binary form*, which is exemplified in the first (and other) movements of many early sonatas, may be observed in Beethoven's op. 2 in the Trios of nos. 1 and 2. *Compound binary form*, in which the scheme just described is extended by the insertion of a central section, is known as 'sonata form' or synonymously as 'first-movement form'. It is used for the opening movements of all three sonatas of op. 2 and will be fully described later. When it has no well-defined central section, as in the Andante of op. 2, no. 1, it is termed 'modified sonata form'.

Ternary form consists of three main sections, the first of which (A) ends in the original key and is repeated, sometimes with superficial modifications, after a contrasting central section (B) written in another key. This A B A form may be seen at its simplest in the Minuet of op. 2, no. 1, in the Scherzo of no. 2 and in both the Scherzo and the Trio of no. 3. The Minuet-and-Trio (or Scherzo-and-Trio) as a complete entity is, however, in itself ternary in form inasmuch as the Minuet (or Scherzo) is repeated after the Trio which forms the contrasting central section. The whole is often rounded off with an independent coda, as in op. 2, no. 3.

This simple threefold scheme forms the basis of many slow movements of sonatas. For instance, the *Marcia funebre* of Beethoven's Sonata in A flat, op. 26, and the Andante of the Sonata in G major, op. 79. It is also exemplified in innumerable single pieces such as some of Schubert's Impromptus and *Moments musicaux*, Chopin's Nocturnes, Brahms's Intermezzos and Grieg's Lyric Pieces.

Enlargement of the ternary structure by accretion leads to the formation of *Simple* or *Older Rondo form*. In this type of form the number of intervening contrasting sections (episodes) is increased, either by the introduction of entirely fresh material, as in the Largo of op. 2, no. 2; or by the repetition in another key of material already used in a previous episode, as in the second movement of no. 3. In theory, there is no limit to the number of episodes or the repeats of the refrain; but in practice, two of the former and three of the latter form the most usual and possibly the most satisfactory scheme. The most impressive example of the older rondo form in the Beethoven sonatas is furnished by the Finale of the 'Waldstein' Sonata. Its already huge proportions are enlarged by long sections that form links between the episodes and the recurrent refrain; the movement is crowned by a magnificent coda in which the inextinguishable principal theme reappears time after time in progressively effective and thrilling variations.

Modern or *Sonata Rondo form*, which is used for many finales, is a blend of the structure of *older rondo* with that of *sonata form*. It is exemplified in Beethoven's op. 2 in the Finales of both no. 2 and no. 3. It may be recognized by the presence of a 'second subject' which later recurs with the customary 'sonata-form' key-change; by the recurrence of the refrain at the end of the first complete section, and by the inclusion of a central section consisting *either* of a contrasting interlude (as in the two Finales just mentioned), *or* of the development of material previously used (as in the Finale of op. 22).

In both binary and ternary forms, exact or approximate repetition, whether of single paragraphs or of whole sections of the music, is a fundamental necessity. Indeed, repetition is one of the most vital and indispensable elements in the whole art of musical composition. To maintain the ideal balance between the quantity of the thematic material, the number of times it is stated and the variety of guises in which it is presented calls for a composer's highest powers of invention. Only by being familiar with the salient features of the recognized musical forms can the music-lover derive the maximum enjoyment from

all the many subtleties of repetition and variation which distinguish the works of any great composer. Most especially is
this so in the instance of sonata form, the late-eighteenth-
century and the nineteenth-century form *par excellence,* which
in the hands of the greatest masters of that long period attained
a nobility of conception and expression perhaps never since
surpassed.

*   *   *   *

Sonata form (or *first-movement form*) consists of three main
sections whose mutual key-relationships are of paramount importance in the organization of the movement as a whole. The
first section, 'exposition', which is generally repeated, comprises
a principal subject or group of subjects in the tonic key,
merging into a short or long passage of transition. It proceeds
towards a fresh key, normally that of the dominant if the sonata
is in the major mode, or the relative major if it is in the minor.
When this fresh key has been reached, a second subject, or
group of subjects is announced. It generally forms a contrast
in character or mood to the principal subject and usually ends
in a distinctive phrase termed the codetta, with a cadence in
the fresh key. Then follows a central section, known as the
development or working-out. During its course some of the
thematic material stated in the exposition recurs in new keys
and in fresh guises, tonal or rhythmic. This procedure is
exemplified in the first movement of the Sonata in A major,
op. 2, no. 2, but sometimes, as in the Finale of the Sonata in
F minor, op. 2, no. 1, entirely fresh material is introduced in
addition to that which has already become familiar.

One of the most important functions of the development-
section is to provide contrast to the surrounding sections by
means of key-change. In op. 2, no. 2, for instance, particularly
strong key-contrast is furnished at the very outset of the development, first by the sudden plunge in tonality from E major
to C major and then by successive modulatory passages through
a number of keys.

The development-section of the movement eventually leads
back to the third and last section, which is known as the re-

capitulation. In this final section, the principal subject re-appears, usually in the original key. It may be decorated or disguised, or it may make a deceptive re-entry in an entirely unexpected key, as it does in the Sonata, op. 10, no. 2, in D major instead of in F. The passage of transition has generally to be modified so as to ensure the return of the second subject in the *tonic* key, in which tonality the movement usually remains until the end. The codetta is sometimes lengthened by a few bars to make a more impressive coda.

The dimensions of this type of movement are at times greatly enlarged by the addition of a separate introductory section, as in the first movement of the 'Lebewohl' Sonata; or of a long, self-contained coda, as in the first and last movements of the 'Waldstein'.

*   *   *   *

Such is the traditional scheme of 'first-movement' form to which Beethoven adhered in principle, although he carried it to a far higher state of development. He transformed it into a closely knit organic whole, bringing the component parts into more intimate mutual relationship. He expanded it into a structure so gigantic and yet so plastic as to make possible the musical expression of an illimitable range of human emotions and abstract ideas.

Among the sonata movements that most strikingly reveal new conceptions of musical architecture are the Allegro of the 'Hammerklavier' Sonata, op. 106, a movement compact of powerful rhythms, a multiplicity of key-changes and intricate fugal texture; and the opening movement of the last Sonata in C minor, op. 111, whose terrific and mysterious introduction preludes a stretch of musical fabric in which distinctive attri-butes of sonata form and fugue are closely interwoven. These are extreme instances of Beethoven's powers of formal organiza-tion. He achieved an opposite effect in the 'adagio sostenuto' of the 'Moonlight' Sonata by eliminating all but the barest essentials of formal structure in favour of creating a supremely poetic atmosphere.

*   *   *   *

As on the single movement, so on the sonata as a whole, Beethoven left his mighty impress. He integrated the individual movements ever more closely, arranging their succession in a variety of ways. Most of the two-movement sonatas comprise strong mutual contrasts in structural design and expressive style. In the Sonata in F major, op. 54, the alternately gracious and recondite opening 'in tempo d'un minuetto', itself a curious blend of rondo and variations, is balanced by an invigorating moto perpetuo of running semiquavers. The feeling of equilibrium established by the suave, well-balanced Allegro of the Sonata in F sharp major, op. 78, is shattered by a quicksilvery 'allegro vivace' that defies exact classification. The anxious mood of the sonata-form movement of the Sonata in E minor, op. 90, is entirely offset by the imperturbable contentment of the rondo Finale in E major. In the great C minor Sonata, op. 111, the towering strength and intricate contrapuntal mechanism of the first movement are perfectly counterpoised by a sublimely restful set of variations on a tranquil theme in the major mode.

The three-movement sonatas, which comprise the largest number of the Thirty-two, display a wide range of planning. The 'Moonlight', op. 27, no. 2, is unique in its threefold succession of movements in contrasted style. The first is a tone-poem so serene that any thought of conscious formal layout is banished by the unruffled continuity of its triplet-quaver figuration; the second, an Allegretto-and-Trio, strictly classical in form but romantic in its delicate chiaroscuro; the third, a Presto whose tameless impetuosity transcends every limitation of its clearly recognizable sonata-form construction.

The earliest sonata in which Beethoven departed from the conventional scheme of three self-contained movements was the 'Waldstein', op. 53 (1804). In this powerful work the opening 'allegro con brio' in symphonic style is followed by a short linking section, *Introduzione*, 'adagio molto' which creates an air of mysterious anticipation before leading without a break into the colossal, brilliant rondo Finale.

The 'Moonlight' and the 'Waldstein' are only isolated

examples of the three-movement sonatas, which also include further differing types. Among these are the large-scale, tragic 'Appassionata' in F minor, op. 57; the picturesque 'Lebewohl' in E flat major, op. 81a, the only one of all the sonatas that purports to delineate specific emotional states; the E major Sonata, op. 109, in which the peaceful flow of the first movement is twice checked by Adagio interludes, and the Sonata in A flat major, op. 110, whose arioso slow movement and fugal Finale are inextricably interlocked.

*   *   *   *

The first seven of the four-movement sonatas, op. 2, nos. 1–3, op. 7, op. 10, no. 3, and op. 22, date from Beethoven's 'first period', during which time he followed traditional structural principles with varying degrees of fidelity. They were succeeded in 1802 by a sonata of an entirely original type: the A flat major, op. 26, known as the 'Funeral March' Sonata. It opens exceptionally with an 'andante con variazioni' instead of the customary Allegro, and unlike all the preceding sonatas has for its second movement a Scherzo-and-Trio, 'allegro molto'. The third movement is the *Marcia funebre*; the Finale, a rondo whose quickly running imitative counterpoint presents an ideal contrast to the heavy chordal texture of the *Marcia funebre*.

This was the first sonata of Beethoven's 'second period' (1802–1814). Its immediate successor, the Sonata in E flat major, 'quasi una fantasia', op. 27, no. 1, is yet another type of four-movement sonata. It was the first of the Thirty-two to be designed as an unbroken whole. All the movements are joined together, either by being marked to be played without a break (Attacca), or by means of linking passages. The recurrence of entire sections, sometimes varied or in a fresh key, lends the whole work a strong sense of unity.

This expedient of restating whole sections of material during the course of a work in cyclic form was employed by Beethoven with dramatic force in the Finales of the Fifth and the Ninth Symphonies. He also resorted to it in the A major Sonata, op. 101, by inserting the tranquil opening phrase of the first movement for expressive purposes just before the soliloquizing Adagio leads into the strenuous Finale.

The last-named Sonata is the first of the five of Beethoven's 'third period'. Of these, the only one in four *separate* movements is the 'Hammerklavier' Sonata in B flat major, op. 106; the longest, the most recondite and the most difficult to play of all the Thirty-two.

*   *   *   *

From the foregoing necessarily brief comments on some of the formal aspects of the Beethoven Sonatas it may be seen that these compositions fall into three distinctive types: the classical, the romantic and the intellectual. The types are by no means mutually exclusive. Classical principles underlie *all* the sonatas, even when they are so romantic in character as the 'Funeral March' Sonata, the 'quasi fantasia' Sonatas of op. 27 and the 'Lebewohl' Sonata. In the intellectually conceived 'third-period' sonatas, too, romantic elements are present in the free organization of the movements and in the improvisatory passages and sections.

We shall meet the classical and the romantic types of sonata again in the works of the later nineteenth-century composers, but not the superlatively intellectual. This type could be successfully cultivated only by a composer whose command of technical resource and whose power of imagination were of an equally high order. In other words, only by the master mind of a Beethoven.

3

The Sonata

(2)

Beethoven's sonatas from the aspects of rhythm, melody, harmony, tonality, contrapuntal treatment, variation technique, colour-effects, expressive qualities.

FOR the pianist, whether or not he is interested in musical architecture, in musical history or in the evolution of the sonata as an art-form, the principal attractions of the Beethoven sonatas are the infinite variety and beauty of their actual musical substance, their limitless range of expression and the supremely effective quality of their pianistic style.

Beethoven was himself a fine pianist. He was not a virtuoso according to the Clementi standard, but a player whose compelling performances, particularly of his own works, made a deep impression upon his hearers. His gift of extemporizing at the keyboard was not only remarkable in itself; it was also the cause of his discovering new pianistic effects. Beethoven had also learned to play the violin, viola, and organ in his boyhood, but he began his musical career as a pianist and teacher of the piano. This close acquaintance during his early years with the realities of keyboard technique resulted in his writing for the piano in a style which, although it calls for the player's utmost skill, seldom makes impossible demands upon his technique.

It was not until after Beethoven's deafness had incapacitated him as a performer that he tended to allow the intellectual aspects of his instrumental music to predominate over the practical. A few of his 'third-period' sonatas, the last five of the Thirty-two, in which emphasis is laid upon the philosophically speculative rather than upon the humanly expressive, are the only ones that are almost beyond the powers of performance of any except professional pianists. Even skilled performers do not lightly undertake to play the 'Hammerklavier' Sonata or the Sonata in C minor, op. 111. Nevertheless, with these few exceptions, the Beethoven sonatas can be played with enjoyment by any reasonably efficient musician. Their inestimable value as music, the beauty and the enthralling interest of the piano writing have ensured their retaining a firm hold upon the affections of players of all grades, professional and amateur, for well over a hundred years, despite a succession of changes in musical fashions.

* * * *

Looking more closely into the musical and expressive aspects of the sonatas we find that one of the principal characteristics of the thematic material is its vitality in rhythm and metre. Many of the actual themes or phrases may have no well-defined melodic outline or commanding harmonic scheme, but they make an indelible impression upon players and listeners by the inner strength of their rhythmic patterns. Beethoven sometimes used short, incisive figures persistently for bars at a stretch or throughout the greater part of a whole movement. They make the effect of the composer's having been obsessed by an inescapable poetic idea which could find equivalent musical expression only in the ceaseless repetition of distinctive groupings of notes and beats or in the maintenance of a uniform figure of accompaniment.

Among the movements which display these features are the Finale of the Sonata in F minor, op. 2, no. 1, a tornado of peremptory staccato crotchet chords and whirling quaver triplets, and the jauntily striding 'vivace alla marcia' of the Sonata in A major, op. 101. Again in the presto Finale of the F major Sonata, op. 10, no. 2, the strongly accented opening theme is reiterated in a number of harmonic and quasi-fugal guises and in a great variety of keys, but never for a moment loses its initial impetus. It furnishes an early example of Beethoven's skill in blending the elements of sonata form and fugue into a con-

c

vincing unity. These movements and others, such as the respective Scherzos of the 'Pastoral' Sonata in D, op. 28 and of the 'Hammerklavier', are all strenuous in character. A movement that exhibits the same type of strongly marked though less emphatic rhythmic features is the rondo Finale of the D major Sonata, op. 10, no. 3. The opening motive of three rising notes, which seems to be forever asking an unanswerable question, pervades the whole fabric and keeps the listener perpetually in suspense as to how and when it will next appear. It is a masterpiece of monothematic organization.

Another movement of this kind is the Finale of the D minor Sonata, op. 31, no. 2, an almost unbroken tissue of six semiquavers to the bar. Despite an occasional syncopation and a breathing-space of a quaver's duration every now and again, it exercises an almost hypnotic effect by its unhurried perpetual motion. In the 'presto con fuoco' of the Sonata in E flat, op. 31, no. 3, the irresistible *élan* of the iambic metre of the dance far outweighs the triviality of the short-breathed melodic outlines, whose clear-cut rhythmic pattern is their principal merit. The Finale of the 'Waldstein' is entirely dominated by the combined rhythmic and melodic pattern of the short opening theme that recurs innumerable times throughout the movement. In the coda it is eventually caught up into a vortex of repetition. Further examples are too numerous to specify. Indeed, they may be found in almost every movement of the Thirty-two.

*   *   *   *

Turning to more purely melodic features we discover many characteristically Beethovenian traits, among which the following are some of the most easily recognizable.

Melodies proceeding mainly scale-wise up or down (or both) include the boldly curving theme of the Presto of op. 10, no. 3 in D major; the second subject of the Allegro of op. 14, no. 1 in E major, in which the scale is alternately diatonic and chromatic; the Trio section (in A flat) of the 'allegro molto e vivace' of op. 27, no. 1 in E flat, where the pianissimo scale in triple time is broken up into units of two crotchets on the weak beats with a rest on each strong beat; and the second subject of the 'allegro con brio' of the 'Waldstein' (from bar 35). The severity of the outline of this theme is emphasized by the strength and simplicity of the chords upon which it rests.

Melodies that proceed arpeggio-wise are exemplified by the forthright opening theme of the F minor Sonata, op. 2, no. 1; by the sprightly, vertiginous codetta and other passages of the 'presto con fuoco' of op. 31, no. 3 in E flat; by the principal subject of the first movement of the 'Appassionata' as well as the chordal section in the coda of the Finale, and by the whole of the Trio of the 'Hammerklavier', first in the right hand and then in canon with the left. Perhaps the most striking of all is the C minor section of the E flat major Sonata just mentioned (op. 27, no. 1). It consists of a steady succession of broken chords tirelessly ascending and descending, and culminates in one last fortissimo plunge down the C major arpeggio into the depths of the keyboard.

Melodies distinguished by recurrent falling intervals consti-tute the opening phrase of the 'adagio cantabile' of the 'Pathétique', the melody of which drops down a fifth three times within the space of five bars, and the theme of the varia-tions in the E major Sonata, op. 109, whose sixteen bars are punctuated no fewer than seven times by falling intervals rang-ing in extent from a third to a sixth.

Themes which start in detached segments before they assume greater continuity of motion form the principal subjects of the Sonatas in C minor and F major, op. 10, nos. 1 and 2, and of the Sonata in B flat major, op. 22. The opening phrase of the Largo of op. 7 is also of this type. Themes such as these make the impression of the composer's being determined to secure the listener's close attention before announcing a more important musical idea.

Entirely opposite in effect are the long, smoothly flowing melodies of the Minuetto of op. 31, no. 3, the 'largo e mesto' of op. 10, no. 3, the 'adagio sostenuto' of the 'Hammerklavier' and the almost moveless theme of the variations forming the slow movement of the 'Appassionata'.

Nevertheless, many of Beethoven's otherwise tranquil themes, especially in the earlier sonatas, are punctuated by sudden accentuation or wayward syncopation. For example, the Minuets of op. 2, no. 1, op. 7 in E flat major, op. 10, no. 3 in D major, the 'adagio con expressione' of op. 27, no. 1, the Adagio of op. 22, the *Marcia funebre* of op. 26 and the 'adagio grazioso' of op. 31, no. 1 in G major. Even a movement so ethereal in character as the Allegretto of the 'Moonlight' Sonata does not escape periodic interruption by impatient sforzandos.

Other distinctive features of Beethoven's melodic invention include two which intensify the expressive character of the material. One is the building of themes by means of sequences (the repetition of a figure or phrase at a different pitch), a device that is exemplified in the Scherzo of the 'Hammerklavier' Sonata and in the second movement of the 'Moonlight'. The other is the use of accented passing-notes (melody-notes extraneous to the supporting harmonies). These abound in the thematic material and the passage-work of all the sonatas. Typical examples may be found in the rondo Finale of op. 7 in E flat, in which accented passing-notes occur on the first beats of the opening bars, imparting great pungency to the melody:

Again, in the 'adagio sostenuto' of the 'Moonlight' Sonata, the accented C natural in the right-hand part in bars 16 and 18 and its equivalent D natural in the right-hand part in bars 52 and 54 are the only disturbing elements in this ineffably peaceful movement. The Adagio of op. 22 is permeated throughout by a motive of a rising semitone which originates in the second bar.

Lastly comes the breaking up of a theme into short sections for distribution over the keyboard at various pitches. Piquant effects arising from this treatment occur at the end of the Adagio of op. 2, no. 3; in the Finale ('allegro vivace') of op. 27, no. 1 between bars 25 and 35, throughout the 'in tempo d'un minuetto' of op. 54 in F major and in the coda of the 'andante con moto' of the 'Appassionata'. This last passage is closely paralleled in the final section of the Allegretto of the Seventh Symphony in A.

* * * *

We have already observed the closeness of the relationship between Beethoven's melodies and their underlying rhythmic schemes. What of their harmonic aspects?

Beethoven's manner of harmonizing his melodic material, especially at its first appearance, was frequently simple in the extreme. He was often content to rely upon the solid strength of plain diatonic harmony, and sometimes he cut down his resources to the primary triads (tonic, dominant and sub-dominant). By these limited means he nevertheless succeeded in investing his themes with the quality of supreme inevitability. Some of the melodies rest the bulk of their weight upon the support of tonic and dominant-seventh harmonies, withdrawing to other, less forcible chords only at intermediate points. Such are the respective opening themes of the rondos of the Sonata in B flat, op. 22 and of the 'Waldstein', the Adagios of op. 27, no. 1 and op. 31, no. 1, and the 'allegro con brio' of op. 2, no. 3, to name only a few.

Other melodies are treated even more simply by being anchored to one bass-note, in this context termed a pedal-point. The note, which is almost invariably the tonic, persists for a few bars while the harmonies change above it. Examples may be found at the openings of the following movements: the 'presto alla tedesca' of the Sonata in G major, op. 79, the Allegro of op. 14, no. 1 in E major, the Adagios of op. 22 in B flat and of op. 31, no. 1 in G major, and in the 'adagio cantabile' introduction of op. 78 in F sharp major. The 'Pastoral' Sonata, op. 28, furnishes an example of the device used for colour-purposes. In the Allegro the tonic pedal-point beats three crotchets in a bar for twenty successive bars and continues to beat almost without interruption either in the centre of the texture or as a bass-note during another nineteen bars. In the recapitulation it persists even longer. The last movement of this sonata, too, begins over a pedal-note which is struck on every strong beat for the first sixteen bars.

An exception to the use of the tonic as the basis of passages of this kind is provided by the short pedal-point on the dominant at the beginning of the Allegretto of the Sonata in A major, op. 101, one of the few movements of the Thirty-two which does not disclose its fundamental tonality at the very outset.

Instances of important themes harmonized with a preponderance of chromatic chords, such as those of the Adagio, the Allegro, and the 'andante espressivo' of the 'Lebewohl' Sonata, are comparatively rare. Beethoven used chromaticisms sparingly in his main thematic material but introduced them freely to perform specific functions. They occur in the development-sections of sonata-form movements and in the episodes of rondos where remote key-changes produce a particularly telling effect. They also play an active part in creating a feeling of suspense before the return of a long-awaited theme or in springing a surprise by presenting fundamentally diatonic material in strikingly fresh versions. A typical instance of the latter occurs in the Rondo of op. 7 in E flat at the last appearance of the refrain. After the theme has first been enlivened with decorative chromaticisms and has come to an impressive pause on a double-octave B flat, it suddenly slips out of gear, so to speak, into a key a chromatic semitone higher. There it pursues its furtive course pianissimo for nearly seven bars until a sudden sforzando jerks it back into the original tonality.

*   *   *   *

The few points just mentioned in connexion with Beethoven's use of diatonic or chromatic harmonic resources are necessarily limited to small-scale operations. His long-range harmonic planning, which includes the determining of key-relationships between the different sections of whole movements and between the several movements of whole sonatas, is a highly technical subject, far beyond the scope of this handbook. Only by analysing complete movements in detail is it possible to come to an understanding of these vital issues, but musicians with a knowledge of harmonic progressions and a strong sense of tonality will almost certainly be able to follow Beethoven's modulations in all their logic and through all their vagaries. Others who are not thus technically equipped may be sub-consciously aware how greatly the very life and interest of a sonata are dependent upon this fundamental matter of key-relationship.

It may be borne in mind that some key-relationships which look extremely remote on paper owe their apparent mystery simply to their enharmonic notation. The seven-bar passage in the rondo Finale of the E flat Sonata, op. 7, just referred to, is a case in point. There, the numerous accidentals denoting the tonality of E major (a sharp key within a flat one) are merely doing duty for the more complicated notation of the implied enharmonic equivalent, F flat major, an impossibly difficult key.

Sometimes whole movements are written with an enhar-monic key-signature for the sake of convenience in reading. The Allegretto of the 'Moonlight' Sonata is written enharmonically in D flat major, the key-signature of five flats being less cumber-some to the sight-reader than the seven sharps of the actual tonic major, C sharp. The third movement of the 'Hammer-klavier' is written in F sharp minor owing to the impractic-ability of using the signature of G flat minor, the key of the lowered sub-mediant (the sixth degree of the scale) of B flat, the basic tonality of the whole sonata. The change in key-signature from A flat to E major during the course of the first movement of the Sonata in A flat, op. 110, is made for the same reason. The second movement of the A major Sonata, op. 101, affords another example of the use of the lowered sub-mediant (F major) for providing strong key-contrast within the framework of a whole sonata, but in this case, there is no necessity for enharmonic notation.

Up till the time of Beethoven the use of any but nearly related keys (relative or tonic major or minor, dominant or sub-dominant) for the inner movements of sonatas was exceptional. In this matter Beethoven showed his independence of tradition. Five other inner movements besides those already mentioned demonstrate his preference for sub-mediant tonality. They are the Largo of op. 7, the Adagios of op. 10, no. 1, and op. 31, no. 2, the 'andante con moto' of the 'Appassionata' and the 'andante espressivo' (Absence) of the 'Lebewohl' Sonata. For the Adagio of the Sonata in C major, op. 2, no. 3 (1795–6) he chose the much less usual key of the mediant (third), E major. It produces a sharp contrast in tonality, but one less sharp than that in Haydn's last Sonata in E flat (1798) (no. 1 in Peters Edition). The central movement of this splendid work is written in the most remote key possible: E major, a chromatic semitone distant. Many years later Schubert used the key of the *lowered* mediant (C sharp, the enharmonic of D flat) with magic effect for the slow movement of his last and greatest Sonata in B flat major (1828).

*   *   *   *

The harmonic, or vertical, interest of the piano writing in the Beethoven sonatas is at least equalled, if not exceeded, by the contrapuntal, or horizontal. Indeed, the pianistic texture of the Thirty-two derives a very large part of its effectiveness and vitality from the devices of counterpoint incorporated within it. This is not the place to discuss the elaborate fugal movements of the later sonatas. They will be referred to in another chapter, but here we may examine a few representative passages in the earlier and middle-period sonatas. At first sight they seem to owe their effectiveness as keyboard music simply to decorative figuration. They prove on closer scrutiny to be compact of canons or canonic imitations between the upper and lower strands of the musical fabric, or to be running in double counter-point.

Such passages occur in abundance in the three Sonatas of op. 2. The Trio in the third movement of the F minor Sonata provides an example of double (invertible) counterpoint: that is to say, of a combination of two themes in which the upper and lower can be reversed without altering the musical sense. In this instance, the right-hand and left-hand parts in bars 1–4 perform each other's functions in bars 5–8, and again at the beginnings of the middle and final sections of the same movement. Three of the four movements of the C major Sonata (no. 3) are rich in contrapuntal devices. In the 'allegro con brio', the right-hand part in bars 5 and 6 is imitated by the left hand in bars 9 and 10, and between bars 47 and 60 the thematic material is tossed from one hand to the other in canonic imitation. Towards the end of the development-section the right hand proceeds in canon at the ninth with the left hand in three short phrases in octaves:

The Scherzo of this Sonata is built up in a series of short canonic imitations. In the Finale some of the most telling passages are those in which the principal theme, the rising scale in staccato chords, at first the prerogative of the right hand, is later transferred to the left hand, freeing the right to provide a decorative counterpoint above it.

In the Sonata in D major, op. 10, no. 3, the pithy subject-matter of the first and last movements affords wonderful opportunities for diverse contrapuntal treatment. In the Presto, the opening descending notes and the concluding ascending notes of the principal subject are reiterated countless times either separately or combined. The initial three-note motive of the Rondo:

appears, either literally or modified, in every section of this movement. It may be found now at the top of the musical texture, now at the bottom, often in the middle, sometimes in combination with its original three accompanying notes, sometimes separated from them, sometimes running in canon below them, as at bars 60 and 61:

or alternating with them, as at bars 100–1:

In the coda, these irrepressible thematic fragments, melodically inverted or re-shaped, are placed deep down in the left-hand part while the right hand executes a counterpoint of chromatic scales or broken chords above them. This Rondo, as well as the Allegretto Finale of op. 31, no. 1, and the Vivace of op. 79 are notable examples of Beethoven's power of constructing a whole movement upon one dominating motive supported by a wealth of subsidiary material.

Contrapuntal treatment of similar and other kinds may be

found in almost every one of the sonatas. The compact fabric
of octaves and sixths in the first movement of op. 54 in F major
abounds in free canonic imitations. The surging scale-passages
in the Finale of the 'Appassionata' are occasionally enriched by
them and the animated texture of the 'Return' section of the
'Lebewohl' is greatly enhanced by highly expressive double
counterpoint. Towards the end of the Scherzo of the Sonata in
A flat, op. 26, the main theme appears first above and then below the same accompaniment in running quavers. A more
closely wrought kind of fugal texture heightens the effectiveness
of the central sections of many movements. In the Finale of the
'Pastoral' Sonata, for instance, a four-bar phrase of ascending
notes is made the subject of a longish phrase in three-part
harmonic counterpoint leading up to a powerful climax.

The fugal devices of augmentation and diminution: i.e. the
presentation of a theme in notes respectively longer or shorter in
value than those of the original statement, were used by
Beethoven for purely expressive purposes. The former, which
conduces to a sense of relative leisureliness, is exemplified in the
Finale of the 'Waldstein' Sonata:

the latter, which has the effect of increasing the musical tension,
in the Finale of the Sonata in E flat, op. 27, no. 1:

In the first movement of the E minor Sonata, op. 90, the three-note figure of descending notes, G, F sharp, E, which is the salient feature of the principal subject, is presented in both diminution and augmentation. Treated thus, it creates a strong feeling of suspense and forms an ideal link between the development-section and the recapitulation. It is, besides, a convincing example of the use of technical means for poetic ends, as is the free canonic imitation between the left-hand and right-hand parts in the 'horn-calls' at the end of the 'Farewell' section of the 'Lebewohl' Sonata. There, the imaginative employment of the contrapuntal device gives rise to exquisitely romantic tone-colouring.

*   *   *   *

Beethoven submitted much of his thematic material to variation. In each of five sonatas, one movement comprises a self-contained set of variations: op. 14, no. 2 in G major, the 'Funeral March' Sonata, the 'Appassionata' and the Sonatas in E major and C minor, opp. 109 and 111. Some of them will be referred to again in the chapter on Variations. Here, we may consider a few points in connexion with Beethoven's *technique* of variation throughout the Thirty-two. It is displayed most particularly in sonata-form movements, when he presented the material first stated in the exposition in a fresh guise in the recapitulation; in rondos, in which he varied the refrain at some, if not all, its subsequent reappearances; and in movements in ternary form, to the opening section of which he imparted an entirely new aspect when he restated it after the central episode.

Variation of this kind was no uncommon feature of Haydn's and Mozart's sonatas, but Beethoven carried it to a fine art. The writing of variations had come to him as easily as had the writing of sonatas. His very first published composition was a set of variations written when he was about twelve years old. Unpretentious though it is in style, it is strongly individual in technique. It points forward unmistakably to the mature Thirty-two Variations in C minor as clearly as does the little F minor Sonata of the same period to the 'Pathétique' and the 'Appassionata'.

A very simple example of variation within a sonata-form movement may be found in the opening Allegro of op. 14, no. 1, in E major. The beating quavers in the left hand which accompany the principal subject at its first appearance (bars 1–4) are replaced in the recapitulation by energetic scales in semi-quavers. The passage of transition also undergoes a change in colour in the recapitulation by being restated pianissimo at a lower pitch than before and in an entirely unexpected key. Another, more effective kind of this essentially straightforward treatment is displayed in the first movement of the 'Appassionata'. The opening section of pianissimo plain octaves, lightly sketched harmonies, and single notes reappears at the outset of the recapitulation with the thematic outline set above a nearly changeless pedal-bass of triplet quavers. It issues in a statement in the *major* of the chordal passage which had previously appeared in the *minor*.

In strong contrast to these easily recognizable metamorphoses is the recapitulation in the slow movement of the 'Hammerklavier' Sonata (beginning at bar 88). The theme of the principal subject 'appassionato e con molto sentimento', one of Beethoven's most peaceful and expressively harmonized melodies, is concealed within a delicate tracery of demisemiquavers in the right hand. The actual melodic outline is distributed capriciously note by note among the four demisemiquavers of every beat; now on the first, often on the second or third, very rarely on the fourth, and sometimes reinforced by the top notes of chords played by the left hand. When, after sixteen bars of this recondite but beautiful figuration, the theme is presented in its original state though enhanced by a syncopated and decorative left-hand part, the feeling is of a descent from the rarefied atmosphere of the mountain-top to the comparative security of the valley below.

Examples of the variation of the rondo refrain are almost too numerous to require comment here. A typical instance of how this treatment can affect the character of a whole movement occurs in the Finale of the Sonata in B flat major, op. 22, Beethoven's first nineteenth-century sonata and the last of his

'first period'. At its first and second appearances the eighteen-
bar refrain is identical in all respects with the first. At the third
entry, however, the first eight bars are entrusted entirely to the
left hand while the right maintains a desultory accompanying
figure above it before resuming its normal functions at the ninth
bar. Thereafter it carries out variations in broken octaves and
ornamental runs. At the fourth and last appearance of the
refrain, the right hand, once again the dominating partner,
sketches the melodic outline in triplets above the nonchalant
left-hand accompaniment. It sometimes omits the first note of
the triplet, thus imparting a feeling of breathlessness to the
otherwise placid final section. The whole movement is distinguished by interesting piano writing, but it is the deft changes
in the recurrent refrain that constitute its especial charm. The
Finale of op. 31, no. 1, is a movement of the same kind. In this
graceful Allegretto, as in the Allegretto Finale (K. 494) of
Mozart's Sonata in F major, the refrain is enchantingly varied
at every one of its several appearances.

The subsequent decoration of the initial section of a movement in ternary form is a feature so usual in the works of all
periods that it is hardly necessary to quote any particular example. One, however, in the 'adagio grazioso' of op. 31, no. 1
(1802), is of especial interest inasmuch as it shows Beethoven
reverting to his most typically eighteenth-century manner. This
leisurely movement with a superabundance of formalized em-
bellishment sounds amazingly antiquated by comparison with
the Adagio in E major and minor in the much earlier Sonata,
op. 2, no. 3, in C major (1795–6). The latter is a movement in
older rondo form throughout which the romantic atmosphere
of a tone-poem is created by the maintenance for many bars at a
time of a mysteriously susurrant accompanying figure between
an expressive bass and plaintive melodic fragments in the treble.
It breathes the very spirit of a Schubert song.

*   *   *   *

It is hardly possible to study the pianistic layout of the Thirty-
two sonatas without being acutely aware of the importance

Beethoven attached to making the left-hand parts musically interesting. In examining some of the passages embodying contrapuntal devices and variations, we have noted how often the left and the right hands exchange their usual functions. Looking more deeply into the matter we find that in very few of the sonata movements is the activity of the left hand limited to that of mere accompaniment. The song-like Andante of the G major Sonata, op. 79, which inevitably recalls the style of a Mendelssohn Song without Words, provides one of the rare instances. In some of the movements which are otherwise predominantly homophonic in character (i.e. consisting of melody and accompaniment), the left-hand part is accorded a certain measure of independence and interest. In the Finale of op. 90, a movement which promises to be one long stretch of accompanied right-hand melody, the left-hand part grows in significance as the movement proceeds. At one point it meets the right-hand part on equal terms. It claims the privilege of announcing both phrases of the rondo refrain in the centre of the keyboard, leaving the right hand to echo each of them in turn an octave higher. The placing of this much-repeated theme just for once in the tenor register, below, instead of above the accompaniment as heretofore, provides an arresting and welcome change in the colouring of a movement which in general tends towards monotone.

*　　*　　*　　*

Beethoven's understanding of the possibilities of imparting distinctive tone-colouring to the texture by differentiating the manner of performance of the left-hand part from that of the right hand is exemplified in the persistent left-hand staccato throughout the greater part of the Andante of the 'Pastoral' Sonata, the Largo of op. 2, no. 2, and the 'allegretto vivace' of op. 31, no. 3. It is also manifest in the ominous little tremolando octaves beneath (and occasionally above) the suave right-hand chords in the Adagio of op. 31, no. 2, and again in the laconic accompaniment of detached semiquavers below the right hand's eloquent, continuous theme in two sections of the 'adagio sostenuto' of the 'Hammerklavier'.

Among other methods by which Beethoven secured unusual colour-tints in the sonatas are the separating of the right-hand and left-hand parts by wide distances, especially in the later sonatas. Examples occur in the Trio of the 'alla marcia' of op. 101, and in the Variations of opp. 109 and 111. In all these passages the combination of extreme heights and depths of pitch imparts a ghostly or an ethereal timbre to the texture. At times, Beethoven created stormy cloud-effects by constantly repeating distinctive figures. The *minore* section of the third movement of op. 7 owes its mysterious tone-colour to the persistent reiteration of undulating broken chords in both hands, beginning and ending pianissimo with stretches of fortissimo between.

Another instance of a different kind occurs near the end of the development-section of the opening movement of the 'Pastoral' Sonata (bars 219–40). Three-note figures in each hand pull against one another time after time in contrary motion and at increasing distances while a pedal-point in varying parts of the texture binds the whole fabric firmly together. For weirdness of effect this sombre cloudscape may well be compared with the famous passage towards the end of the first movement of the Seventh Symphony in A. There, the lower strings seem to be straining away from the upper strings throughout a series of repetitions of a two-bar phrase, while the wood-wind and brass remain static upon a dominant pedal-point, sublimely indifferent to the strings' agonized struggle for liberation.

*   *   *   *

In surveying the inner structure and the outer surfaces of the Thirty-two sonatas we have incidentally made closer acquaintance with Beethoven's unrivalled manner of using technical resources for the purposes of creating poetic atmosphere and of expressing many different states of mind. We have studied movements that depict moods of excitement, serenity, tragic gloom or careless rapture. We have not as yet taken any opportunity of revelling in his wit.

Beethoven's wit is manifested less frequently in the musical material itself than it is in the unexpectedness of the treatment to which it is submitted. In the midst of a smoothly running passage the music may suddenly come to an abrupt pause and then, possibly after one or two false starts, the argument may be resumed as though nothing unusual had taken place. Again, an important theme may without warning dart out of its native key and the listener may be kept in a state of anxiety as to how and when it will be able to regain its basic tonality.

Illustrations of both these points may be found in the third movement, Allegro, of the Sonata in E flat, op. 7. The counter-statement of the opening eight-bar phrase stops suddenly at bar 12. After a pause, the last three beats are repeated sequentially a tone lower, and after another pause, the same little figure is repeated (amplified) four times in succession, temporarily delaying the progress of the phrase, which eventually succeeds in coming to a cadence. It is as though a machine had un-accountably ceased working, and on being restarted, could not be made to stop. In the recapitulation of this whole section, the original length of twenty-four bars is extended to fifty-three by several series of repetitions and by various circumlocutions. Most particularly, however, by an unexpected translation into the key of C flat whence the return to the original tonality of E flat occupies several bars and even necessitates a whole bar's rest for recovery from the effort.

* * * *

These are small-scale manœuvres. Sometimes Beethoven exercised his wit throughout an entire movement by arranging whole sections in unusual order and keys, deceiving the listener at every turn. Such a movement is the light-hearted 'allegro vivace' of op. 31, no. 1, in G major. Its true inwardness can best be realized and enjoyed by players or listeners who are able to follow and relish the oddities of its construction. The thematic units include perfunctory runs and jerky syncopated chords for the principal subject and a singularly undignified little tune at the beginning of the second subject-group. They are witty in themselves, but it is the treatment, constructional and expressive, to which they are submitted that determines the whimsicality of

D

the movement. The principal subject, or a portion of it, appears no fewer than six times—or nine times if the exposition is repeated. Immediately after its first announcement in the tonic it is restated, complete, in the key a tone lower. It recurs, incomplete, in the tonic at the very moment when the announcement of the second subject seems to be imminent. Still in the tonic, it opens the development section. It reappears in its normal place at the beginning of the recapitulation, preceded by thirty-one bars' elaborate preparation consisting of dominant harmony. Lastly, telescoped into the transition theme, it heralds the longish coda. Its ubiquity is the most distinctive feature of a movement whose eccentricities of construction and of mood are emphasized by the unusual keys chosen for the second subject: mediant major in the exposition and submediant major and minor in the recapitulation.

The Finale, too, contains further examples of the composer's proclivities for poking fun at his musical material. They reach a climax in the coda, where the rondo refrain is eventually bisected and presented alternately allegretto and adagio, with uneasy pauses between. After the theme has been stretched to its utmost limits and the music has come almost to a standstill, the opening figure is suddenly detached and whirled, presto, from top to bottom of the keyboard.

*   *   *   *

Beethoven extracted the very last ounce of effectiveness from his musical subject-matter. Economy of thematic material, wealth and diversity of treatment are the characteristics that most clearly distinguish his sonatas from those by his younger contemporaries, Weber and Schubert, which we shall study in the next chapter.

4

The Sonata

(3)

Weber as a composer for the piano; his four sonatas described individually and their musical qualities summarized. Schubert's sonatas as a whole collection; the eleven best known selected as the basis of a survey of their distinguishing formal and expressive attributes: the Sonata in A minor, op. 164 discussed in detail for purposes of comparison; invasion of the sonatas by the elements of the song and the dance; style of the piano writing.

WE have already seen that Beethoven's very first printed works for the keyboard revealed the youthful composer's phenomenal understanding of the instrument for which he was soon to write masterpiece after masterpiece. They gave more than an inkling of the characteristic style of his mature production.

Not so Weber's. The thumbnail Opus 1 which the future composer of wildly romantic operas and grandiloquent piano music printed in his twelfth year comprised six of the shortest, driest and most naïve little fughettas that can ever have issued from the pen of a composer who was ultimately to achieve lasting fame. This opuscule written in 1898, Weber's only piano composition in the 'severe' style, is the only survivor of the numerous prentice works he wrote before the turn of the century. The others, which included several sonatas, were destroyed by fire. All his now well-known published compositions for the piano: variations, dances, concertos and sonatas, date from after 1800. The four sonatas with which we are concerned in this chapter were written during the decade ending 1822 and are thus roughly contemporary with Beethoven's last six sonatas: op. 90 and the five of his 'third period'. But the difference in style between the two composers' works in this category is immeasurable.

Weber was a virtuoso pianist whose individual style of playing was largely determined by his long slender fingers and by an unusually large stretch. He could play widely extended chords and florid passage-work and could leap from one note to another far distant on the keyboard with the utmost ease. These circumstances encouraged him to write music to suit his own abnormally brilliant capabilities as a performer rather than to consider the limited skill of the average pianist. Moreover, as a composer of extremely colourful orchestral music he not unnaturally attempted to transfer orchestral effects to the piano. As pre-eminently a composer of operas, he was more inclined to write melodies of a singable type with conventionally flowing accompaniments than he was to invent the terse, pregnant themes capable of infinite development such as abound in the Beethoven sonatas.

It will readily be understood that Weber was not ideally endowed for the composing of abstract music for the keyboard; nor does he seem to have been strongly drawn to it or to have found it easy. Only two of his sonatas were written within a short space of time: the First in C major between April and July 1812, and the Third in D minor (the shortest) during three weeks in November 1816. The Second Sonata in A flat major, occupied him at intervals from 1814 to 1816 and the Fourth in E minor, which he began to write in 1819, was not completed until 1822. Nevertheless, despite the desultory manner of their composition, the four works are poetically and imaginatively conceived. In effect they are both picturesque and dramatic. While following in the main the accepted principles of classical sonata form they display a freedom from formal restraint and an exuberance in style that bring them within the category of the early romantic. Weber's constant preoccupation with opera may have made it almost inevitable that he should have a narrative in his thoughts when he was composing instrumental music. Indeed, he himself made known the romantic story upon which he based his *Concertstück* for piano and orchestra, and he also described the varying states of mind he sought to depict in the Fourth Sonata, now known as the 'Programme' Sonata. The other three sonatas, although they have no avowed programmatic background, seem to portray stirring events, deeply felt emotions and inescapable moods. One of them, the Third Sonata, has thereby acquired a descriptive title; it is known as the 'Demoniac'.

In Weber's lifetime his piano compositions were highly prized. In 1824 one critic, Adolph Bernhard Marx, went so far as to write that, next to Beethoven's, they were the most important and valuable of their period, and that in respect of grandeur and elaboration they sometimes even surpassed those of the older master: an opinion no one would dream of holding to-day.

The sonatas have unfortunately fallen into neglect. The heavy and specialized demands they make upon performing technique place them beyond the reach of amateurs and even deter the majority of concert pianists from including them in their programmes. But if these resplendent works cannot be adequately interpreted by any but highly accomplished performers, they are not too difficult to be played through and enjoyed by musicians technically less well equipped who take a delight in exploring unfamiliar music.

*   *   *   *

Weber wrote three of his sonatas, the First, the Second and the Fourth, in four movements, and the Third in three movements without a minuet-and-trio. The opening movement of each is in sonata form; three of the four slow movements and every one of the finales are rondos and all the minuets-and-trios are of the lively, Beethovenian scherzo type. Yet the sonatas are far from uniform in style or design. Each is differently planned as a whole, either in the order of the movements or their mutual key-relationship, and no two movements of the same kind of form resemble one another at all closely in outline. The works are fascinating to study on account both of the many structural irregularities they display and of the composer's unending resourcefulness in treating his musical ideas.

Weber's gift for thematic development was not comparable with Beethoven's but he possessed extraordinary facility in re-arranging his themes in unexpected sequence. He was adept in varying them melodically, harmonically and rhythmically and in weaving them jointly or severally into highly effective pianistic texture. The thematic material of the sonatas is strongly marked and well differentiated in character; it impresses itself so readily upon the memory that its adventures throughout a movement can generally be followed without difficulty. It must be borne in mind, however, that in the Weber sonatas, as in Mozart's, phrases, subjects and even whole sections are just as likely to recur in haphazard fashion as they are to take their places according to established custom. Portions of the music which seem to be essential to the argument in the early part of a movement may sometimes not be referred to again. Conversely, an apparently insignificant figure may later assume an important role. As we make a brief survey of the four sonatas we shall find examples of all these features, and of others which are equally characteristic of Weber's production.

*   *   *   *

Before he wrote the First Sonata in C major, op. 24, in 1812, Weber had already composed his First Piano Concerto and several sets of variations. These activities left traces in the pianistic style of all the sonatas which may straightway be observed in the concerto-like brilliance of the first and last movements of the C major Sonata and in the variation technique of the Adagio.

Among points of interest in this sonata the following may be specially noted. First, that the descending diminished-seventh arpeggio played by the left hand at the very beginning of the Allegro is not merely the preliminary flourish that it appears to be, but in reality, an integral figure which takes an important part in the codetta and the coda and is referred to in the development. Secondly, that the recapitulation of this movement opens most exceptionally in the key of the lowered mediant, E flat, and only gradually works its way round to the tonic.

The Adagio is in ternary form. In place of the customary repeat of the whole opening section, however, only the first four bars reappear. This most easily recognizable fragment of the thematic substance is restated four times in succession, each time in an entirely fresh guise. A resumption of the closing bars of the opening section and a brief coda bring the movement to a quiet end. This Adagio, which is in F major, is immediately followed by a minuet-and-trio in the tonality of E (minor and major); a rare choice of keys for adjacent movements.

The Minuet, short and quick, is in miniature sonata form. It abounds in brief phrases, lively cross-rhythms and neat canonic imitations, whereas the Trio contains a flowing accompanied melody and a triplet motive of repeated notes that sounds like a fairy horn-call. An enchanting feature of the ending of this section is the recall of the opening sentence, attenuated to become a distant, ghostly echo of its former self. The Finale is the Moto perpetuo in C major, well known as a separate piece. The superficial glitter of the passage-work conceals the ingenuity of the structure, in which the main part of the rondo refrain is stated four times note-for-note, but subsidiary figures appear in new keys, major and minor, throughout the movement, causing a succession of surprises. Even so, this effective quicksilvery movement is perhaps the least imaginative in design of all the four rondo finales.

*   *   *   *

The Second Sonata in A flat, op. 39, is altogether more intimate in style. The passage-writing is less spectacular, the texture richer and the tone-colours are infinitely more varied. The 'allegro moderato' in 12/8 time is the most expansive of all Weber's first movements. It is also the most vivid in narrative quality and the most subtle in suggesting orchestral colouring. The Andante, too, is written in the style of a ballad which grows in fervour of expression during its recitation. The 'menu-etto capriccioso' and the Finale both evoke the rhythms of the dance.

As in the opening movement of the First Sonata, the intro-ductory phrase of the A flat Sonata reappears in the codetta, though not in the coda. The recapitulation is little more than a summary of the salient features of the exposition, for the development-section contains so much repetition and elabora-tion of the many themes that their reappearance would be redundant.

The following movement, Andante in C minor, which pur-sues its way with cumulative effectiveness as the sparse crotchet and minim beats are broken up into groups of progressively smaller note-values, is fundamentally simple in thematic con-tent but complex in its irregular rondo structure. It opens with a threefold statement comprising a first phrase with the melody in the treble, a second phrase with the melody in the tenor or bass, and a varied counter-statement of the first phrase. The haunting character of the melody is intensified by its presenta-tion in single notes, legato, accompanied by light detached chords. This threefold statement of the refrain never recurs complete. On its next appearance it is limited to the first two phrases, this time with the melody in octaves in the left hand below a decoration of semiquaver triplets. Later it is reduced simply to the first phrase, which is varied with fresh, chromatic harmonies. A 'second subject' in E flat which begins to unfold at bar 35 displays its thematic outline in demisemiquavers first in the left hand and ten bars later, slightly modified, in the right hand. When it returns in C minor towards the end of the movement it is shortened by the telescoping of the long left-hand and right-hand phrases into one short phrase divided bar by bar between the two hands. The only other important theme, beginning in E flat major at the end of bar 57, is later re-introduced, varied, in C major to become the dynamic climax of the whole movement. It is eventually tapered to form the coda.

After the spacious Andante comes the impetuous, stimulating

'menuetto capriccioso' which bears little resemblance to the traditional minuet but is capricious beyond a doubt. It is compact of short rhythmic figures continually repeated at varying pitches and in fresh keys. The greater part of the main section in A flat major consists of figuration in quavers, whereas in the whole of the central episode in D flat major, every bar comprises three beating crotchets. The two sections are ultimately linked together by the sudden return of the quaver figuration, which combines with the crotchets to form an exciting passage leading to the repeat.

Anticipatory links of this kind were a speciality of Weber's, particularly in his rondo movements. Examples may be found in the Moto perpetuo, and more notably in the Finales of the Third and Fourth Sonatas. The sensitively pianistic layout of the 'menuetto capriccioso' of the Sonata in A flat, which recalls that of the sparkling prestissimo *Momento Capriccioso* in 5/4 time composed by Weber six years earlier, undoubtedly served as a model to Schumann when he came to write *Carnaval* in 1834–5. The endings of 'Préambule' and 'Marsch der Davidsbündler' contain a figure that strongly recalls the one immediately following the first double-bar of the 'menuetto capriccioso'.

Unlike the finales of the other three sonatas, the last movement of the Sonata in A flat major is moderate in tempo and graceful rather than nimble. The refrain creates a pleasant feeling of stability owing to the first of its two phrases being habitually tethered to a tonic pedal-bass. The changes in harmony throughout the whole movement are inclined to leisureliness but the melodic outline is rich in variety. The dovetailing of the sections is even more ingenious than in the Moto perpetuo, which movement it resembles in both rhythm and texture though not in speed or brilliance.

*   *   *   *

Weber wrote the Second Sonata in two instalments: the *last* two movements in the early part of 1814 and the *first* two in October 1816. These two highly poetic movements were immediately followed in November the same year by the whole of the Third Sonata in D minor, op. 49 (the 'Demoniac'). Its dynamic forcefulness furnishes an astonishing contrast to the dreaming beauty of its predecessor. The first movement, 'allegro feroce', has a Beethovenian tinge in the determined statement and the strongly marked rhythms of the principal subject-group and in the purposeful fugal texture in the development section. The second subject, 'tranquillo e lusingando' with gracious melodic curves, is written in a style typical of Weber's operatic arias. A noticeable feature of the movement is the treatment of two of the musical ideas as motto themes: the initial phrase and the one first announced in octaves in bar 36. The former, having made two appearances in the minor at the very outset, returns in the major to inaugurate the development-section, and to introduce the recapitulation in conjunction with the octave theme that forms the mainstay of the development-section. It finally dominates the coda.

The ensuing 'andante con moto' in B flat in older rondo form is the least complex in structure of all Weber's slow movements but is the most lavishly decorated. The tranquil sixteen-bar refrain, at whose first announcement the melody is accompanied by simple chords, is immediately varied twice in succession. The second time, its melodic contours are softened almost beyond recognition, and at each of its two subsequent appearances it is still more richly embellished. Both the episodes are dramatic in expression and even the refrain is punctuated by sudden and violent changes in dynamics which contrast strangely with its placid character. The concluding rondo in D major, 'presto con molto vivacità', differs in three important respects from those in Weber's other sonatas. It is in triple instead of duple time; the continuity of the semiquaver figuration is several times broken by the insertion of contrasting sections in quavers, and one of the themes is an expressive cantabile in waltz rhythm such as the composer had not previously introduced into his finales. Although the movement is known alternatively as 'Allegro di bravura' and is sometimes played separately, it is no empty piece of virtuosity. Structurally it is a blend of older and modern rondo and is full of interesting points in design and layout. The waltz section, which appears twice in different keys, may be regarded as the second subject, but there are at least five distinctive themes, which recur in irregular sequence. Some of them eventually combine in pairs, to the great enriching of the texture and to the building up of a highly effective climax.

* * * *

The 'Programme' which Weber is reported by his biographer, Sir Julius Benedict, to have had in mind when composing the Fourth Sonata in E minor, op. 70, is as follows. It tells of an unhappy sufferer who passes through various stages of mental disturbance, from acute depression, by way of rage and insanity, to exhaustion and death. The musical outcome of this melancholy tale is, however, far from oppressive in character. The first movement is by no means unrelievedly sombre, while the Minuet-and-Trio are alternately bracing and hypnotically enchanting. The 'andante quasi allegretto, consolente', which is intended to portray the temporary alleviation of the sufferer's distress by the sympathetic ministrations of his friends, is only occasionally interrupted by stormy outbursts. The inspiriting rhythms of the Finale go far to counterbalance the feeling of inescapable torment suggested by the feverish repetitions of the thematic material.

The first movement is built almost exclusively upon two contrasting ideas which may well be termed motto themes. They are a descending passage that constitutes the most distinctive feature of both the first and the second subjects, and an agitated passage in ascending semiquavers that first appears in the transition. The latter plays a prominent part in the development and recapitulation sections and finally supplies the purling accompaniment to the descending scale theme as it gradually falls to silence in the coda.

The tonality of E minor and major respectively for the Minuet-and-Trio, the syncopations and crisp texture of the Minuet recall the corresponding movements of the First Sonata. The Trio, 'leggiermente murmurando', is unlike those of the other sonatas either in texture or in character. A repetitive pattern of pianissimo quavers, which seldom leaves the centre of the keyboard, floats so lightly above a waltz-like accompaniment that the individual notes form a web of delicate sounds. Eventually the pattern is worked up into a long crescendo and diminuendo, but no sooner is the pianissimo reinstated than the precipitate crotchets of the Minuet return to dash the murmuring quavers brusquely from their path.

The third movement, Andante, bears the distinguishing marks of a rondo: a recurrent refrain (sometimes varied) and episodes in contrasting keys. In actual construction, however, the movement is a mosaic into which every unit of the musical material is deftly fitted to form a convincing design. The refrain is of the same simple folk-tune character as are the themes upon which Weber's other slow movements are based; a type of melody which is hardly to be found in Beethoven's sonatas but which often occurs in those by Schubert, Schumann, and Brahms.

The Prestissimo of the Fourth Sonata, entitled *La Tarantella* and also known as *Jet d'eau*, is the only one of Weber's finales in the minor mode, and the only one, too, in which the majority of the themes are in dotted rhythms. It is dominated by the opening phrase, whose strongly-marked triplet figure and dotted notes recur again and again in each single strand of a texture so fine-drawn that every melodic fragment stands out in relief.

*   *   *   *

Weber's sonatas occupy a midway position between the classical and the romantic. They combine something of the rhythmic urge of Beethoven's with the virtuosity of Clementi's and Dussek's and the lyricism of Schubert's. They anticipate to no small degree the vivid colouring of Schumann's, the sensuousness of Chopin's and the rhetoric of Liszt's. To play them is to be transported to a glowing world of sound, in which immediacy of expression counts for more than formal balance and the systematic development of thematic material.

*   *   *   *

Weber began to write his First Sonata when he was twenty-six, and he spread the composition of the series of four over a period of ten years.

Schubert compressed the writing of twenty-one sonatas into the space of thirteen years. He designed many on an altogether smaller scale than Weber's and he left a number in various stages of incompleteness. Nevertheless, Schubert's sonatas stand in the centre of his production for the piano. He composed the first when he was eighteen and the last in the year of his death at the age of thirty-one. The whole series consequently displays the growth of his pianistic style from early to late in his career.

Among the earliest sonatas, a few in three movements begin in one key and end in another, as though Schubert could not decide upon a satisfactory type of finale to complete each work. These, and the several unfinished fragments, reveal that he did not arrive easily at the style of sonata-writing which he cultivated during his last years. Had he lived longer, he would very likely have developed it in fresh directions, for every one of his most important sonatas differs from its predecessor in some essential aspect of form or style.

Few pianists know or play all the Schubert sonatas. The earlier ones are not altogether easy to obtain; the unfinished fragments, which are even more difficult to acquire, are of interest only to the historian. Among the eleven which in the course of time have come to be considered the most valuable and which are readily obtainable, few appear regularly in recital programmes. Disparity in musical value between the individual movements of some of the sonatas may be one reason for the infrequent performance of these works in public. Another, the composer's preoccupation with the thematic content at the expense of its presentation in terms of grateful piano writing.

Unlike Weber, Schubert was not a virtuoso of the piano, nor was he equipped with a powerful technique as was Beethoven. His hands were small. He could not easily play heavy chordal passages or extended stretches, but his fingers could run swiftly and lightly over the keys and his exquisitely sympathetic touch made him an incomparable accompanist. These attributes as an executant, together with his superlative genius as a composer of songs, were largely responsible for his writing a kind of piano music which seldom indulges in brilliant and effective passage-work. Wealth of melody, profoundly interesting harmonies and compelling rhythms are its most distinctive features. While it is technically less difficult to perform than Beethoven's or Weber's, it calls for particularly sympathetic understanding if it is to yield its deepest secrets to the performer.

*   *   *   *

When playing Beethoven's sonatas we are constantly aware of the compelling personality behind the music. We recognize the fineness of the balance maintained between the several component parts of each movement and between the individual movements of each sonata and we realize that we are following the workings of the mind of a great symphonist. When we play the Schubert sonatas we are more often led to think of the inspired song-writer and the composer of Impromptus and *Moments musicaux* than we are of a born symphonist. Whereas Beethoven treated his musical ideas with extreme economy and evolved large-scale movements from slender material, Schubert was leisurely and discursive. In some movements he repeated or elaborated a few themes as if he could hardly bear to part from them; in others, he filled the musical structure to overflowing with melody after melody. His sonatas are lyrical rather than dramatic, but that is not to say that they are ineffective in performance or that they do not repay study in respect of their architecture and workmanship quite apart from their deeply expressive qualities. As the basis for studying them here, the eleven best-known and most easily-available sonatas must suffice: the ten included in the standard practical editions, and the 'Fantasy or Sonata' in G major, op. 78. This latter work was first published as 'Fantasy, Andante, Menuetto and Allegro', an ambiguous title that led to its being classified as a Fantasy and printed in the same volume as the 'Wanderer' Fantasy. It is, however, essentially a sonata, of the same large dimensions as the composer's last three sonatas, op. posth.

Although this necessarily incomplete collection leaves out of account the sonatas that Schubert wrote in earlier years, it is truly representative of his sonata-production in general. While his style in composing sonatas deepened immeasurably, it did not change fundamentally. The difference between his very first sonata, the slight but expressive E major (1815) and his last, the magnificent Sonata in B flat major (1828), is one of degree rather than of kind. For this reason we shall find it simpler to consider the sonatas as a whole series instead of in groups according to periods as we did when studying Beethoven's. The eleven will first be enumerated in the order in which they were written and a short survey will be made of Schubert's methods of planning whole sonatas and designing single movements. Thereafter we shall explore one complete sonata, comparing its movements with those of the other sonatas which exemplify similar distinctive features in different fashion. In this way we shall have opportunities of becoming acquainted with each of the eleven sonatas in respect either of its structural features, its expressive style or of points which are specially interesting to pianists.

The opus-numbers of Schubert's works, some of which were affixed indiscriminately by his publishers, do not represent the date-order in which they were written. As, however, they form the most practical means of identification they have remained in general use, deceptive though they are.

*   *   *   *

The earliest in date of the eleven sonatas of the present study is the Sonata in A minor, op. 164, in three movements, composed in 1817 when Schubert was twenty. During that year he composed six sonatas, two of which he left unfinished. Only two of the others are included in the practical editions: the sonatas in E flat major, op. 122 and in B major, op. 147, each in four movements. A long period was to elapse before he completed another whole sonata, the 'little' A major, op. 120, in three movements in 1819. This in turn was separated by nearly four years from the next sonata, the A minor, op. 143, composed in 1823, also in three movements. Thenceforward Schubert wrote *all* his piano sonatas in four movements, with an increasingly sure hand and with a greatly enlarged conception of the sonata as an art-form. The sonatas in A minor, op. 42, and D major followed in 1825, the 'Fantasy or Sonata' in G major in 1826. And then in 1828, the year that saw the composition of his 'Great' Symphony in C major, the Mass in E flat, the String Quintet in C, the so-called 'Swan-song' collection of songs, and many other works, he wrote his three greatest sonatas. The C minor, the A major, and the B flat major (opp. posth.) were composed in the incredibly short space of one month, only a few weeks before he died.

*   *   *   *

Schubert was twenty-seven years younger than Beethoven. For this reason alone it might be expected that he would have manifested stronger leanings towards romanticism than did his senior. Yet although his sonatas are no less romantic in colouring and expression than are Beethoven's, they are more classical in structural principles. Beethoven's innovations in the planning of whole sonatas seem to have exerted no perceptible influence upon Schubert's own style of musical architecture. For whereas Beethoven occasionally chose a less usual type of form for the first movement: a set of variations or a 'tempo d'un minuetto', Schubert never deviated from using sonata form. While Beethoven sometimes joined two or more movements together, as in the 'Appassionata', the 'Lebewohl' and others, and while he once composed a whole sonata (op. 27, no. 1) in an almost unbroken sweep, Schubert wrote every movement throughout his twenty-one sonatas as a separate unit.

Unlike Beethoven, and Haydn, too, Schubert composed no sonatas in two movements. The early work in E minor (1817), printed in some editions in only two movements, actually comprises three if not four movements and has only recently been published in full. In the eight completed four-movement sonatas he invariably placed the Minuet-(or Scherzo-)and-Trio as the third movement, whereas Beethoven several times placed it as the second. (In op. 27, no, 1. op. 31, no. 3, and in opp. 101, 106, and 110.) In Schubert's solitary five-movement sonata, known as *Fünf Klavierstücke* (1816), the scherzo-and-trio comes fourth in the scheme. He designed only one movement as a set of variations, the 'andante poco mosso' of the Sonata in A minor, op. 42. But like Beethoven, he frequently submitted his thematic material to variation, especially in the recurrent sections of rondos, notably in the Adagio of the Sonata in C minor and in the 'con moto' of the D major. He used the same treatment in movements in ternary form, such as the Andante of the Sonata in B major. Although he was a highly experienced contrapuntist he hardly ever combined the elements of fugal construction with those of sonata form as did Beethoven. Instead, he wrote numberless passages, as it were subconsciously, in an enchantingly fluent kind of double counterpoint. We shall look more closely into the subject of Schubert's piano writing later, but first we must consider a few points in connexion with the architecture of the sonatas.

*   *   *   *

Schubert composed nearly all his sonata movements in traditional forms, often modifying them to suit his highly individual style of presenting his musical ideas. In sonata-form movements,

E

for instance, he often elaborated the thematic substance so copiously in the exposition that it could hardly stand further working-out. The development-section had consequently to assume the function of a contrasting episode of entirely, or almost entirely fresh material. He occasionally opened the second subject-group irregularly in an unrelated key before letting it swing round into the accustomed tonality. For example, in the exposition of the 'molto moderato' of the B flat major Sonata, the second subject begins in F sharp minor, and in the recapitulation, in B minor: the enharmonic keys of the flattened sub-mediant and the flattened super-tonic respectively. In a few movements to be referred to later, he opened the recapitulation in the key of the sub-dominant instead of in the tonic. In others, he intensified the effectiveness of this part of the movement by presenting the subject-matter in a succession of keys, thus creating a feeling of growing excitement. In the Moderato of the Sonata in A minor, op. 42, the original tonality and mode are not re-established beyond a doubt until a tonic-and-dominant coda decides the issue with resounding finality.

Sometimes Schubert varied the succession of the thematic units at their second appearance. One of countless examples occurs in the 'andante molto' of the Sonata in E flat major. In this romantically-coloured movement in modified sonata form he excluded the passage of transition (bars 20-26) from the recapitulation but held it in reserve to make a more telling effect in the coda.

Schubert imparted a strong feeling of homogeneity to some of the movements by maintaining similar types of figuration or persistent rhythm throughout their course. The long Finales of the Sonatas in A minor, op. 42, and in C minor, and the much shorter, sonata-form Finale of the B major Sonata convincingly illustrate this point. An intensely poetic example of the same kind of treatment applied to the individual sections of a movement in ternary form is comprised in the second movement of the B flat major Sonata, the 'andante sostenuto' in C sharp minor. The accompanying figure in the left hand (♪ 𝄾 ♫♩ 𝄾) is repeated in all except nine bars of the entire opening section,

and again, slightly varied (♪♫♪ ♪ ♩♫) in all but three bars
of the final section. The flow of twelve or eighteen semiquavers
in a bar in either one hand or the other during the central
episode is never for a moment interrupted. This movement and
the Andantino in F sharp minor of the Sonata in A major, op.
posth., are tone-poems which recall the most expressive of the
composer's Impromptus.

For the slow movements or finales of his sonatas from the first
to the last, Schubert employed both older and modern rondo
form. A rarely-used type that he made particularly his own was
a long rondo in which the two episodes are alike in thematic
content but not in key, and in which there is no development-
section as there is in modern rondo form. In a few of his later
sonatas he found its ample proportions, which conduce to a
sense of great spaciousness, ideal for slow movements. The 'con
moto' of the D major Sonata, the Andante of the G major, and
the Adagio of the C minor are among the most sublimely restful
he ever wrote.

*　　*　　*　　*

The Sonata in A minor, op. 164 (1817), in three movements,
is the one we shall explore in detail. It may be considered
typical of Schubert's sonata-writing in that it includes two
movements in traditional forms treated in a strongly individual
manner, and a third in a form of his own devising. Each movement displays characteristic features of his style. The opening
'allegro, ma non troppo' shows his fondness for the repetition,
either exact or sequential, of short figures and whole phrases. It
also provides a concrete instance of his tendency, already
mentioned, to 'develop' the subject-matter prematurely in the
exposition. The reiteration of the dotted figure of the principal
subject and the varied repetition of the first phrase of the second
subject-group serve to focus so much attention upon this
thematic material as to necessitate its exclusion from the
development-section. In this part of the movement a paragraph
of new material in a fresh key is the salient point.

The movement also exemplifies a procedure the composer
favoured on several occasions: the opening of the recapitulation

in the key of the sub-dominant. He had already employed it in the two sonatas preceding the A minor, and he was to resort to it again in the first movement of the B major Sonata and the Finale of the 'little' A major, op. 120. In the movement under discussion, as also in the Finale just mentioned, he restored the balance by re-introducing the principal subject in its native key in the coda. Another distinctive Schubertian touch, several times exemplified in the Allegro of the A minor Sonata, is the occasional insertion of a bar's rest as if to call the listener's attention to the coming announcement of a fresh theme or an unexpected change of key.

This first movement also gives a preliminary idea of Schubert's unrivalled powers of modulation and of his partiality for introducing a series of chromatic harmonies into a predominantly diatonic context. During the exposition, transient modulations to distantly-related keys diversify the tonal colour-scheme, and the main episode in the development-section opens in the far-away key of A flat major.

Few, indeed, are the movements that contain no striking modulations. The music either slips in and out of keys with lightning rapidity, notably in the Finale of the B major Sonata; or it proceeds gradually from one key to another by way of a rainbow of chromaticisms. Throughout the whole twenty-one sonatas there is no more remarkable modulatory passage than the long and breath-taking series of swiftly-changing chromatic harmonies that fills the central part of the development-section of the 'molto moderato' of the Sonata in B flat major and leads with miraculous inevitability into a stretch of comparatively stable tonality.

Returning to the discussion of the A minor Sonata we find that the second movement, 'allegretto quasi andantino' in E major, composed in older rondo form, is typically Schubertian in many respects. Among them are the following. The vocal quality of the air of the refrain and the gently ambling staccato bass over which it is poised; the choice of distantly-related keys: C major and D minor respectively for the two episodes and F major for the first restatement of the refrain; the variation of the refrain each time it recurs; the graceful curves of the melody as well as the reiteration of its component figures; the expressive left-hand accompaniment and the leisureliness of the modulatory link to the final section. The movement exemplifies Schubert's unparalleled gift for incorporating an artless, song-like melody within an intricate musical structure. Another more highly-developed example of the same procedure occurs in the long Finale of the A major Sonata, op. posth., written eleven years later; likewise an Allegretto, but in *modern* rondo form. These two movements are closely connected. The refrain of the one is a variant of that of the other, but the later movement affords an even more striking instance of the integration of the melodically simple and the structurally complex.

The Finale, 'allegro vivace', of the A minor Sonata, op. 164, stands alone among the movements of Schubert's piano sonatas although it has parallels in the second and last movements of the 'Trout' Quintet. It is cast in an entirely individual mould and cannot be assigned to any definable class, even though it possesses some of the attributes of modified sonata form and of rondo. It falls into two main divisions, each made of similar material. The second is merely a reflection of the first, which is seen from a fresh angle by being transposed into a different set of keys. The appearance of the introductory paragraph for a third time to form the coda suggests the planning of the whole as a rondo.

*   *   *   *

Other sonata movements for which Schubert evolved individual types of form include the Finale, 'allegro vivace', of the Sonata in A minor, op. 143 (1823), the Andante of the same work, and the Andante of the A major Sonata, op. 120 (1819). The Finale of op. 143 shares with the movement just described the distinction of being composed in repetitive panels; this time three instead of two. The panels themselves are threefold in construction. Each comprises a whirling introduction in triplet quavers, a passage of transition in crisp chords and quick runs, and an episode in lilting dance rhythm. Fundamentally, the panels are similar, but each differs in some way from the others.

The introduction always *begins* in the tonic, but at its second
appearance suddenly flies off at a tangent into a fresh key. The
episode in dance rhythm appears each time in a different key.
The passage of transition is omitted from the last panel but is
reinstated to form a link between the episode and the coda, in
which the triplet quavers return in double octaves to whirl the
movement to its close. More telling even than the originality of
construction is the pervasive sense of urgency and continuity
and the marked contrast between the pianistic styles of the
three species of thematic material. The first two are almost
Beethovenian in intensity of expression. The third represents
the Schubert of the *Valses sentimentales* composed the same year.

The two deeply expressive Andantes mentioned at the beginning of the last paragraph are the very antithesis of the two
Allegros just described, both in conception and in musical substance. The tranquil course of the Andante (in D major) of the
Sonata in A major, op. 120, seems to be predetermined by the
restricted thematic substance of which it is composed. Melodically, the distinguishing feature is the interval of a falling second
which opens every phrase. Rhythmically, it is a pattern of
beats, one crotchet and four quavers in a bar (♩ ♫♫), which
recurs in either the right-hand or the left-hand part in thirty-
nine of the seventy-five bars and is implied in sixteen others.
The piece is virtually monothematic and mono-rhythmic, and
harmonically it seldom ventures beyond the confines of nearly-
related keys. In range of expression, however, it is anything but
monotonous.

The melodic outline and the piano writing of this Andante
in D major are essentially instrumental in style. Those of the
Andante (in F major) of the Sonata in A minor, op. 143, pertain
to the sphere of the song. This last-named movement is written
in the style of an arrangement of a song for piano solo. The
quietly expansive voice-part is entrusted first to the right hand
in octaves over a sparse chordal bass, and, after a brief but
passionate interlude, to the left hand in the centre of the keyboard between supporting harmonies and a canopy of triplet
quavers far above. For the opening phrase of the melody,

which finally reappears to round off the movement, Schubert
borrowed the last few bars of his song 'An den Mond' (To the
moon) (Schreiber) composed five years earlier. The little
serpentine figure, which is inserted pianissimo between every
phrase of the melody and which eventually detaches itself to
become an independent episode, is entirely new. The piano
writing throughout this deeply expressive piece of music is
imaginative. It possesses an ethereal quality in the passages
where the texture is widely spaced and pianissimo trills vibrate
in the upper reaches of the treble.

*   *   *   *

The player of the Schubert sonatas who is acquainted with
the composer's songs is frequently reminded of their supremely
beautiful piano accompaniments. Pieces such as the Andante of
the B major Sonata, the first movement of the 'little' A major,
op. 120, and the Andante of the G major Fantasy contain pages
of the kind of music of which many Schubert songs are made.
Two extreme instances are the second episode (in G major) of
the rondo Finale of the Sonata in D major, and the central
section (in A major) of the 'andante sostenuto' in the B flat
major Sonata. With their continuous streams of melody and
ceaseless accompanying figures they might well be transcriptions
for piano solo of typical Schubert songs. Sometimes a strong
rhythmic likeness may be traced between a sonata movement
and a specific song. The 'con moto' of the D major Sonata is
distinguished by the recurrent figure ($\frac{3}{4}$ ♩. ♫♪ |♩. ♫♪)
which, together with the rich chromatic harmonies, brings the
movement into close relationship with the song 'Fülle der Liebe'
(Abundance of love) (F. Schlegel) which Schubert composed
the same year (1825).

*   *   *   *

In studying even these few movements we have already found
that the vocal style of much of the thematic material is one of
the most distinctive features of Schubert's sonatas. Another,
equally distinctive feature is their invasion by the rhythms of
the dance. In movement after movement, whether in quick or

slow tempo, in the major or the minor, in triple or in quadruple time, dance measures are immanent. They often determine the character of the second subject-group in a sonata-form movement and cause this thematic material to stand in acute contrast to the principal subject. In the 'molto moderato e cantabile' of the G major 'Fantasy or Sonata' the mysteriously hushed opening is followed by a long section in unabashed waltz rhythm. In the Sonata in E flat, nearly the whole of the extensive second subject-group of the opening Allegro is written in the style of dance music. The Finale of this work, also in sonata form, preserves the spirit of the dance throughout its more than two hundred bars in 6/8 time, and although the beginning and ending of the Minuet are almost Mozartian in their classical preciseness, the series of dotted beats in the central section lends it a pastoral air. The Trio is unfeignedly a 'ländler', a type of national dance that Schubert had been accustomed to writing from boyhood, either as separate short pieces or in groups.

In all but one of the eight minuet- (or scherzo-) and-trio movements which come within our purview, the lilting rhythm of the trio evokes the ländler or the waltz and the music could well serve as an accompaniment to dancing. In this respect the little pieces are unlike those in the Beethoven sonatas. They bear a resemblance to some of Haydn's and to that of Weber's Fourth Sonata in E minor, though none of Schubert's is so large in dimensions as the last-named. The Trio of the Sonata in D major differs from all the others by being composed in an almost unbroken succession of semi-staccato chords in both hands. They lessen the rhythmic plasticity of the movement but lend it a distinctive and romantic tone-colour.

The minuets, three in number, are mutually very different in style and mood. That of the E flat Sonata is the only one in which the style and the tempo (Allegretto) conform to the older, more stately type. The Allegro of the C minor is restless in gait and the 'allegro moderato' of the 'Fantasy or Sonata' in G major moves briskly, like a scherzo.

Contrarily enough, one of the five scherzos, that of the Sonata in B major, is marked Allegretto, but its lightly-tripping metre sets it apart from the more dignified Allegretto in E flat. The other four scherzos are all marked 'allegro vivace'. Those of the Sonatas in A minor, op. 42 and D major make an impression of vigour by their respective syncopations and sforzandos. The former is alternately explosive and equable in temper; it possesses no definite characteristics of the dance although the Trio is ländler from the first note to the last. The latter swings robustly along in a series of phrases in dotted beats punctuated by heavily accented chords.

The two remaining scherzos, those of the posthumous Sonatas in A major and B flat major, display in varying strength and different fashion the typical features of the waltz: two-bar rhythm and the persistence of one harmony throughout the bar. The variety in the piano figuration is greater in the A major than it is in the B flat major scherzo, but the latter movement, which seldom rises above a pianissimo, displays an elfin lightness of spirit unparalleled in all Schubert's sonatas. The Trio, the only one in the minor mode and the lowest of all in pitch, is tinged with a feeling of anxiety which is noticeably absent from all the others.

*   *   *   *

The musical style of the Schubert sonatas is more expansively tuneful than that of Beethoven's and the piano texture much less complex. Yet even in movements where the melodic outline claims the principal attention, the layout of the accompaniment, however simple, is seldom lacking in interest. The Finale of the Sonata in A major, op. posth., is a case in point. It witnesses to Schubert's skill in placing the melody in any part of the texture and in surrounding it with a never-failing variety of decorative figuration. The movement also shows the full use Schubert made of the whole compass of the keyboard. It contains no passage, however, in which the entire texture is placed so deep in pitch as it is at the ending of the Andantino of the same Sonata, nor as high as momentarily in the central section of that movement. The pre-eminently tuneful and expressive 'con moto' of the Sonata in D major remains more consistently in the centre of the keyboard, but the sensitive style of the piano writing and the great diversity of figuration lend the movement intense fascination for the player.

Schubert sometimes left very wide gaps between the parts for the two hands, as we noted when studying the Andante of op. 143. In the development-section of the first movement of this sonata they create a feeling of extreme attenuation during the ghostly pianissimo phrases in which the right hand breaks up the melody of the second subject into dotted beats while the left hand preserves the rhythmic pattern in chords. Wide gaps of this kind also impart an eerie character to the passage-work towards the end of the development-section of the Allegro of the Sonata in C minor. Entirely opposite in effect is the compact part-writing of the theme of the variations, 'andante, poco mosso', in the A minor Sonata, op. 42 and the close but luxuriant texture of most of the Andante of the Sonata in B major; a type of layout familiar in the composer's string quartets. A more florid kind of part-writing is maintained almost continuously throughout the Finale of the Sonata in E flat major.

In striking contrast is the decorative, supremely instrumental style which sometimes characterizes whole movements or portions of movements, such as the dashing Finale of the Sonata in C minor with its never-flagging rhythm, swirling scale-passages and cross-hand leaps; the development-section in quasi-Hungarian style in the Allegro of the Sonata in A major, op. posth. and the weirdly impressionistic central episode of the Andantino of the same work. In both the two last-named, the exotic colouring and rhapsodic style bring the movements into close relationship with the composer's Impromptus and *Moments musicaux*. At the other extreme are the short pianissimo phrases in tenuous plain octaves or single lines which seem to express some of Schubert's deepest thoughts: the openings of the two Sonatas in A minor, opp. 42 and 143; the interpolations in the Andante of the latter, and the descending scale and long low trill in the Allegro of the Sonata in B flat major. In all of these there is an infinitude of meaning.

5

The Sonata
(4)

Brief survey of post-classical sonatas from Clementi to Grieg.
Sonatas by individual composers; Clementi, Mendelssohn,
Chopin, Schumann, Brahms, Liszt, Tchaikovsky, Grieg.

AFTER Schubert's death in 1828 the piano sonata was no longer to maintain the central position it had occupied for so many years in the output of serious composers, nor was it to preserve its original characteristics as a framework for the expression of abstract ideas. Beethoven had already greatly enlarged its structure and intensified its expressive possibilities. Weber had imparted to it some of the attributes of operatic composition. Both had also enhanced its purely pianistic qualities and Schubert had made it more intimately lyrical. In the hands of their successors it was first to undergo further modification and then to suffer neglect. Where the classical composers had counted their sonatas in tens, the romantic and neo-classical composers were to count theirs in units, but their smaller piano pieces in legions.

The Romantic period, which is reckoned as dating from about 1830 to 1900, was preceded by a period of transition during which classical composers were becoming more closely drawn to romantic ideals, and the coming romantic composers were still under the influence of classical principles. Beethoven had composed his one programme sonata, the 'Lebewohl', in 1811. In 1821, Clementi, who had produced a long series of predominantly classical sonatas from 1770 onwards and who was then in his seventieth year, published his last five works in this category. Two of them, which were far from being regular in form and which contained connecting movements, were issued as Caprices. Another, the third Sonata of op. 50, bore the title *Didone abbandonata; scena tragica*, for which reason it may be considered as definitely romantic in intention.

In the same year (1821), a boy of twelve, who was later to win renown as a romantic composer, completed a Sonata in G minor whose opening and closing movements showed a strong affinity with Clementi's earlier style, but whose mellifluous central Adagio unmistakably prefigured the Songs without Words which the composer came to write far more naturally than he ever did sonatas. Six years later, a Polish youth of seventeen produced as his op. 4 a Sonata in C minor in which the treatment of classical form, unconventional though it was, foretold nothing of the power and the originality of conception he was to display about ten years later in the 'Funeral March' Sonata in B flat minor. Only the sensitive piano writing revealed the future poet of the keyboard.

*   *   *   *

Mendelssohn wrote three sonatas early in his career and then turned to other forms of piano composition which were more congenial to him. His last sonata and Chopin's first coincided in date (1827) and both are now equally forgotten by the practising pianist; the one because it is faded in style, the other, because it is immature. The piano sonatas written by the principal composers during the next few decades, however, have not only survived. Some of them have become indispensable to recitalists and have won the affection of amateurs. Schumann's three were composed during the 1830s, as were the two other large-scale works he conceived as sonatas but published under different titles: the Fantasy in C, op. 17 and *Faschingsschwank aus Wien*, op. 26. In 1837 came Liszt's 'Dante' Sonata. The same year saw the completion of the Funeral March that was to become the third movement of Chopin's Sonata in B flat minor; the other movements were composed in 1839. Chopin wrote his third and last Sonata in B minor in 1847. When Liszt had written his Sonata in B minor a few years later, the sonata-production of this generation of composers, all of whom were born between 1809 and 1811, came to an end.

A composer of the younger generation stepped temporarily into the breach. The young Johannes Brahms, born in 1833, wrote three sonatas in quick succession during 1852 and 1853, but then eschewed the composition of piano sonatas for the remainder of his life. Not until 1865 was the species continued in varying styles by two composers from countries with musical traditions very different from those of their sonata-writing predecessors. Grieg, who was twenty-two when he painstakingly wrote his Sonata in E minor, op. 7, did not pursue this type of piano solo composition any further. Tchaikovsky, who wrote a Sonata in C sharp minor the year he left the St. Petersburg Conservatoire at the age of twenty-five, returned once more to the fray thirteen years later with the Sonata in G major, op. 37. Both these works of his have disappeared from the average performer's repertory and from publishers' catalogues in this country. The Grieg Sonata, however, has never lost its charm for the amateur pianist, although recitalists do not consider it sufficiently solid fare for public performance.

*   *   *   *

The sonatas of the post-classical period are so widely contrasted in style that it will be easier to consider those of each composer in turn than to group them for study according to their dates of composition. For instance, Mendelssohn's Sonata in G minor and Clementi's *Didone abbandonata* Sonata, which both date from 1821, have little in common beyond being in the same key and in three movements each. As for Brahms's Sonata in F minor and Liszt's in B minor, a more irreconcilable difference between two works ostensibly in the same category and written in the same year (1853) can hardly be imagined.

*   *   *   *

Clementi, the senior composer of the period under review, did not break fresh ground as regards structure when he wrote *Didone abbandonata* (1821). The form is no more irregular than that of Beethoven's 'Lebewohl' Sonata (1811); in fact, it is rather less advanced than that of Clementi's own Sonata in B minor composed in 1804. In the last-named work, which is in two movements, not only is the first, 'allegro con fuoco', preceded by a long Adagio introduction. The second movement, also an Allegro, is preluded by a short Largo section, the languorous central phrase of which becomes the energetic principal subject of the ensuing Allegro. The other thematic material of the Largo is re-introduced in its original tempo as an interlude before the presto coda.

It is chiefly the greater expressive power and the passionately earnest mood of *Didone* which distinguish it from Clementi's other sonatas. That he was carried away by enthusiasm for his tragic subject is implicit in his choice of the same dark key (G minor) for *all* the movements; by his complete renunciation of virtuoso passages and by the graphic performing-directions ranging in intensity from 'languente' to 'con furia'. The 'introduzione largo patetico' is heavy with foreboding. The two Allegro movements, 'diliberando e meditando' and 'con disperazione' are filled with agitated reiterations of the thematic content. The 'adagio dolente' leading into the Finale is a continuous, almost improvisatory intermezzo, conceived in very different style from the slow movement in cut-and-dried ternary form of the first sonata of the same opus (50). Clementi, whose style of writing for the piano was often more effective than was Beethoven's, did not always succeed in subordinating technical means to artistic ends. While Beethoven's expressive canonic imitations of the 'horn' theme in the 'Lebewohl' Sonata add picturesque touches of colour, Clementi's ingenious strict canons in *Didone* sound academic and out of place in their dramatic context.

Other nineteenth-century composers wrote programme sonatas for the piano. Among them were Karl Loewe of ballad fame and our own Sterndale Bennett. Neither holds a key position in musical history as does the 'Father of the Piano'. The sonatas of both have been doomed to obscurity, whereas many of Clementi's are still current 'classics'.

*   *   *   *

Although Mendelssohn's sonatas are less generally familiar than are many of his other piano pieces, they are by no means lacking in interest for musicians. For one thing, they are among his earliest published works. He wrote all of them between the ages of twelve and eighteen and they reflect both his precocity and the remarkable maturing of his style during the years that separate the first one from the last two. For another, they show uncommon features of construction and they contain stretches of lively, imaginative piano writing. Characteristically enough, it is in the scherzos that the composer reveals himself at his most likeable. In their fairy lightness of touch they approach the magic of the Overture to *A Midsummer-night's Dream* written at the same period.

The two outer movements of the first Sonata in G minor are conceived in the style of the eighteenth rather than the nineteenth century, structurally as well as pianistically. They would hardly sound inappropriate on the harpsichord. The first movement is short and sectional; both halves are marked to be repeated and there is a separate coda. As in some of Haydn's sonata movements, the chief theme of the second subject-group is practically identical with the principal subject, except that it is in the relative major. Mendelssohn made such strenuous use of its most characteristic figure that the movement tends to sound wearisome. The spirited presto Finale, also in precise sonata form but with a contrasting second subject, consists of a nearly unbroken succession of two-bar phrases, the monotony of which is occasionally relieved by deft cross-hand passages.

It is the slow movement, Adagio in E flat major, that displays the composer's later well-known lyrical style and his ingenuity in arranging his subject-matter. The piece falls into three main divisions, each shorter than its predecessor, roughly as follows. The first division, which is made up of five thematic units, ends in the key of the dominant; the second works gradually back to the tonic, using only three of the units, abbreviated and in fresh keys; the third is simply a partial restatement in the tonic of the opening phrases. The whole is an interesting cross between ternary form and the simplest kind of sonata form. It stands in effective contrast to the other movements in which the structural outlines are notably clear-cut.

* * * *

The Sonata bears a late opus number (105) because it was not published until after Mendelssohn's death. While it is only natural that the composer should have declined to print this boyish work during his lifetime, his witholding of the third Sonata in B flat, op. 106 (1827), from publication is less understandable. The work is of much the same calibre as the E major Sonata, op. 6 (1826), which he thought fit to publish at the time it was written.

Each of these two sonatas is in four movements with interconnexions between the movements. In this respect the works show Beethovenian influence, though in actual pianistic style they are far closer to Weber's sonatas than to Beethoven's. The Sonata in E major is a continuous whole. The first movement, an easy-going Allegretto in 6/8 time in sonata form, is straightway followed by a 'tempo di minuetto' in F sharp minor, 'staccato e leggiero' with a legato Trio in D minor, 'più vivace'; a pair of movements displaying all the accustomed sprightliness of a scherzo. Instead of the conventional slow movement, a twice-repeated panel, consisting of a stretch of recitative-like 'adagio e senza tempo' in fluid tonality, a single chordal phrase, andante and a section of passage-work, allegretto, leads into the Finale. This last movement, 'molto allegro' in E major runs its headlong course until rounded off unexpectedly with the opening phrase and codetta of the first movement. Pianistically, one of the most striking features in the whole work occurs in the miniature development-section of the first movement. The attempted statements of the principal subject are interrupted by the mocking goblin laughter conjured up by low staccato octaves played by the left hand. It is a passage that finds a counterpart in mood in Brahms's early Ballade in B minor, op. 10, no. 3.

Mendelssohn's Sonata in B flat is less continuous than the one in E major. Only the third and fourth movements are actually linked together, but the passage that joins them contains a reference to the principal subject of the first movement. A portion of the second (Scherzo) is interpolated and developed in the Finale, giving an effect of unity which is, however, more artificial than organic. The rushing passages appended to the third movement, a placid 'barcarolle' in the remote key of E major, merely for the purpose of attaching it to the Finale, sound incongruous in this context. The interruption of this last movement by an excerpt from the imaginative, light-footed Scherzo only serves to emphasize the purely bravura quality of the surrounding passage-work.

The most interesting piano writing in the sonata occurs in the Scherzo. The wide gaps in the layout of staccato semiquavers cause some piquant sound-effects, particularly in bars 14 and 15, and in the parallel passage later, where the right hand's high G flat and the left hand's low F natural produce a bizarre semitonal clash across the intervening distance of four octaves. The composer's indication pianissimo for the playing of almost the whole of this movement and of many virtuoso passages in the first and last movements, adds immensely to the effectiveness of the music.

Mendelssohn's own performing technique was distinguished by great fluency and extreme lightness of touch. His flexible hands were not unusually proportioned as were Weber's; his writing for the piano is consequently less exacting to the performer. The piano of his time had not as yet attained any great resonance in the lower octaves, so the passages he wrote to be played in the depths of the keyboard can hardly have sounded confused, as they are apt to do on the full-toned instrument of to-day.

Brilliant pianist though he was, Mendelssohn did not give the deepest expression to his musical ideas in his compositions for the piano. The writing of orchestral, choral and concerted instrumental music exerted stronger claims upon his interest. It was in these spheres that he achieved his finest work.

*   *   *   *

F

To Chopin, the piano was the be-all and end-all of his existence. He found it nearly impossible to conceive music in any other terms than in those of the keyboard, and he spent his whole life in exploring its possibilities and evolving new and original methods of writing for it. His manner of playing was as distinctive as was his style in composing. No one could equal him in the interpretation of his music. During his lifetime he acquired almost legendary fame as a performer of his own works; since his death his compositions have come to be recognized as one of the treasures of the whole literature of piano music.

Despite the tremendous popularity of the 'Funeral March' Sonata in B flat minor Chopin's sonatas are not among his most representative works. He was seldom at his happiest in pouring ideas into traditional moulds. In writing large-scale works he preferred to invent new forms, such as the 'ballade' and the 'polonaise-fantasy'. The first Sonata in C minor, op. 4, for which he did not succeed in finding a publisher at the time of its composition and which was first printed after his death, is never performed in public. Yet it cannot justifiably be passed over by anyone who is interested in studying the growth of this composer's style. The intrinsic musical worth of the Sonata may be extremely slight. As an example of Chopin's youthful production and as a record of his standard of performing-technique at the age of seventeen, op. 4 is historically valuable. It gains in interest, too, if it is studied side by side with the two sonatas of the composer's maturity, with which it has several points in common: its composition in the minor mode, and the arrangement of the four movements in similar order, with the minuet-and-trio or scherzo as the second movement and the slow movement as the third.

*   *   *   *

Unlike the opening movements of the Sonatas in B flat minor and B minor, in which the clear outline of the rich thematic content and the definite key-changes at focal points cannot be missed by even the most inattentive listener, the 'allegro maestoso' of the C minor Sonata is sparse in subject-matter and indeterminate in key-relationships. The short chromatic curve which is the characteristic feature of the opening paragraph and virtually the motto theme of the whole movement is practically the only fragment of melody that the ear can readily seize. A second subject can hardly be detected, for during the whole movement, although short-term modulations occur by the hundred, there is little fundamental or abiding change of key. Moreover, the resulting monotony is increased by the lack of rhythmic variety. Two-bar rhythm prevails and there is little intermission in the pattern of eight quavers to the bar. Nevertheless, the movement is undeniably attractive on account of the interesting part-writing and the decoratively beautiful passage-work of which it largely consists. The pianistic layout bears the Chopin imprint from the opening phrase, which is placed in the most expressive register of the keyboard, to the last few bars, during which a chromatic scale descends from the high treble to meet a rising bass; a passage that faintly adumbrates the immeasurably more striking close of the Ballade in G minor.

Chopin's sonata-form movements are alike in the irregular opening of the recapitulation. In the Sonata in B flat minor this section starts with the second subject. In the B minor, the principal subject is shorn of its first sixteen bars, and in the C minor Sonata the opening phrase appears in the key of the flattened leading-note, a whole tone lower than at its already deep-pitched original statement.

*   *   *   *

Strangely enough, the second movements of the three sonatas begin, and two of them end, in the tonality of E flat, major and minor, and the key-signature of E flat major reappears in the Finale of the B minor Sonata. The choice of the key of the relative major for the Sonata in C minor and of that of the subdominant for the Sonata in B flat minor is in accordance with established practice. In the B minor Sonata, however, the signature of E flat does enharmonic duty for D sharp, the much

less usual key of the mediant major. The ending of the Scherzo
of the last-named Sonata on E flat and the beginning of the
succeeding Largo on D sharp may be interpreted as a subtle
justification of the unusual tonal procedure.

The so-called Minuet-and-Trio of the C minor Sonata is less
far removed in spirit than it is in dimensions from the scherzos
of the later sonatas. The sudden sforzandos on weak beats, the
coruscating triplet figures in double notes that flash up and
down in the Minuet and the waltz rhythm in the centre of the
Trio all go to impart a rhythmic vitality that is absent from the
preceding movement. Yet they hardly presage the terrific energy
of the main section of the Scherzo of the Sonata in B flat minor.
Nor are the broad expanses of melody in the 'più lento' interlude of the latter foreshadowed by the limited melodic curves of
the early Minuet-and-Trio. The Scherzo of the B flat minor
Sonata also differs in all except structure from that of the B
minor Sonata, whose self-repeating pattern of running quavers
and central section of furtively-moving inner melodies in crotchets and minims are the very reverse of the former's crisp
staccato octaves and cantabile accompanied melody.

The slow movement of the Sonata in C minor, Larghetto in
A flat major in 5/4 time, is the most individual in style of all the
movements in this youthful sonata. It is not conventional in
build as are its two famous successors in ternary form; the
music flows almost continuously throughout the forty-two bars.
The movement is vague in contour but it makes an impression
of unity by being opened, closed and twice punctuated by a
phrase containing an easily memorable harmonic progression:

The most distinctive feature of the Larghetto is the piano writing. The division of the beats into irregular groupings of notes, the occasional cross-bar rhythm, the delicate tracery of broken chords in the right hand and the flowing melodies in the left hand combine to intensify the atmosphere of languor already created by the unhurried quintuple metre.

It is in the rhythmic even more than in the structural aspect that the Larghetto differs so profoundly from the Funeral March of the Sonata in B flat minor, where the character of the music demands a steadily recurrent beat. A comparison of the last-named movement with the *Marcia funebre* of Beethoven's Sonata in A flat major, op. 26 reveals how differently the two composers conceived the respective central portions: Beethoven, as a short, dramatically explosive insertion with strong accentuation; Chopin, as a spacious interlude in which the heavy tread and muffled drums of the surrounding sections are entirely forgotten. In a Funeral March in C minor which he composed eight years earlier when he was nineteen, Chopin had differentiated the style of the two sections very little, apart from changes in mode and tonality.

The Largo of the Sonata in B minor also comprises two kinds of musical material, but they stand in much less acute contrast than do those of the Funeral March in B flat minor. The whole movement is serene in character. The cross-rhythm of the central episode is counter-balanced by liquescent figuration; the jagged edges of the dotted beats in the left-hand part throughout the opening section are ironed out, so to speak, into gentle curves during the shortened reprise.

Although a period of seventeen years elapsed between the composition of the first and the third Sonatas, Chopin designed the two presto Finales on similar lines. Each consists primarily of two long panels, the second displaying the copious original material in a fresh light, and each movement ends with a last statement of the opening subject and a coda. In the type and the treatment of the musical subject-matter and in the style of the piano writing the contrast between these two Finales is immeasurable. The short-breathed, frequently repeated phrases

and the monotonous figuration in quavers of the early movement in C minor are replaced in the B minor by subject-matter
that is rhythmically and melodically convincing, and by
superbly variegated pianistic texture. Yet the contrasts in the
conception and workmanship of the two movements so widely
separated in date are as nothing compared with the complete
antithesis in style that exists between their large dimensions,
intricately-woven fabric and virtuoso passages, and the masterly
conciseness of the movement in ghostly plain octaves that brings
the 'Funeral March' Sonata to its terrifying close. With this
darkling cloudscape of scurrying chromatic notes Chopin wrote
one of the most remarkable movements in the entire history of
the piano sonata, and at the same time, a tone-poem as compelling in effect as it is simple in the musical means it employs.

*   *   *   *

Chopin's powers as an executant were so phenomenal as not
only to determine the style of his own creative production but
to set an entirely new standard of performing-technique. Much
of his music is unmanageable by the average pianist on account
of its great technical difficulty.

Schumann's equipment as a performer was of a different
order. In his youth he was an excellent pianist. It was not until
he damaged his right hand at the age of twenty-two that he
renounced his intention of adopting the career of a virtuoso and
decided to devote himself to composition. At that time he had
already written the 'Abegg' Variations, *Papillons* and a few
other pieces. As he always composed at the piano, his now
decreased command of the keyboard might well have led him
to simplify his manner of writing for the instrument. On the
contrary. The style of his pianistic texture became progressively
more intricate, the chords more widely extended and the
passage-work more complex. For although Schumann could no
longer play his own compositions adequately, he could entrust
them to an incomparably finer executant: Clara Wieck, his
future wife, who was from girlhood the ideal interpreter and the
champion of his music. The exceptionally wide span of her

hands and her skill as a performer were responsible for many of
the technical difficulties in Schumann's piano music that have
ever since beset the inexpert player.

Like Chopin, Schumann did not find the writing of sonatas,
or of any works in established large-scale forms, wholly congenial. His musical ideas were of a kind that did not lend
themselves so well to development as they did to statement in
alternating paragraphs or to repetition in fresh guises. He
expressed himself at his most typical in successions of short
pieces such as *Papillons*, *Carnaval*, *Kinderscenen*, and *Davidsbündler*.

Before he began the composition of any of his three sonatas
Schumann made several attempts at writing movements in
sonata form. Only two of these survived to be printed as separate
pieces: the well-known Toccata in C major, op. 7 (1829, revised
1832) and the Allegro in B minor, op. 8 (1831). The composition
of the three published sonatas, all of which are in four movements, proceeded in desultory fashion.

The First Sonata in F sharp minor, op. 11 was begun in 1833,
when the opening movement was constructed out of a revised
version of an allegro Fandango which Schumann had written
the year before as a single piece. He prefaced it with an Adagio
introduction, incorporating a melodic fragment from it in the
ensuing 'allegro vivace'. The second movement, 'Aria', which
also contains a theme from the Adagio, was simply a transcription, in another key and with a few alterations, of a song, 'An
Anna' (To Anna), that he had written four years previously.
The remaining movements, 'scherzo ed intermezzo' and Finale,
were composed of fresh material and the whole was completed
and published in 1836. It appeared under Schumann's duple
pseudonym 'Florestan and Eusebius', to the origin of which
reference will be made in a later chapter.

Lengthy as was this process of composing the First Sonata,
it was spread over a shorter period than was that of the Second
in G minor, op. 22. From start to finish it exercised Schumann's
mind during the space of ten years. The first movement and the
third (Scherzo) were written in 1833. For the second movement,
Schumann used a greatly enhanced transcription of yet another

of his songs of 1828, 'Im Herbst' (In autumn) which he had already remodelled as an independent piano piece in 1830. The Finale as we know it to-day was not composed until 1838, and then as a replacement for another written three years earlier with which Schumann was dissatisfied. Meanwhile, his Sonata in F minor, now known as the Third, had been published in 1836. Schumann wrote it originally in five movements, but in view of its elaborate style his publisher urged him to cut out the two scherzos and to let it appear in three movements as *Concert sans orchestre* (Concerto without orchestra). The composer consented, though evidently without conviction. When he revised and republished the work in 1853 he included one of the discarded scherzos as the second movement.

From the foregoing it is plain that Schumann did not conceive his sonatas as organic wholes. From a study of the principal movements it is also apparent that although he was never at a loss for musical ideas, he found great difficulty in arranging them in logical sequence and in submitting them to development for which they were fundamentally unsuited. Few of the sonata-form movements display either a sufficiently definite contrast between first and second subject-groups as wholes, or a satisfactory balance between exposition, development and recapitulation; attributes which are among the prerequisites of sonata form. Schumann's 'subjects' often consist of a series of self-contained paragraphs which are restated intact or in instalments in unorthodox keys at points during the movement where their occurrence obscures the scheme of tonality and destroys the formal proportions. Sometimes the development-section is repeated in the recapitulation and the movement is lengthened still further by a third statement of the principal subject before the coda. The development-sections themselves contain repetitions rather than fresh workings of the various thematic units; often, however, with ingenious canonic treatment.

These shortcomings in technical procedure are to a very large extent offset by the expressive and vivid character of the musical material itself. Schumann's long opening and closing movements are like great tapestries filled with incidents depicted in glowing colours. They are a delight to play and to listen to as sheer music.

The slow movements of the First and Second Sonatas, which as we have already seen are based upon Schumann's own songs, are of the same lyrical type as some of his shorter pieces such as the Intermezzos of op. 4. The Andantino of the F minor Sonata, 'quasi variazioni' (on a theme by Clara Wieck), is an interesting example of the composer's great skill and inventiveness in writing variations; a branch of his art that we shall study in the next chapter.

The three Scherzo movements are of varying size and shape. The shortest, in the G minor Sonata, is a miniature rondo in which the refrain is accented regularly but both the episodes are strongly syncopated. The 'scherzo ed intermezzo' (Allegrissimo) of the F sharp minor Sonata opens conventionally but breaks off suddenly into an 'intermezzo alla burla, ma pomposo', lento, in which the composer burlesques the extravagances of the 'galant' style, winding up with a mock-heroic recitative. Longest, most continuous, most difficult though most rewarding to play is the Scherzo of the F minor Sonata. It exhibits to much greater advantage than do the sonata-form movements Schumann's genius for arranging his material in alternating paragraphs. This interesting Scherzo includes a typical example of his fondness for repeating subject-matter in a key only one semitone distant: in this instance, in D and D flat. It also contains some of his more intricate cross-hand passages, here combined with unusual pedal-effects.

* * * *

Schumann's two other large-scale works in several movements, the Fantasy, op. 17, and *Faschingsschwank aus Wien*, op. 26, which as we noted he designed originally as sonatas, will be considered in the present chapter, for they throw a different light upon his conception of sonata style.

Like the three works just examined, these two were not brought into being without alterations in their planning. Schumann had at first intended the Fantasy to be a contribution from 'Florestan and Eusebius' to the proposed Beethoven monument at Bonn in 1836. He named it *Grand Sonata* and gave the titles, 'Ruins', 'Triumphal Arch', and 'Starry Crown' to the three movements respectively. Then he changed his mind and published the work under his own name simply as *Fantasy*. He omitted the titles, added four lines of a poem by F. W. Schlegel to indicate the poetic basis of the composition and dedicated the work to Franz Liszt.

It is only in their main outlines that the three pieces of the Fantasy approach established types of sonata-movement. The opening Allegro in C major and minor is approximately in first-movement form. The central section, 'alla leggenda', which is in the nature of a self-contained interlude with a different time-signature and in slower tempo, performs the function of a development-section as it is based largely upon a theme first heard in the opening pages:

The rhapsodic style of this movement is intensified in the next, 'moderato ma energico' in E flat. It is a piece in free rondo form, notable in pianistic layout for the fantastically widespread chords and terrific leaps which accompany and decorate the invigorating thematic substance. In the Finale in C major, which is also the slow movement of the work, all the technical difficulties of its two predecessors are smoothed away in a piece of calmly flowing music in 12/8 time, not without powerful climaxes. The movement is distinguished by a great wealth of melodic ideas in all parts of the texture which are presented with sonata-form key-relationships in two long panels between an introduction and a coda. The Fantasy as a whole composition is typical of Schumann's very finest production for the piano.

Faschingsschwank aus Wien (Carnival jest from Vienna) in five movements, four of which were composed while Schumann was on a long visit to Vienna in 1839, recalls the mood of *Carnaval* which was written a few years earlier. He designed it as a 'Grand Romantic Sonata,' but the descriptive title it now bears conveys a far truer idea of the picturesque nature of its musical content. Only the Finale, the most conventional in structure, is in sonata form. The three central movements are hardly of the same calibre as those of the sonatas. The second movement, a brief Romance comprising a few meditative phrases, ends inconclusively though it does not lead without a break into the Scherzino, an assemblage of lively, scrappy themes which are constantly repeated. The fourth movement, an 'intermezzo con molto energia', which Schumann printed separately before he decided to include it in *Faschingsschwank*, is a short moto perpetuo of speeding semiquavers: a 'song without words' very similar in style to the first of the composer's well-known Three Romances, op. 28. The kaleidoscopic first movement in quasi-rondo form, the *pièce de résistance* of the whole work, exemplifies Schumann's most vivid style of composing. It consists of a collection of variegated episodes grouped round a recurrent short section. The forceful metric pattern and the straightforward harmonic scheme of this section are thrown into strong relief by the surrounding episodes. Some of them contain long stretches of chromatic progressions and passages or whole paragraphs characterized by persistent syncopation. Among the last-named is a hardly-concealed allusion to the Marseillaise— at that time forbidden in Vienna—which occurs about halfway through the episode beginning in F sharp major.

*   *   *   *

With the writing of *Faschingsschwank* Schumann had almost completed the long series of piano compositions, large and small, which occupied him throughout his earlier years when his romantic tendencies were at their strongest. As time went on, his admiration for Mendelssohn led to a modification of his own musical outlook. Mendelssohn's romanticism was only a youthful phase from which he emerged as a neo-classical composer, more interested in perfection of form and fine craftsmanship than in evocative tone-painting, and less ready to give free rein to his imagination and fancy. Schumann himself gradually shed his ultra-romantic traits and turned more readily to the writing of abstract music. He did not altogether renounce the composition of imaginative short pieces such as the *Album for the Young*, *Waldscenen*, which contains the favourite 'Vogel als Prophet', and collections of highly fanciful piano duets, all of which will be discussed in later chapters.

*   *   *   *

When Brahms began his career as a composer his classical and romantic tendencies were fairly evenly balanced. Later, when he came to write large-scale chamber and orchestral works, he was more inclined to follow classical procedure. In the smaller piano pieces and songs that he wrote all his life his deeply-rooted romantic characteristics found their natural musical outlet. In the three sonatas, which are among his earliest extant compositions, signs of romanticism appear in the use of folk-songs as the basis of the slow movements of the First and Second Sonatas, and in the quotation of a few lines of poetry at the head of the Andante of the Third Sonata.

We noticed earlier in this chapter that both Clementi and Mendelssohn continued Beethoven's later practice of introducing a phrase or a whole section from one movement into another, and that Schumann made connexions by means of mutual thematic quotation. Schumann was to proceed much further in the direction of thematic metamorphosis in his symphonies, which he began to write when he was over thirty. Brahms, his junior by a whole generation, was already using this device at the age of twenty. We shall find evidences in every one of his three sonatas. In the Sonata in F sharp minor, which was the first to be composed (in 1852) although it is numbered op. 2, the Scherzo is based upon a rhythmic variant of the theme of the slow movement. The first and last movements of the Sonata in C major, op. 1 (1852-3), are similarly related, and in the F minor Sonata, op. 5 (1853), there are cross-references between all five movements. The most obvious is the recrudescence in the fourth movement, Intermezzo ('Retrospect'), of part of the opening theme of the second movement, Andante.

Brahms's sonatas differ strongly from Schumann's in being much more firmly knit. The relationship between the movements of each sonata is integral; the form of the individual movements, which is far from being rigid, is clearly-defined and purposeful. There is a vast difference between the Finales of the two composers' Sonatas in F minor. Schumann's is a brilliant toccata with hardly a break in its uniform pattern of twelve restless semiquavers to the bar; Brahms's, a sectional rondo characterized by great rhythmic variety, broad sweeps of melody and many contrapuntal ingenuities. Only one movement in the Brahms sonatas, the Andante of the F minor, makes the impression of not having been conceived as a whole but of having developed in unexpected directions during the course of its composition. It begins in one key and ends in another, the time-signature is changed five times and there are four different tempo-indications. The movement seems to be drawing to an end when a longish final section of fresh character is added. Even a last allusion to the opening theme, greatly slowed down in the closing bars, does not achieve a convincing unification of the whole. The beautiful music itself, however, corresponds perfectly in feeling to the moonlit rapture expressed in the lines of poetry prefixed to the movement.

This poetic Andante and the fourth movement, 'Retrospect', of the same sonata, together with the Andante of the C major Sonata and the Trios of all the sonatas are the only ones which do not make heavy demands on the player. The others bristle with difficulties in the shape of strenuous chord-passages, awkward skips, and intricate part-writing. Brahms was himself a magnificent pianist with large, powerful hands. When he wrote for the piano he spared neither himself nor his interpreters. The very look of some of the pages is intimidating to the average performer. The Sonata in F sharp minor contains tempestuous cascades of octaves (furioso) in the first movement, single-handed double tremolos wider than an octave in the Scherzo and complex writing on three staves in the Andante and the Finale. Non-stop passages in thirds abound in the Finale of the Sonata in C major. In the Sonata in F minor there are acrobatic leaps from deep bass to high treble in the first movement, long upsurging arpeggio ornaments in the Scherzo, and quicksilvery semiquaver passages of alternately rising and falling sixths ('molto agitato') in the Finale. The difficulty of all these passages, as well as other impediments to easy sight-reading, may debar the pianist of limited attainments from performing the sonatas, but they need not deter him from studying them as music.

And indeed, it is as music rather than specifically as *piano* music that they yield their greatest fascination. Brahms's musical style was more intellectual than sensuous. He bestowed greater interest upon the formal than upon the colourful presentation of his material. His writing for the piano takes far less account of the distinctive attributes of the instrument than does that of Chopin, whose compositions seem to emanate from the piano's very soul. It is rare in the Brahms sonatas to find passages which sound as if they could not possibly be performed as effectively on some other instrument or group of instruments.

Leaving aside all strictures on the pianistic style of these works of the composer's youth, we find that the actual musical material is clear-cut and attractive. In the sonata-form movements the respective subject-groups are so well differentiated in character that they are easily followed. Brahms had undergone a rigorous training as a composer. The chief formative influences in his early production were the works of Bach and Beethoven, and German folk-songs. In the sonatas, the fruits of his studies may be seen in the Beethovenian terseness of idiom in some of the principal subjects, the notably melodic outlines of subsidiary themes and the recondite contrapuntal treatment to which the material is at times submitted.

*   *   *   *

A few of the numberless instances of contrapuntal treatment may first be studied with the eye before they can easily be apprehended by the ear. In the 'allegro non troppo ma energico' of the Sonata in F sharp minor the return of the principal subject in its own key (bar 131) is signalized by the running of the theme in canon between the two hands. In the Finale of the same work a short fugato is based on a variant of the principal subject. The opening notes of the theme (itself easily recognizable by the twice-repeated interval of a falling fifth) are announced in augmentation in the bass-part, which is written (in C major) on the lowest of the three bracketed staves just before the coda. In the first movement of the Sonata in C major, the principal subject is soon broken up into fragments for treatment in canonic imitation. The tuneful second subject opens the development-section in canon at the octave. Examples of double counterpoint occur during the section with the key-signature of two sharps and again in the Trio of the third movement.

The texture of the Sonata in F minor is less scholastically contrapuntal except in the rondo Finale, in which, once the chordal theme of the second episode in D flat has been announced, its opening curve seems to take charge of the remainder of the movement. This figure of three whole tones descending followed by the fall of a fourth reappears in single notes in canon between the two hands. Later, at 'più mosso', a longer section of the theme appears by diminution in quavers in the left hand and is soon combined with its original self in dotted crotchets in the right hand. Lastly, at 'presto', the four-note figure emerges triumphant in diminution in the right hand, and before finally disappearing, runs momentarily in canon with the left hand.

*   *   *   *

This is perhaps the most intellectual of the sonata-movements. At the other extreme stands the melodically and harmonically straightforward Andante of the C major Sonata. It comprises free variations on a theme which Brahms believed to be a genuine folk-song but which was later shown to be an imitation composed by A. W. Zuccalmaglio, a collector and editor of German folk-songs. By printing the words of the first verse against the notes of the theme at its announcement, Brahms made clear his intention that the movement should be understood as portraying the romantic sentiments and the atmosphere of the poem. The extreme simplicity of outline, the warm harmonies, occasional little enclaves of colour-effects (the demi-semiquaver passages, *una corda*), the change from minor to major for the last variation, and the tranquil coda above a tonic pedal-point carry the poetic intentions into effect.

The variations which form the slow movement of the Sonata in F sharp minor are more complex. The much longer theme is less direct in expression. First, because the melody ranges over a wider compass and wanders outside the key. Secondly, because during the variations it is for the most part kept mysteriously in the lower strands of the texture. It only occasionally rises to the surface, and even then, heavily disguised. The theme itself ends indefinitely on the dominant, in which respect it resembles the slow movement of Schumann's F minor Sonata. If these two sets of variations are compared it will be seen how much more freely Schumann treated his theme than did Brahms. Schumann re-arranged the three sections of the theme in different order in each variation. In the third variation he broke it up so rigorously that recognizable fragments are far to seek; in the last, he compressed its salient features into a recurrent motto phrase. As if to convince the listener of the finality of this variation he appended no fewer than nine successive tonic chords to bring it to a close. Brahms, however, ended his last variation faithfully upon the dominant harmony prescribed by the theme. He marked the Scherzo to follow without a break, as if to emphasize the fact that the new movement was based upon a variant of the same theme.

The Trios of the Scherzos in all the sonatas display the composer at his most genial. That of the F sharp minor Sonata moves briskly in short repeated segments over a simple harmonic foundation. Those of the Sonatas in C major and F minor unfold in great arcs of melody soaring above firm basses and radiantly variegated harmonies. These movements, together with the glowing Andantes of the Sonatas in C major and F minor and the Intermezzo of the last-named, a brief tone-poem in the composer's much-loved key of B flat minor, go far to clear Brahms of some of the many charges brought against him of being a predominantly academic composer.

* * * *

In following the fate of the sonata from Beethoven to Brahms we have noticed that the modifications it underwent during this period were more pronounced in style than in structure. None of the examples we have studied is so unusual in shape as to be unrecognizable as a sonata. The traditional division into two, three or four movements was only rarely set aside; by Schubert and Brahms in their respective five-movement sonatas and by Schumann in his quondam sonata *Faschingsschwank*. The linking together of two or more movements, a practice initiated by Emanuel Bach and followed once by Haydn and more frequently by Beethoven, was only occasionally adopted by the composers of the post-classical period. Our most recent study, the Brahms sonatas, has shown us that two of these works by the composer furthest in date from Beethoven are actually more classical in form and style than are those of the Bonn master's 'third period'.

* * * *

Our next study concerns a startlingly new, though certainly only short-lived phase in the history of the sonata.

With his Sonata in B minor composed in 1852-3 and performed by his pupil Hans von Bülow on the first Bechstein grand piano in 1856, Franz Liszt broke down the barriers of established form. He produced a single piece of music comprising within its scope some of the distinguishing characteristics of the

traditional movements, the structural principles of first-movement form and the elements of variation and fugue. It was a
mighty feat, to which even Liszt's detractors, and they are
many, are loth to deny greatness.

Liszt, the contemporary of Mendelssohn, Chopin, and Schumann, all of whom he long outlived, was a romantic who did
not shed his romanticism with the passing years. He clung
firmly to its tenets. For the composition of his original works he
was singularly dependent upon external stimuli, either literary,
pictorial or scenic. He made extensive use, too, of music by
other composers, which he submitted to highly imaginative and
elaborate treatment in the form of fantasies, paraphrases, and
transcriptions, examples of which we shall study in later
chapters. His pieces of abstract music are few and far between.
The two piano concertos, the piano sonata, and one or two
largish pieces for organ are among the most important. He was
an unparalleled virtuoso of the piano and was possessed of an
invincible performing-technique. His compositions for his instrument, even more than those by Chopin, form a turning-
point in the history of piano music. Yet Liszt could be austere
and intellectual as well as amazingly brilliant. His intellectuality
is manifest in the thematic metamorphosis and complex structural organization of the Sonata in B minor.

Although this composition was the only one upon which
Liszt conferred the title 'Sonata', it does not stand entirely alone
in his output. It had two predecessors which may be regarded
as preliminary studies; one written as long as fifteen years
before, and the other, only three years previously. The first is
the so-called 'Dante' Sonata, the most substantial piece in the
Second Book ('Italy') of the *Années de Pèlerinage* (Years of
pilgrimage). It was sketched in 1837 and was first performed by
Liszt in Vienna in 1839. The title it bears, *Après une lecture de
Dante* (After a reading of Dante), is that of a poem by Victor
Hugo in which the writer compares the horrific visions seen by
Dante on his journey through the infernal regions, with the
inescapable torments experienced by man during his mortal
life. Based as it is upon a literary subject, the piece should

rightly be placed in the category of programme music. The sub-title *Fantasia quasi Sonata* (which recalls that of Beethoven's two sonatas of op. 27, though in reverse) justifies its consideration in the present chapter.

The vestiges of sonata form are not as easily discernible in this piece as they are in its two successors. They consist less in the division of the whole into mutually balancing sections than they do in the continual development of a few themes, strongly-contrasted in character like those of a typical first movement. The subject-matter is frequently restated in varying sequence in a wide range of keys and tempi, and in an even wider range of pianistic figuration. The thematic metamorphosis which takes place throughout the piece often assumes the character of elaborate variations.

The music itself is amazingly evocative of the subject it portrays. The peremptory opening motive hurtling downwards in diminished intervals, the passages of chromatic octaves and chords sighing, shuddering, and shrieking throughout the whole length of the keyboard, and the outstandingly melodic theme which slightly alleviates the prevailing despair are welded into a cumulatively effective movement. It is equally fascinating as piano music and as an experiment in form. And this is to omit all reference to the harmonic daring which characterizes the whole work. In the latter respect, even more than in the luxuriant piano writing, Liszt's style differs most essentially from that of all his predecessors except Chopin. It was by his untiring efforts to expand the boundaries of tonality, rather than by his innovations in structural principles that Liszt exerted his most profound influence upon the subsequent development of the art of music.

*　　*　　*　　*

The 'Dante' Sonata was succeeded by the Grand Concert Solo which Liszt wrote in 1849 and which he later arranged for two pianos as *Concerto patetico*. In recent years another arrangement of the work, this time for piano and orchestra, has come to light and has been performed. The original version for piano solo may be regarded as the most authentic, and it is as the immediate predecessor of the Sonata in B minor that the piece possesses its greatest interest.

The Concert Solo is a little longer than the 'Dante' Sonata and comprises a larger number of significant themes. One, which contains the falling interval of a diminished seventh, actually prefigures one of the most important themes of the Sonata in B minor:

Diminished intervals and prominent themes in semibreves and minims are characteristic features of the musical substance of all these three large-scale works. A feature common to the 'Dante' Sonata and the Concert Solo is the quadruple time-signature which prevails unchanged throughout both. The B minor Sonata, however, which begins and ends in quadruple time, contains several sections in triple time which heighten its rhythmic interest and simulate the effect of division into separate movements. This Sonata and the Concert Solo being, at least nominally, independent of a programmatic background, are less fantastic in style and pianistic layout than is the 'Dante' Sonata, although each is interrupted from time to time by little passages of brilliant 'quasi cadenza' or thoughtful 'quasi recitativo' character such as Liszt could seldom forbear from introducing into his compositions.

*   *   *   *

In the Sonata in B minor Liszt carried the device of thematic metamorphosis to far greater lengths than heretofore. Few portions or even single passages can be found that do not bear some relationship, close or distant, to the several basic themes, which constantly reappear in new and unsuspected guises.

Only bar-to-bar analysis, which any musician would find engrossingly interesting to make for himself, would be effective in tracking down all these thematic interconnexions and affinities. Here, we must be content to seek out a few instances, easily identifiable by the reader, of notable transformations in the expressive style of the most significant among these malleable themes.

The contemplative theme in descending crotchets, 'lento assai' (sotto voce) with which the Sonata opens and closes, assumes a firmer character when it recurs (pesante) in minims between pulsating octaves during the section in E flat. Again in its original notation, it is all fire and energy as the dominating bass of the vigorous semiquaver passages preceding the change to the signature of B major 3/2.

The most immediately striking theme (x)

first announced impressively in the eighth bar ('allegro energico') is soon accelerated in busy single notes in diminution ('forte e sempre agitato'), but reverts to its original note-values when it is exultantly hurled forth in double octaves with canonic imitations in the section in B flat major. It seems to be invested with magic import when presented (espressivo) first in awed single notes and then in flowing curves over a slow-moving chordal accompaniment at the end of the Grandioso section in D major. It regains its forceful character and takes on new meaning in the Fugato (in B flat minor) where it is combined with the insistent figure containing five repeated quavers (y)

which originated as the bass of bar 14. The latter figure develops almost beyond recognition into the cantabile melody beginning with four repeated crotchets which recurs in a succession of different keys throughout the whole sonata. It makes a final emphatic appearance in the 'stretta quasi presto' near the end, where it is sometimes distributed in fragments at different pitches in typically Beethovenian style.

The ubiquitous themes so far mentioned are all in quadruple time. Two others, equally prominent, in triple time, appear less frequently. Although they are presented in different keys and with fresh types of accompaniment they do not undergo any such violent rhythmic or metric metamorphosis as do their fellows. One, which heralds the grandioso section (3/2) with the melody principally in minims and crotchets, is restated in crotchets and quavers (3/4) in a slower section of the sonata. The other, which opens and plays a determining part in what may be regarded as the slow movement, 'andante sostenuto' beginning in F sharp major, returns in the tonic major only just before the end of the sonata. It establishes a sense of tranquillity before the last uneasy mutterings of (y), the subdued plaint of the once commanding (x) and the measured descent of the opening 'lento assai' theme bring the tumultuous work to an almost inaudible close.

No analysis in words can give any adequate idea of the splendour or the pathos of the B minor Sonata, or of its superb piano writing. Only a playing or a hearing will suffice.

*   *   *   *

Liszt's individual conception of sonata form went almost unheeded by his contemporaries. The B minor Sonata, which was dedicated to Schumann, awakened an immediate echo in the now almost forgotten Sonata in B flat minor by Liszt's pupil Julius Reubke, who died in 1858 at the age of twenty-four. Thereafter, the one-movement sonata went out of cultivation during the remainder of the century. The next piano sonatas to appear were written in the conventional four movements. Tchaikovsky's Sonata in C sharp minor, which he composed in 1865 at the end of his student days, was not published until after his death and is little known except to specialists. Neither this work nor its successor in G major, op. 37 (1878) made any essential contribution to the evolution of the sonata. The Sonata in G major is not sufficiently convincing as a sonata to hold a secure place in the recitalist's repertory. The piano writing, with its heavily chordal passages and awkward left-hand parts, makes such severe demands on the player's technique that the work is beyond the reach of the average pianist. Some of the thematic material, especially in the slow movements of both the sonatas, displays features typical of Russian folk-music. From this aspect the two works may be compared with Grieg's only Piano Sonata, op. 7 (1865), which is faintly tinged with characteristics of Norwegian folk-music. But the Grieg Sonata possesses practical advantages over Tchaikovsky's: it is much shorter, more concise, and comparatively easy to play. Hence, perhaps, its survival, for it is by no means representative of the composer at his best.

*   *   *   *

Grieg, who was a fine pianist though not a magician of the keyboard like Chopin or Liszt, was pre-eminently a miniaturist. He was neither endowed by nature nor equipped by study to develop his small-scale musical ideas to fill large-scale formal structures. His music is sectional rather than continuous. The early Piano Sonata, like the sonatas he subsequently wrote for violin and piano and cello and piano, maintains its interest by the vividness and charm of the subject-matter rather than by any great skill evinced in its arrangement and organization. At the time Grieg composed it his musical style was not as deeply permeated by the characteristic traits of Norwegian folk-music as it was to become a few years later. Nevertheless, definite traces of folk-idiom may be found in the two inner movements of the Sonata: particularly in the Andante, at 'poco più vivo' and in the whole of the 'alla menuetto'. In this third movement Grieg struck a new note. The piece is neither an elegant minuet-and-trio of the classical school nor a lively scherzo-and-trio of the romantic type, as are those of Tchaikovsky's sonatas. It is a robust, dignified and rhythmical Norwegian peasant dance in the minor mode with a wistful trio in the major: a forerunner of many of the Lyric Pieces that we shall meet in the later pages of this book.

Grieg's strength as a composer lay in the freshness of his melodies and the extreme originality of his harmonies. The latter facet of his art is displayed at its most convincing in the Ballade, op. 24: a set of variations which will be discussed among the compositions of this type in the next chapter.

— 6 —

Variations

*Origin, types, and styles of variations described and exemplified.
Variations by Beethoven, Weber, Schubert, Chopin, Mendels-
sohn, Schumann, Brahms, Liszt, Tchaikovsky, Dvořák, and
Grieg.*

THE writing of variations was one of the earliest methods of
composing pieces for the keyboard. It afforded almost the only
means of securing length and continuity in music at a period
when the longer and more elaborate instrumental forms we
know to-day were either non-existent or in a rudimentary state
of development. Moreover, variation form never fell out of
favour with creative musicians. It gradually assumed proportions which could never have been foreseen by the early composers of instrumental variations, the Elizabethan virginalists.
Their efforts in this category sometimes consisted simply of a
single variation upon each of two or more consecutive tunes,
as in Giles Farnaby's 'A Toye', John Bull's Courante, 'Jewel'
and in hundreds of pieces of this type. Sometimes they wrote a
chain of increasingly elaborate variations on one theme.
William Byrd's 'Carman's Whistle' and 'Sellenger's Round' are
two of the best known.

We made acquaintance earlier in these pages with short sets
of variations written by Beethoven, Schubert, Schumann, and
Brahms to form individual movements in their sonatas. We
noticed, too, that these composers employed the technique of
variation in other movements, particularly in rondos at the
recurrence of the refrain. Now we shall look more closely into
the art of variation itself. After making a rapid survey of the
several different types of variations we shall study some of the
most interesting sets composed during the nineteenth century.

Variation form is by nature static, consisting as it does of a series of repetitions of the same stretch of music. The finest composers of variations have nevertheless always been able to find means of counteracting the monotony inherent in the type. Among these are the making of radical changes in key, tempo, rhythm, and dynamics; the writing of several consecutive variations in groups alternating in expressive style so as to create well-defined units within the larger design, and the grouping of these units to engender a sense of progress towards a climax.

The two principal kinds of variations are the melodic and the harmonic. In the former, the air of the theme is submitted to decorative treatment, as in most of Mozart's, Weber's, and Schubert's, and in some of Beethoven's earlier sets of variations. In the latter kind, the bass and the harmonic scheme remain more or less constant while the upper and middle parts of the texture undergo all manner of transformations.

The harmonic variation includes the 'ground bass' or 'basso ostinato', in which a short melodic phrase placed in the bass is repeated beneath a continuously changing decorative superstructure. An early example is Purcell's 'Ground in Gamut' (late seventeenth century). A much later and extremely picturesque specimen is Liszt's *Trauermarsch* (Funeral march) (1885). The chaconne and the passacaglia are more elaborate species of the same genus. They are exemplified in conventionally direct fashion in Handel's two Chaconnes in G major with twenty-one and sixty-two variations respectively (1733) and in the Passacaglia in G minor from his Seventh Suite (First Collection, 1720). On an infinitely more impressive scale are Beethoven's Thirty-two Variations in C minor (1806) and Bach's 'Goldberg' Variations (1743), the last-named being one of the most important sets of keyboard variations ever written.

These are the classical kinds of variations. A third, more modern kind is the symphonic variation, in which the treatment of the theme is altogether freer. It may include variations based on short motives detached from the theme and the entire series of variations may be interrupted by the insertion of a free interlude and finally rounded off with a coda. Such a set of variations is Schumann's Impromptus on a Theme by Clara Wieck, op. 5 (1833). Another work of this kind but on a much larger scale, with a longish introduction and without any well-defined breaks to destroy the sense of continuity, is César Franck's Symphonic Variations for piano and orchestra (1885).

Sets of variations cannot, however, be rigidly classified into exact categories. Many of them are apt to display the distinguishing marks of two or more kinds. For instance, in Handel's set known as *The Harmonious Blacksmith*, the opening variation is purely melodic, but all the variations are strictly harmonic in preserving the chordal structure throughout the whole series. They represent the early kind of variations termed 'Divisions', in which the beats are divided into increasingly florid scale and arpeggio figuration in smaller note-values. In Schumann's Impromptus just mentioned, some of the variations are founded upon the bass of the theme (nos. 1, 2, and 4), others on the melody (nos. 5, 7, and 9). As the set also includes a longish interlude (no. 10) and a free, fugal Finale, the whole may be accounted melodic, harmonic, and symphonic at the same time.

*   *   *   *

From the artistic and expressive aspects, variations can be described as intellectual, virtuosic, or romantic. In this sense, too, a set may exhibit more than one of these characteristics. Bach's 'Goldberg' Variations, which are predominantly contrapuntal in conception and are filled with recondite technical devices, are highly intellectual but they also possess a strong element of keyboard virtuosity. Brahms's 'Paganini' Variations (1862–3), which are virtuosic in the extreme, are intellectual in the sense of being the result of elaborate calculation rather than of spontaneous expression. Beethoven's 'Diabelli' Variations (1823) blend these two qualities in almost equal degree. They are intellectual in their passacaglia foundation and in their inclusion of a fughetta and a fugue which form the twenty-fourth and the thirty-second variations respectively; they are virtuosic in the piano style of the majority of the variations. Moreover, in expression, many of them are profoundly romantic.

None of these large-scale compositions is played very often in public. They impose tremendous intellectual demands upon listeners and present forbidding technical difficulties to per-formers. But acquaintance with them is essential to pianists, for each is a compendium of the styles of keyboard technique cur-rent during its own period, and each in its own way is a land-mark in the history of the variation. To study them at the key-board with the aid of Tovey's superb descriptive analyses is not only a valuable musical experience in itself, but is also a means of acquiring a greater understanding of variations in general.

*   *   *   *

Strictly speaking, to qualify for the epithet 'romantic' a set of variations should be the outcome of inspiration by some external stimulus, pictorial, literary or poetic. It may even be pro-gramme or descriptive music, as is Strauss's orchestral tone-poem in free variation form, *Don Quixote* (1898). Keyboard variations tentatively foreshadowing this kind were written long before the dawn of the Romantic period. The 'King's Hunting Jigg' com-posed during the sixteenth century is descriptive of the bustle of the chase and its echoing horn-calls. An 'Aria Allemagna' with twenty variations written by the seventeenth-century Ital-ian composer Alessandro Poglietti contains variations bearing titles to show that the pieces are intended to depict respectively the noisy chatter of market-women, the exquisite manners of the French, the feats of a tight-rope dancer, the characteristic sounds of the musical instruments typical of several nations, and so on.

In these two sets of variations the romantic elements are blended with the virtuosic. A blend of the romantic with the intellectual is to be found in Brahms's pianistically simple Romance, op. 118, no. 5 (1893). The title gives no indication of the fact that variation-technique is employed from beginning to end of this expressive little piece. The opening Andante section consisting of four varied statements of the same basic theme is followed by an interlude, 'allegretto grazioso'. It comprises a tiny chaconne in a fresh key, during which a four-bar phrase is six times repeated with variations over an almost changeless left-hand part above a tonic pedal-point. At its conclusion the opening Andante returns, shortened, to form the final section. In the method of its construction the movement is not unlike the Elizabethan type of variations upon two tunes.

Among other short romantic pieces conceived in the sense of variations, though not so entitled, is one of the studies in Clementi's *Gradus ad Parnassum*: no. 94, 'Stravaganze' (*c.* 1817). It is made up of four continuous sections, in the first three of which the same eight-bar phrase in the bass is presented note-for-note but in different keys, with a decoratively varied right-hand part. In the fourth section the musical argument is summed up in brilliant passage-work. Another, immeasurably more poetic piece of this kind is Chopin's *Berceuse* (1843), throughout fifty-four of whose seventy bars the same harmonic progression, tonic—dominant, is repeated beneath a treble part which rises and falls in patterns of delicate pianistic filigree. Only in the last sixteen bars does the harmonic foundation undergo slight modification, and not until the final cadence does the bass sever its connexion with the tonic pedal-point. The *Berceuse* is a series of continuous variations upon the most minute 'theme' it is possible to conceive.

Perhaps the most original and imaginative of all the sets of nineteenth-century variations is Schumann's *Carnaval* (1834-5). It is a sequence of short movements strongly contrasted in character but nevertheless closely related to one another by their common derivation from a motto theme. The sub-title of the work is 'Scènes mignonnes sur quatre notes'. The four notes in question, A (A flat), E flat, B and C represent the musical letters in Schumann's name and those of the place-name ASCH in Bohemia, the home of his inamorata at the time he wrote *Carnaval*. (The German symbols for A flat, E flat and B natural are respectively As, Es and H). The three short thematic figures which Schumann devised from these notes, or their enharmonic equivalents, are printed under the heading 'Sphinxes' as the ninth section of the whole work. They may be identified, generally in the upper part of the texture, in all the pieces except

'Préambule' and 'Paganini'. The element of variation is present in the subtle alterations in outline, rhythm, harmony, and expression which these tiny segments of theme undergo. For this reason, and because of the placing of the movements between a long introduction and a finale, *Carnaval* may be considered a set of symphonic variations.

*   *   *   *

From the aspect of nineteenth-century keyboard technique, Schumann's and Brahms's works in variation form, other examples of which we shall examine later, are possibly of greater interest to pianists, but Beethoven's are the more universal in expression. Apart from the five sonata movements in variation form, he wrote twenty-one independent sets for piano solo. Many of these were composed before the turn of the century and do not fall within this study, but we may look into a few of them as predecessors of the later, more important works of this kind.

Beethoven's earliest composition in this category, the Variations on a March by Dressler (1782–3) is of particular interest, inasmuch as in tonality, mood and style it is clearly the ancestor of the Thirty-two Variations in C minor that he was to compose more than twenty years later (1806). Like this well-known work, the 'Dressler' set is a chaconne. It maintains the same harmonic structure throughout, except in the last variation, where the minor gives way to the major and the change of mode necessitates a rearrangement of the harmonies. This final variation is double the length of the others, as each bar of the theme is spread out to become two bars of variation. It is not, however, a 'double variation': a term used to denote the varying of the *repeat* of each half of the theme. For example, in the third variation in the slow movement of the 'Appassionata' Sonata and in variations nos. 2 and 3 of the Finale of the E major Sonata, op. 109.

A few points of interest in Beethoven's pre-nineteenth-century variations may be noted before we consider those belonging to our prescribed period. The 'Righini' Variations (1790), based

on a theme of great simplicity, are most notable for their effective ending. The last (twenty-fourth) variation develops into a
free, modulating fantasy upon motives from the theme. It ends
with a Presto in which the theme, once more in its original key,
is gradually attenuated to a pianissimo nothingness, the fading
horn-calls evoking the romantic ending of Schumann's
Papillons.

The set of thirteen Variations on Dittersdorf's air 'Es war
einmal ein alter Mann' (1791) includes an Arioso, a Capriccio,
and a March, thus anticipating the 'Diabelli' Variations. It is
characterized by numerous changes of tempo and abounds in
witty touches arising from the superabundance of repetition in
the theme itself. The Finales of the sets of variations on 'Das
Waldmädchen' (1797), 'Kind, willst du ruhig schlafen' (1798)
and 'La stessa, la stessissima' (1798) incorporate prolonged
workings of motives detached from their respective themes. That
of the last-named, marked 'all'Austriaca', maintains the triple
rhythm of a dance throughout many of its bars. 'Tändeln und
Scherzen' (1799) is distinguished by a certain sense of continuity. Some of the variations lead into their successors without
a pause and the work ends with a brisk fugato Allegro (2/4)
sandwiched between two stretches of 'molto adagio ed espressivo' in 3/8.

Beethoven's variations show a remarkable diversity of type.
For instance, in one and the same year (1802) he composed the
Variations in G on an original theme, op. 15 which comprise
melodic variations, most of them as simple in style as the early
'divisions', and a brief coda based on a characteristic motive;
the Variations in F, op. 34, of which the first five are all in
different keys and the last (in the tonic) is succeeded by a long,
highly ornate Adagio; and the Variations in E flat, op. 35 on a
theme from his own ballet *Prometheus*. This last-named set, the
most important of all, is intellectual in type. It is made up of
fifteen variations upon both the bass and the melody of the
theme; it includes canonic workings and ends with a fugue. One
of the most original features is the Introduction, during which
the bass of the theme is stated, first in plain octaves and then

successively in two, three and four parts, after which the melody takes its rightful place above the bass and the variations begin. A point of great interest is the connexion of this set of variations with the 'Eroica' Symphony which Beethoven composed the following year. The Finale of the Symphony is based upon the same subject-matter treated in incomparably more expansive fashion.

Beethoven himself considered his opp. 34 and 35 to be different in style from his previous sets of variations, as indeed they are. When he came to write the Thirty-two Variations in C minor four years later, he reverted to a more conventional style in the actual pianistic treatment of the sparse eight-bar theme, but he planned the work as a more powerful and convincing whole than any of its predecessors. It falls into four main sections as follows: Variations 1–11 in the minor; 12–16 in the major, beginning with a quiet chordal variation; 17–30 again in the minor, including one (no. 22) in strict canon in double octaves; and lastly, after a solemn statement of the theme in chords (var. 30), a Finale (nos. 31–32) filled with violent contrasts in dynamics such as characterize the entire work.

In after years Beethoven spoke slightingly of this composition, but his opinion has not been endorsed by pianists. The Thirty-two Variations are frequently played in public; far more frequently than Beethoven's own most favoured sets in F and E flat, opp. 34 and 35.

Between the time he wrote the Variations in C minor (1806) and his last and greatest set, the 'Diabelli' Variations (1823) already referred to, Beethoven composed two sonata movements in yet another style of variation form. The sets of variations that constitute the Finales of the Sonatas in E major, op. 109 (1820) and in C minor, op. 111 (1822) are distinguished by great continuity. The theme of each is tranquil in the extreme; it inspires meditative rather than virtuosic treatment. The liveliness of two variations in the E major Sonata (no. 3, a double variation with double counterpoint and no. 5, which is fugal in texture), is more than compensated by the reflective mood of the others. The set comes to an end with a calm restatement of the theme preluded by a long section of delicate pianistic embroidery abounding in trills. The almost continuous variations (in C major) of op. 111, whose predominantly demisemiquaver figuration blackens the pages with unmanageable-looking passage-work, are musically clear-cut, and as piano music, by no means overwhelming in difficulty. Whereas the 'Diabelli' Variations are resplendent with their alternations of amazingly ingenious, profoundly intellectual and poetically expressive variations, the 'adagio molto semplice e cantabile' of op. 111 is one long quiet ecstasy of radiantly beautiful sounds.

*   *   *   *

The eight sets of variations for piano solo which Weber wrote from the age of fourteen onwards add little or nothing to the history of the form. They are for the most part decoratively melodic and extremely sectional in treatment but the piano writing, when it is not merely superficial in style, is attractive and rewarding to the pianist. A few sets include variations in the dance rhythms that abound in this composer's works. The 'Castor and Pollux' Variations, op. 5 (1804) and those on 'Vien quà Dorina bella', op. 7 (1807) end with a mazurka and a polacca respectively. The 'Schöne Minka' Variations, op. 40 (1815) end with a long 'Espagnole' in which the prosaic theme is transformed into a graceful and spirited movement in triple time. Among the Variations on an original Theme, op. 9 (1808) is a 'Spagnuolo' (var. 4) a genuine characteristic piece with Spanish atmosphere. Variation 6, Fantasia, largo, composed in alternating chordal phrases and passages of dramatic recitative, is typical of Weber's operatic style. The *Samori* Variations, op. 6 in B flat major (1804), contain a *Marche funèbre* (var. 6) in the tonic minor, notable for its deep pitch (both staves bear the bass clef throughout) and for romantic tone-colouring, especially at the end, where a free linking passage leads into the Finale.

The Variations on an Air from Méhul's *Joseph*, op. 28 (1812) are predominantly virtuosic in type. They exemplify the brilliant piano technique already familiar to us in the composer's sonatas. The fifth variation of the set, 'presto con fuoco', is a

H

moto perpetuo recalling the abandon of the Finale of his Fourth
'Programme' Sonata. The last variation, another Presto, 'leggiermente staccato', seems to foreshadow the glittering finger-
work of Schumann's Toccata in C major, op. 7. Only in the
sixth, Largo, does Weber renounce technical brilliance and
present the theme as if in orchestral guise, with strong contrasts in pitch, colour and dynamics.

*   *   *   *

Schubert's variations are of a different calibre. They are predominantly lyrical in character although the pianistic figuration
is occasionally as exuberantly decorative as Weber's. Of his four
sets for piano solo only one, the Variations in A minor, is
based on a theme not his own. All are distinguished by interesting harmonic progressions, a wide range of tonality and beautiful part-writing. The two earliest sets: the F major (1815) and
the A minor (1818) are independent. The third, in C major,
forms the slow movement of the Sonata in A minor, op. 42
(1825) and the last is the Impromptu in B flat major, op. 142,
no. 3 (1827). Almost midway in date between these two pairs
comes the single variation written in 1821 at the request of the
publisher and composer Anton Diabelli upon the same waltz
that inspired Beethoven to the writing of his Thirty-three Varia-

tions, op. 120. Schubert's transformation of the sturdy waltz-tune in the major mode into a gently-swinging ländler in the minor with all the obvious harmonic sequences smoothed out into subtle modulations is a perfect example of one aspect of his conception of the art of variation.

*   *   *   *

A distinctive feature of Schubert's earliest set of Variations in F major is the irregular phrase-construction. The theme consists of twenty-one bars divided into two main sections of nine bars and twelve bars, these in turn being sub-divided into four plus five and seven plus five bars respectively. The themes of the sonata movement and the Impromptu run in phrases of regular bar-lengths. Yet in both these pieces Schubert found ways of obviating rhythmic squareness. In the former, by devising echo-effects between short sections of the theme; in the latter, by extending the final phrase with a double repetition of the last bar, the second time an octave lower.

A comparison between the F major Variations, which date from Schubert's nineteenth year, and the sonata movement written ten years later shows that whereas in his early days the composer designed the ornamental passage-work in a purely conventional manner, in the later composition he conceived it in the sense of romantic tone-colouring. The demisemiquaver passages in the second variation of the sonata movement spring, as it were, like delicate overtones from the harmonic basis; those in the fourth variation form an enveloping cloud around the theme. The semiquaver triplets in the last variation and the coda make the impression of a great wave of sound eventually subsiding in the far distance. The effect of these picturesque touches is enhanced by the unbroken continuity of the whole set of variations and by the many changes in tonality. In the Impromptu in B flat, which Schubert composed the year before he died, the third variation in the tonic minor and the fourth in G flat major are romantically impressionistic in a style that seems to anticipate many of Schumann's and Chopin's compositions. The brief allusion to the theme at the very end of the piece is as deeply expressive in its restraint as are the preceding variations in all their wealth of colourful figuration.

The two early sets, although much less subtle both in the style of variation and in the keyboard technique, are charming as piano music. Especially rewarding to players of the ten Variations in F major are the flowing contrapuntal harmony of the fourth; the melodic left-hand part of the fifth; the distribution of the theme between the different strands of the texture in the ninth and the diversity of virtuosic figuration in the Finale. The set of thirteen Variations in A minor is based upon a shorter theme in dactylic metre from a string quartet by Schubert's friend Anselm Hüttenbrenner. In pianistic style it is less florid, though hardly less attractive than its predecessor. In tonality it is much more interesting. Variations in the major alternate with those in the minor. In the last variation the music hovers indecisively for a long time on the borderline between C sharp minor and C major before it swings back to the tonic, whose radiant major mode is finally contradicted by an unanswerable cadence in the minor.

The sets of variations that Schubert wrote for piano duet will be considered later in these pages, as will also one of his longest and most important works for piano solo, the unclassifiable 'Wanderer' Fantasy. The technique of thematic metamorphosis employed in this composition brings it within the sphere of works in variation form, but its title 'Fantasy' marks it out for inclusion under that heading in the following chapter.

*   *   *   *

As a writer of variations Chopin is remembered principally because the first of his two compositions of this type called forth an enthusiastic article by Schumann in the *Allgemeine Musikzeitung* in 1831 hailing the little-known composer as a genius. The work in question, Variations on Mozart's 'Là ci darem la mano', op. 2, which was written in 1827 when Chopin was seventeen, was designed for piano and orchestra, but can also be played with the orchestral accompaniment incorporated in the piano part. It was followed in 1833 by the *Variations brillantes* on a Theme by Meyerbeer, op. 12, for piano solo.

The two works differ from most of their forerunners in each being prefaced by a long improvisatory introduction based on motives from the theme and leading up to the first complete statement of the theme itself. Weber had written a stately introductory Largo, twenty-five bars in length, to his 'Schöne Minka' Variations in 1815, but Chopin's prelude to the 'Là ci darem' Variations extends to well over sixty bars. It is filled with brilliant though delicate passage-work and culminates in a long and highly decorative cadenza above a dominant pedal-point. The piano writing in both Chopin's sets of variations contains features of interest to the student of his style. In op. 2 the combination of melody and accompaniment in the same hand throughout the first variation, and the leaping staccato figuration in the fourth point forward to some of the *Études* and Preludes. The detached chords in close formation in the Scherzo variation of op. 12 and the passage of flickering demi-semiquavers at the end of the Lento seem to presage the picturesque writing of the Nocturnes.

Like Weber's Variations on 'Vien quà Dorina bella', Chopin's 'Là ci darem' Variations end with a polacca. A comparison of the two Finales shows that though Weber's piano technique was little less fluent than Chopin's, his skill in modulation and his command of chromatic resource were infinitely less. Apart from one longish section in the key of the flattened sub-mediant, Weber's polacca remains principally in its home tonic. Chopin's ranges at will through a series of keys, and the passage-work shimmers with chromaticisms. A comparison, too, between the sixth variation of Weber's 'Castor and Pollux' and the fourth of Chopin's 'Là ci darem' Variations displays the last-named composer's far deeper understanding of the possibilities of keyboard effect. Throughout both these variations the melody of the theme forms the surface of the texture. In Weber's it runs 'leggiero e piano' in single notes in broken-octave formation over an uneventful left-hand part, but in Chopin's, the broken octaves are galvanized into life by a bravura accompaniment of light staccato chords springing to and fro in resilient contrary motion.

Weber borrowed most of his variation-themes from other composers; Chopin took his from Mozart and Meyerbeer, but Mendelssohn relied on his own invention. He wrote three sets of variations upon original themes within a short space of time in 1841 and did not return to the form again. All these compositions are still extant, but only one has escaped oblivion: the *Variations sérieuses* in D minor, op. 54. Its survival in the concert-room may be attributed in part to the superior quality of the theme as compared with those of the other two, and in part to the large-scale, convincing plan of the whole work. The theme, which is distinguished by cross-bar suspensions and chromatic progressions, gives rise to variations of greater musical interest than do the rhythmically more straightforward and harmonically less eventful themes of the Variations in E flat and B flat respectively.

The seventeen *Variations sérieuses*, though mainly self-contained, are virtually continuous in effect. Only the fourteenth, an Adagio in the major mode, is preceded and followed by a well-marked pause. Another halt for breath occurs at the end of the fifteenth variation, after a meditative allusion to the theme has created an expectant atmosphere for the final summing-up in a whirlwind of presto quavers.

Among the individual variations which stand out from the others by reason of their more intellectual conception or their poetic quality are the fourth, which runs in sparkling two-part canon, alternately strict and free; the fifth, whose changing harmonies are tethered to a tonic pedal-point; the tenth, a fugato upon a motive derived from the theme, and the fifteenth, throughout which the rhythmic implications of the theme are carried to their logical conclusion by the placing of the salient melodic features entirely upon the weak beats. The eleventh variation manifests close affinity of style and expression with some of Schumann's short pieces. Pianistically, the thirteenth variation is the most rewarding. The theme winds its way legato in the very centre of the keyboard surrounded by a quivering accompaniment of staccato demisemiquavers in the right hand and detached quaver beats in the left. Mendelssohn used the same extremely effective figuration for the whole of the first variation of the set in B flat (op. 83) and again, at the beginning of the fifth of the Variations in E flat (op. 82). But there he modified the design by allowing the theme to escape every now and again from the inner to the outer parts of the texture.

Slighter in dimensions and different in overall construction are the Variations in E flat and B flat. The two works have several points in common. The respective themes are exactly the same length (twelve bars plus eight); each set comprises five variations with a longish finale attached to the last, and in both, the fourth variation is equally romantic in the tone-colouring evoked by a persistent metrical figure which is maintained throughout each by the left hand. These two poetic variations are 'characteristic pieces' in the most typically Mendelssohnian style.

*   *   *   *

Among the romantic composers, early and late, Schumann and Brahms practised the art of variation with the deepest understanding of its musical and technical possibilities. Where Weber's, Schubert's, Chopin's, and Mendelssohn's sets of variations are decorative or lyrical, Schumann's are supremely imaginative and Brahms's are intellectual and closely reasoned. These two composers went far to restoring the form to the important position which it had attained in Beethoven's hands and from which it had fallen through being cheapened by 'pianist-composers' such as Czerny, Cramer, Moscheles and other adepts in superficially brilliant writing for the keyboard.

Schumann's first published composition was a set of variations written when he was twenty. It had already been preceded two years earlier by another, now lost. It was followed by a series of works in the same category (a few of the earliest incomplete and unpublished) which Schumann wrote at intervals throughout his whole life. His very last composition was a set of Variations on an original theme in E flat which he was unable to complete, but which has been published in recent times just as he left it.

In his opus 1, the 'Abegg' Variations, Schumann immediately displayed features of style which were to characterize some of his more mature works of the same kind. He based the whole work on a musical motto, as he did *Carnaval* and the much later Fugues on the name BACH. The theme itself is derived from the name ABEGG, the surname of a real person; a much-admired girl whom Schumann had met at a ball at Mannheim. The 'Countess Pauline von Abegg' to whom he inscribed the Variations was simply a figment of his imagination.

Schumann used the letters of the name not only for the opening notes of the theme: A, B flat, E, G, G (B is the German symbol for B *flat*), but also in reverse order (melodic inversion) for the beginning of the answering phrase. Moreover, he 'varied' the theme itself at its original statement by repeating each half with slight alterations in the pianistic layout. He developed rather than embellished it in each of the four variations and the rondo-form Finale. In none of them can the melody be recognized as a whole entity, and even the harmonic framework is heavily disguised. The first three variations are all 'double' in the first half. The fourth presents the theme expanded in one place and contracted in another, and in the Finale it almost completely loses its identity. The uncommon and effective piano writing includes two features which are characteristically Schumannesque. The crossing-over of the left hand in bars 9–16 of the cantabile second variation to play the bass part of bars 1–8 two octaves above the stationary right hand; and the gradual releasing of the notes of a chord in the Finale (thirty-two bars before the end), a device Schumann employed with much more telling effect at the end of *Papillons*.

Schumann's free interpretation of the term 'variation' is manifested even more clearly in the slow movement of his Sonata in F minor which we discussed in the previous chapter, and in the two works mentioned near the beginning of the present chapter: the Impromptus, op. 5, of which he wrote and published two successive versions (1833 and 1850) showing considerable mutual differences, and *Carnaval*, op. 9 (1834–5).

The *Études symphoniques* in C sharp minor, op. 13 (1836)

furnish another proof of his unusual conception of the form. The work comprises a series of pieces which are variations in a stricter sense than those he had published hitherto, but which are at the same time concert-studies exemplifying the finest aspects of his many-sided keyboard style. The variation technique and the pianistic figuration stand on equal terms. For instance, the third variation is theoretically a strict two-part canon based on the theme; practically, it is a study in the playing of detached chords whose rhythmic scheme calls for a different system of accentuation in each hand. The fifth variation, which follows the theme equally closely, gives the pianist's lfet hand gruelling practice in executing rapid leaps across intervals wider than the octave, starting each time a demisemiquaver beat earlier than the regularly accented and less vertiginous right-hand part. The seventh variation, throughout which a metrical pattern (♩♪♪♪ ♪♪♪) runs furtively in every bar and in every part of the texture in succession, is as much a *Fantasiestück* as are any of Schumann's movements bearing descriptive titles. The ninth variation in G sharp minor, with a long-drawn-out melodic line poised over an accompaniment of murmuring demisemiquavers, is a meditative tone-poem. The Finale is written in the enharmonic tonic major (D flat) in free rondo form. It is as exuberant in mood, though not quite so exacting in piano technique, as the second movement of the composer's Fantasy in C which we considered in the preceding chapter among his sonatas.

Schumann's fertility, both in writing variations and in devising novel kinds of pianistic figuration, is exhibited in five additional variations, which are printed in most editions of the *Études symphoniques* although the composer rejected them from his own final version. Further examples of his art of variation, conventional and otherwise, will be referred to later in this book among transcriptions, concert-studies, pieces for beginners and piano duets. They show how strongly his creative work as a whole was influenced by this particular form and style of composition.

* * * *

With Brahms, the writing of variations was almost as much a science as it was an art. Nearly all his works in this category teem with recondite devices, and for the greater part compel admiration rather than affection. Only the continuous variations comprising the slow movement of his Piano Sonatas in C major and F sharp minor are sufficiently straightforward to yield most of their secrets at a first hearing or playing.

In the Variations on a Theme by Schumann, op. 9 (1854) some of the variations reproduce the melody or the bass of the theme so clearly that it is immediately recognizable. In nos. 1 and 3 the melody is assigned to the left hand and in no. 16 the bass proceeds solemnly in legato notes three times their original value. In other variations the theme is disguised with great ingenuity. In the second, the twenty-four-bar bass is compressed to a quarter its length and the resultant six-bar phrase repeated to make good the loss in extent. A distinctive feature of this whole composition is the prominence given to canonic treatment. Three of the variations are two-part accompanied canons, each strikingly different in effect. In the eighth, the canon runs between the treble and the bass, an octave or more apart and at the distance of two bars. Again, in the fifteenth, it runs between the two outside parts, one bar distant and at the interval of a compound sixth below. It is accompanied by flowing arpeggios, whereas in the eighth variation the space between the two canonic parts is filled by chords. These two examples of comparatively straightforward canonic treatment are supplemented by another more abstruse. In the fourteenth variation the right hand has to play a decorated version of the melody as well as its canonic reflection a tone higher at two bars' distance. The left hand is let off lightly with a single-line arpeggio accompaniment.

Despite these forbidding characteristics Brahms's op. 9, which is based upon the first of Schumann's *Five Album Leaves* from *Bunte Blätter*, op. 99, is pianistically gracious. In several aspects it recalls Schumann's own fundamentally more imaginative type of writing. The elliptical style of the seventh variation reminds us of his mysterious utterances in *Kreisleriana*. The ninth variation actually adopts the key and the figuration of the second 'Album Leaf' in B minor, and thrice reproduces some of its bars note-for-note (e.g., Schumann's bar 1 becomes Brahms's bars 2, 6 and 16).

*   *   *   *

The two sets of variations, both in D major, to which Brahms gave the same opus number (21) although he wrote them at different times, are rhythmically more interesting and are grouped with greater subtlety than are those in the work just discussed. As piano music they are less satisfying.

The theme of the first set (1856), the only one of all the composer's piano solo variations that he wrote himself, is typically Brahmsian in the uneven bar-lengths (nine plus nine) of its two phrases. The first six variations maintain the triple time of the theme, the next four are in duple time and only at the eleventh is the 3/8 time-signature restored. This last (double) variation, to which the Finale is attached, surpasses even the fifth in the intricacy of the smoothly-flowing part-writing. The right hand is in sole charge of two strands of decorative texture which are often far apart in pitch, while the left hand performs an unbroken trill on a series of different bass-notes throughout the whole thirty-six bars.

The Hungarian song on which Brahms based the second set of variations of op. 21 (?1853) has a peculiar rhythmic constitution. It is composed of eight bars containing alternately three and four beats and bearing the unusual time-signature of 3/4 C which persists during the first eight variations. After the next variation in 9/16, the time changes to 2/4 for the remaining four variations and until the end of the Finale. The theme is then restated fortissimo in the original time-signature and is extended by one bar to make a more impressive close. The rhythmic eccentricity of the theme called for perceptive treatment if it were not to lose its distinctive flavour in the ensuing variations. Brahms secured the desired effect by writing the first eight without deviating one hair's-breadth from the eight-bar pattern. When he changed the time-signature to 2/4 he still preserved the feeling of rhythmic mutability by means of syncopation and cross-bar accentuation, or by combinations of irregular groups of notes (three against two in the twelfth variation and four against three in the thirteenth). In the Finale he made many changes in key, mode and figuration.

*   *   *   *

These several sets of variations, all of which Brahms wrote before he had completed his twenty-fourth year, are of great interest musically and technically. Their rare appearance in the concert-room is due less to any intrinsic shortcomings than to the unchallenged superiority of their successors, the 'Handel' and the 'Paganini' Variations, which rank among the finest keyboard variations of all time. The two large-scale works are utterly different from one another in conception. The 'Handel' Variations, op. 24 (1861), twenty-five in number, follow the Beethoven tradition. They are arranged into groups designed to produce a feeling of growth towards a climax and they end with a fugue, in which respect they resemble the 'Eroica' and the 'Diabelli' Variations. The 'Paganini' Variations, op. 35 (1862–3), comprising two completely independent sets which were never intended to be played consecutively, are in reality concert-studies, one outdoing another in virtuosity until all the resources of the keyboard seem to be exhausted.

Different as are these masterpieces by Brahms in point of style and expression, they have two features in common. Each is written upon a theme with an exceptionally clear-cut melodic outline and a straightforward harmonic basis, and each theme had already been subjected to variation by its own composer. The Handel theme comes from his Suite in B flat major, no. 1 of the Second Collection, where it figures as an Aria with five variations. Paganini's, with twelve variations, constitutes the twenty-fourth of his *Caprices*, op. 1 for solo violin. This same theme was later to attract other composers of variations. Liszt used it for the last of his *Paganini Études*. In our own time it inspired Rachmaninov to the composition of his 'Paganini' Rhapsody for piano and orchestra (1934), the most variegated in style, and in point of performing-technique the most difficult of all these formidable tests of the pianist's skill and endurance.

The very simplicity of the themes themselves, and the determination with which Brahms adhered to their structural design throughout his most daring adventures in variation, are largely responsible for the overwhelmingly powerful effect both sets make in performance. Even at their most decorative the variations create an impression of being concerned only with essentials. The variation technique is less recondite than in the composer's earlier works in the same category. The piano writing is bolder and the contrapuntal devices are used with greater skill.

*   *   *   *

In the 'Handel' Variations, which are more purely musical in interest than the 'Paganini' set, the 'learned' variations are introduced only sparingly among others whose principal attraction is their pianistic layout. The contrasts between successive variations are particularly finely planned. The chromatic fluency of the second comes with startling freshness after the solidity of the primary harmonies of the first; the brisk chordal fanfares of the seventh follow gratefully upon the laborious canonic progress of the sparse octave passages throughout the sixth. The closely concentrated texture of the ninth, every two bars of which are held in the inescapable grasp of a pedal-point, is quickly forgotten in the light staccato chords that bounce up and down the keyboard in the tenth. The powerful fugue with a subject based upon the theme introduces the element of continuity and magnificently sums up the protracted series of short, fascinatingly diverse variations.

*   *   *   *

The theme of the 'Paganini' Variations is less melodic than that of the 'Handel' set and is, in a sense, mechanical in character. Every bar, except the last of each of the two phrases, contains exactly the same metrical pattern (♩. ♪♪♫♫), and the melodic line proceeds entirely in cut-and-dried sequences. This apparently unpromising musical substance nevertheless forms an auspicious basis for variations of the most brilliantly virtuosic type. It also yields to more gracious treatment in the eleventh variation of the first set and in the fourth (almost a waltz), the twelfth and the thirteenth of the second set. In contradistinction to the 'Handel' Variations, in which the quadruple time of the theme is retained throughout the whole work, the 'Paganini' Variations exploit the device of rhythmic metamorphosis. In the first set, the 2/4 time-signature of the theme is changed in some of the variations to 6/8 and 12/8, and in one, to 2/4 in the right hand with 6/8 in the left. In the second set, rhythmic complexity is more pronounced. The time-signatures of 3/8 and 6/8 appear in some of the early variations; and in the seventh, the right-hand part is written in 2/4, the left-hand part in 3/8 and vice versa. The final variation, which begins in 2/8 time, proceeds through sections in 2/4 and 6/8 to end with the right hand in 2/4 and the left hand in 6/8.

The combination of different rhythms or metres is a strong characteristic of Brahms's music as a whole. It is especially noticeable to pianists, whose two hands sometimes have to cope simultaneously with four lines of texture each running in a different metrical grouping. Brahms even went to the length of writing special finger-exercises to perfect his own technique in this particular respect. We shall consider them in a later chapter, among piano studies.

*   *   *   *

Closely contemporaneous with, but entirely different in style from, Brahms's greatest sets of variations is Liszt's large-scale set of Variations on a Theme by Bach from the Cantata *Weinen, Klagen* (1862). It is a passacaglia, constructed upon a theme which is used predominantly as the bass, but also, alternatively, as the treble or as one of the inner parts throughout a succession of over fifty almost continuous variations interspersed with free interludes. The theme in F minor, a line of semitones descending from F to C and returning direct to F, is short and distinctively

chromatic in character. Its ceaseless repetition could easily conduce to monotony were it not for Liszt's inexhaustible resource
in submitting it to changes in accentuation, tonality and pitch
and in decorating it with a wealth of effective figuration. The
whole piece is fascinatingly interesting to the player.

The thematic metamorphosis recalls that of the composer's
Sonata in B minor, but the work is less powerful in effect. The
basic musical material is comparatively limited in extent and
the whole lacks an overwhelmingly convincing climax. The
much-needed element of contrast is introduced at the end by the
presentation of a chorale in the major mode with simple diatonic harmonies strongly differentiated in style from the preceding welter of chromaticism. Musically, it forms an anti-climax
although the procedure is fully justified in an extra-musical
sense. The antithesis between the words associated with the
theme: 'Weinen, Klagen, Sorgen, Zagen' (Weeping, mourning,
sorrow, fear) and those of the chorale, which forms part of the
cantata itself: 'Was Gott thut, das ist wohlgetan' (What God
does, is well done), is reflected in the music which portrays the
respective opposing moods. The Variations are accordingly romantic by reason of their literary basis.

*   *   *   *

Next in chronological order to Liszt's Variations is Tchaikovsky's set in A minor written in 1863–4. It was not published
until after his death and is now very difficult to obtain. Another
set in F major which forms the last item of his Six Pieces, op. 19
(1873) has recently been published in this country as a separate
piece. The distinctive feature of the theme is a short melodic
curve of seven notes rising and falling between C and the F
above it. Not only is it introduced three times into the theme
itself, but it forms the introductory phrase of all the twelve
variations and of the separate coda, each time in either a fresh
rhythmic pattern, a new key or in a different part of the texture.
The ninth variation is a strongly syncopated mazurka in B flat.
The eleventh, 'allegro brillante', is headed 'alla Schumann', the
principal Schumannesque elements being the repetition in

every single bar of the same metric figure and the heavy accentuation of the first beat in many of the bars.

*   *   *   *

Dvořák's Variations in A flat major, op. 36 (1879) are based on a 'tempo di minuetto', forty-five bars in length, which includes so many repetitions of short figures and phrases that it is itself almost a variation. In some of the eight variations the element of repetition becomes still more prominent, and it is perhaps for this reason that the work has disappeared from the pianist's repertory despite the attractive style of the keyboard writing.

*   *   *   *

The most important survivor of the period in question, Grieg's Ballade, op. 24 (1875), is actually the composer's only large-scale piano solo still to be heard from time to time in the concert-room, whence his Piano Sonata has long since vanished.

By the time Grieg came to write the Ballade he was thirty-two. He had composed the Piano Concerto seven years earlier, his command of keyboard resource was already highly developed and his musical style had assimilated many of the most striking characteristics of Norwegian folk-music which he had been studying enthusiastically for about ten years. He was fully qualified to compose a work in which the typical features of Norwegian folk-music should find expression in apt and effective pianistic terms. He based the Ballade on a folk-song in the minor mode, to whose simple and repetitive melodic outline he supplied harmonies chromatically so rich as to render further harmonic development difficult. Indeed, a few of the variations, notably the fifth, sixth and seventh, simplify rather than elaborate the chordal structure underlying the theme. Some of the most telling effects in others, especially towards the end of the work, are produced by unexpectedly remote modulations.

The variations, which are arranged to form a succession of strong contrasts in mood and style, are extremely individual in character. The third, Adagio, is a duet in which the melody of

the theme is sung in thirds in the middle register of the keyboard between an undulating accompaniment above and below.
The fifth is an ardent dialogue; the eighth, a funeral march
accentuating the melancholy inherent in the theme. The sixth
and seventh variations, 'allegro scherzando', are written in
canon but are the reverse of academic in their pianistic style.
The tenth is a peasant dance in 12/8 time.

Although Grieg's strongest gift was for composing short
lyrical pieces, his planning of the Ballade as a large-scale whole
work is completely convincing. The first eight variations follow
the theme fairly closely but the remarkable diversity of their
figuration precludes any sense of monotony. The ninth variation, an interlude based on fragments of the theme, is twice
interpolated by delicate arpeggios based on the notes of a
chromatic dominant-ninth chord which are unfurled in a flexible double line in the treble and are merged into an opalescent
cloud-effect by means of the sustaining-pedal. Up to this point,
the triple time and the tonality (G minor) of the theme have
remained unchanged. From the tenth variation onwards to the
end of the twelfth, the time alternates between quadruple and
duple (simple and compound) and the music, which now runs
without any break, passes through several keys, major and
minor. Only in the thirteenth and fourteenth variations is the
key of G minor definitely re-established.

For the conclusion of the work Grieg followed an old tradition
which is exemplified in Bach's 'Goldberg' Variations, in the last
movement of Beethoven's Sonata in E major, op. 109 and in
Brahms's 'Hungarian' Variations. He restated the theme in its
original version, as if to remind the listener of the simplicity and
the elegiac character of the music which gave rise to such an
abundance of brilliant and passionate argument.

7

Rondo, Fugue, and Fantasy

Other established forms: rondos by Beethoven, Weber, Mendelssohn, Chopin, and Schumann. Fugues and works in contrapuntal style; definition of fugue; works by Beethoven, Mendelssohn, Schumann, César Franck. Fantasies by Beethoven, Schubert, Liszt, Mendelssohn, Chopin, Balakirev.

IN nineteenth-century piano music the dividing-line between classical and romantic is seldom very firmly drawn. The majority of the large-scale works already studied in these pages have been found to follow classical principles in their main outlines, but frequently to display romantic characteristics in conception, or in the details of their structure. In some, the romantic element is predominant. For instance, in Beethoven's 'Lebewohl' Sonata and in Clementi's *Didone abbandonata*. Their titles denote an extra-musical basis and on this account they come within the category of romantic programme music. Liszt's 'Dante' Sonata is also of this type, but his Sonata in B minor, which boasts no descriptive title, is not a whit less romantic in effect for it comprises an equally fundamental transformation of the recognized structure of the sonata.

This one-movement sonata of Liszt's is an extreme example of the romantic treatment of a classical form. Schumann's *Carnaval* is another. Although it is based on the principle of variation form it displays the greatest possible freedom, both in the whimsical method employed for varying the motto theme and in the construction of the whole as a set of miniatures. Moreover, it bears a comprehensive title and the individual pieces carry superscriptions denoting that they are the musical likenesses of personalities, real or fictitious, and their doings in

Schumann's world of imagination. *Carnaval* is programme music
in the truest sense of the term.

The sonata and the variation were not the only types of
established form to be remodelled by romantic composers. The
rondo, the fugue, and the fantasy also underwent basic alteration in their hands and emerged in some case almost unrecognizable in structure or style. Schumann's *Blumenstück* and
Humoresque demonstrate the rondo principle of recurrent sections although they strain the conventional resources of the form
to their utmost limit. Beethoven's and César Franck's fugues,
with their ornate keyboard writing and passionately rhetorical
style, constitute a remote if logical development of the intellectual contrapuntal technique of the Baroque period. Schubert's
Fantasy in C major known as the 'Wanderer' even inaugurated
a new type of composition: the symphonic poem.

*   *   *   *

The rondo, like the variation, led an independent existence
long before it was incorporated in the sonata as an individual
movement. Among the simplest examples still current in the
concert-room are the *rondeaux* by the early eighteenth-century
clavecinistes, Rameau, Couperin and others. These exquisitely
wrought compositions consist merely of a number of short sections or couplets interspersed with repetitions of the opening
paragraph. The more developed, less sectional type known as
older rondo, in which the episodes are often linked to the refrain
by passages of transition and the whole is completed by a coda,
is exemplified by Mozart's well-known Rondo in A minor,
K.511 (1787). Beethoven's Rondo in C major, op. 51, no. 1
(1796) conforms to this type, but his Rondo in G major (1801),
no. 2 of the same opus, is in *modern rondo* form. Neither of these
pieces compares in interest with the early *Rondo a capriccio* in G
major, 'Rage over a lost penny vented in a Caprice'. Unconventional as it is in title and in style it is vividly expressive with
its furious repetitions of the recurrent theme, or fragments of it,
presented stolidly in the tonic, furtively in remote keys, and
with occasional chromatic displacement of the diatonic material.

It is, in effect, a rondo combined with variations. In this sense it shows an affinity in structure with Haydn's only independent piece of this kind: a little-known but fascinating Capriccio in G major published in 1789. The difference in mood, however, between Haydn's delicate wit and Beethoven's grim humour is immeasurable.

*   *   *   *

Weber's *Rondo brillante*, op. 62 (1819), in modern rondo form, although it is of the same calibre as the finales of his sonatas, is distinguished from all of them by its lilting rhythm. In tempo and mood it bears a likeness to the rondo of the composer's Second Sonata in A flat, but the figuration in demisemiquavers lends it an altogether more buoyant character. His *Invitation to the dance*, another rondo, belongs equally to the provinces of programme music and dance forms, in both of which connexions it will be referred to later.

*   *   *   *

Mendelssohn's *Rondo capriccio* in E minor, op. 14, a presto movement with a longish andante introduction in the tonic major, is free in construction and light-footed in style as are the scherzos of his sonatas. Chopin's three rondos, which are also irregular in the organization of their component sections, make an entirely different impression owing to their all-pervading dance-rhythms. The first in C major, op. 1 (1825) and the third in E flat major, op. 16 (1832) are both in duple time, but the latter is preceded by a long introduction in quadruple time. The second, *Rondo à la Mazur* in F major, op. 5 (1826), written in the triple time native to the mazurka, resembles the Rondo in E flat in its construction in two long panels with a final statement of the refrain and a coda. At the same time, it displays stylistic features that differentiate it sharply from both its fellows. The wistful theme of the refrain in the Lydian mode (with the sharpened fourth degree of the scale) is woven surreptitiously, though unmistakably, into the texture several times by the left hand. Insistence upon the distinctively modal flavour of the musical material, and the constant repetition of short thematic figures, which is also a characteristic of Polish folk music, emphasize the romantically national style of the piece and prove the strength of the sixteen-year-old composer's affection for the folk-idiom of his homeland.

*   *   *   *

The three works in rondo form, all with fanciful titles, that Schumann wrote in 1838-9, are successively more complicated in build. They are alike in being composed of a series of independent sections, each neatly railed off from the next by double-barlines and headed by a specific tempo-indication. The first, the well-known *Arabesque*, op. 18, is the only one in clear-cut older rondo form with episodes in contrasting keys linked to the recurrent opening section. It ends, as do others of Schumann's piano works such as the *Humoresque* and *Kinderscenen*, with a valedictory section in which the composer seems to give the listener a final message to turn over in his mind. In the *Arabesque*, this section, which is much slower than any of the preceding, is clearly marked 'Zum Schluss' (In conclusion).

Blumenstück (Flower piece), op. 19, is divided into five numbered sections. Schumann described the movement and its successor *Humoresque* as 'variations, but not on a theme'. The element of variation in *Blumenstück* may be recognized in the presentation of the thematic units in different keys and in the appearance of the melodies in different threads of the texture. Section II, which is first stated in A flat major, recurs in B flat minor and later in D flat major, and the melodic line of section I becomes the tenor part of section IV. The whole piece is more notable for structural ingenuity than it is for convincing musical expressiveness. With its monotonous figuration and narrow range of tonality it repels rather than attracts the player.

Humoresque, op. 20, which is over three times as long and is incomparably more intricate in musical architecture, is profoundly interesting to performers. It demonstrates almost every distinctive feature of Schumann's pianistic style. Long cantabile melodies in every part of the texture, persistently lively rhythmic patterns, paragraphs in flowing contrapuntal harmony, short canonic imitations, outrageously difficult cross-hand passages and picturesque colour-effects all find their place in this glowing music. The rondo plan is only faintly apparent in the restatement of some of the earlier sections of the piece, but the generally loose organization of the musical substance is to some extent offset by the vividness of the piano writing. Even so, *Humoresque* is far more satisfying to the player than to the listener, who may well feel bewildered by the superabundance of the thematic content.

*   *   *   *

The writing of keyboard fugues as independent pieces, except for didactic purposes, languished during the latter half of the eighteenth century and the earlier part of the nineteenth owing to the growing importance of the sonata as an art-form. Neither Haydn nor Mozart composed fugues for piano solo except as portions of larger works. Nor did Beethoven or Schubert. But they, and other nineteenth-century composers showed their awareness of the unsurpassably telling effect that could be produced by a fugue, either as the culminating section of a long composition or as an insertion in a musical context completely antithetic to it in style.

The fugal Finales of Beethoven's 'Hammerklavier' Sonata and the Sonata in A flat, op. 110 form the most perfect endings to these profoundly expressive works by reason of the sheer contrast of their argumentative style to all that has gone before. On the other hand, the fugue comprising the development-section of the sonata-form Finale of the Sonata in A major, op. 101 is little differentiated in character from the contrapuntally wrought opening and closing sections. The energetic fugue in the major mode which serves as the penultimate variation of the 'Diabelli' Variations is placed to the very greatest advantage. It stands between three extremely leisurely variations in the minor mode, and before the concluding 'tempo di minuetto' whose fine-spun chords and placid runs still the torrent of discussion that was let loose in the preceding pages. The 'Eroica' Variations culminate in a fugue whose subject is derived from the *bass* of the theme. It constitutes the most fitting prelude to the ultimate statement of the *melody* of the theme which follows hard upon it and brings the whole work to an end.

The fugue which terminates Brahms's 'Handel' Variations gathers up all the threads of the theme and weaves them into a texture glowing with brilliant colours. The fugato of Liszt's Sonata in B minor is introduced at a point where its terse treatment of the motto theme shows up most vividly against the luxuriant style of figuration which has previously surrounded it. The five-part fugal interlude in the Finale of Schumann's Impromptus on a Theme by Clara Wieck effectively rehabilitates the theme which has forfeited so much of its identity during the adjacent variations. The energetic fugue that concludes Schubert's tremendous 'Wanderer' Fantasy not only counteracts the meditative languor of the variations on the 'Wanderer' theme and the light-hearted grace of the Scherzo-and-Trio. By ultimately presenting the fugal subject in a style of piano writing similar to that of the opening movement it seems to form the last arc in a great musical circle.

*   *   *   *

It was Mendelssohn, Schumann, and Liszt, all of them enthusiasts for Bach's music and pioneers in its revival, who resuscitated the independent fugue for the piano and for the organ. Chopin stood aloof from this movement. The one fugue still extant under his name is thought to have been written by Cherubini.

Among Mendelssohn's Six Preludes and Fugues, op. 35, which were written between 1832 and 1837 when he was in his twenties, the first in E minor is the only one that is still a regular item in the pianist's repertory. The flexible melodic line threading its way through the ceaseless arpeggio figuration of the Prelude, the expressive, dignified character of the Fugue, and the strong sense of climax in both movements make them particularly rewarding to players. The first, second, fourth, and fifth Preludes are in effect 'songs without words'. The melody running through each is essentially vocal in type and never goes beyond a singer's compass. The third Prelude is a typically

Mendelssohnian will-o'-the-wisp prestissimo scherzo; the sixth is weighed down by a heavy chordal accompaniment. The six Fugues of this opus follow the main structural outlines of the fugue according to Bach and incorporate the contrapuntal mechanism which he perfected. A brief description of these phenomena is appended to serve as a standard of comparison in studying the various methods of fugal composition practised during the nineteenth century.

*　　*　　*　　*

A fugue is essentially a musical discussion of a subject by a stated number of voices (instrumental parts)—generally three, four or five—in turn and in combination. The opening section known as the exposition adheres to an accepted formula in the manner of presenting the subject. In a four-part fugue, the first voice announces the subject in the tonic, the second answers in the dominant with the first running against it in counterpoint. The third voice then enters to reaffirm the subject in the tonic and the fourth joins in to repeat it in the dominant. The four-part mechanism having been set in motion the voices are free to proceed more independently. The central or modulatory section is inaugurated by the entry of the subject in a fresh key. There-after, the subject can be introduced by any of the voices, in any key and any number of times. It is also allowed to rest during short periods while fresh musical material, often derived from it, is interpolated in paragraphs of varying length known as episodes. The return of the subject in the original key usually marks the opening of the final section, in which the tension of the fugal argument is tightened by entries of the subject follow-ing one another so closely (stretto) as to overlap. The whole fugue is brought to a close with a coda which sometimes com-prises a last statement of the subject in a full panoply of triumphant chords.

These are the barest outlines of a type of composition which ac-knowledges no hard and fast rules and whose length and charac-ter are determined largely by the subject itself. A fugue may have two, or even three subjects, each of which may undergo separate exposition before being combined with the other. Sometimes, as in Mendelssohn's Fugue in E minor, the second of the two subjects may be the melodic inversion of the first.

When there is only one subject, the opening section of the fugue may be extended by a counter-exposition in which the voices enter in reverse order from that of the exposition.

The fugue is a texture rather than a form; it is essentially continuous and unified in character. The learned contrapuntal devices, canon, stretto, augmentation, diminution, inversion, and double-counterpoint, which may be introduced severally or collectively into its texture, are of the same kind as those we have already observed in many of the sonata movements and sets of variations discussed in the earlier chapters of this book.

*   *   *   *

Beethoven's fugal movements, while observing most of the conventional technicalities of fugue, seem to transcend all its inherent limitations. Mendelssohn's Six Fugues convey the impression of consciously preserving the letter rather than the spirit of Bach's fugal style. Their contrapuntal technique is impeccable, but they make no fresh contribution to the evolution of the fugue. Beethoven's evince an entirely new conception of its expressive possibilities. The fugue of the 'Hammerklavier' Sonata, to take the longest and most original, is designed on a colossal scale. It has three subjects and a wide range of tonality. The first subject, which is distinguished by the initial interval of a rising tenth followed by a trill, pervades the entire movement like a leit-motive. Yet at the end of nearly four hundred bars it sounds ever-new in its final guise of bare octaves. The whole armament of Beethoven's contrapuntal technique is brought into action in this fugue; even the stratagem of *cancrizans* (the playing of the subject backwards). It is, however, the immense driving force of the musical material itself, rather than the ingenious treatment to which it is subjected, that produces the cumulatively powerful effect of this long movement. Utterly different in style is the much shorter fugue of the Sonata in A flat, op. 110, which is both preluded and interpolated by a leisurely Arioso. The subject, after being conducted through many varieties of learned contrapuntal procedure, is finally exhibited in an entirely fresh light, embodied in chords and floating above or below a purely decorative accompaniment of scales and broken chords.

Another aspect of Mendelssohn's contrapuntal production is displayed in two of his Seven Characteristic Pieces, op. 7, no. 3, 'Energetic and fiery' and no. 5, 'Seriously, with increasing animation'. In design and texture they are strict fugues, but their titles and their inclusion in a set of pieces portraying various moods denote that they were conceived as romantic, rather than as absolute music. The sparkling no. 3, a model of grateful and effective piano writing, is possibly the most enjoyable to play of all Mendelssohn's fugues. Incidentally, it reveals in every bar the composer's familiarity with Bach's keyboard works. A pattern of chords towards the end of no. 5 instantly conjures up the ubiquitous figure in the first movement of the Third Brandenburg Concerto.

*   *   *   *

The romantic conception of fugue as a 'characteristic piece' is also exemplified in Schumann's works of the same type. With this composer, the writing of complete fugues was a phase rather than a lifelong preoccupation. The five-part fugal Finale of his Impromptus mentioned earlier in this chapter was an isolated phenomenon in his early production for the piano. Not until later in his career, in 1845, did he concentrate his energies for a time upon writing contrapuntal works for the keyboard. In his eagerness to enlarge the scope of his piano compositions he had a pedal-board attachment fitted to his own piano.

Of his five works in this category, only the Four Fugues, op. 72 and the Seven Pieces in Fughetta form, op. 126 were intended for the piano. The Six Studies, op. 56 and the Four Sketches, op. 58 were written for the now almost extinct pedal-piano, while the most important and enduring of all, the Six Fugues on the name BACH, op. 60 were designed 'for organ or pedal-piano'. Although these three last-named compositions do not actually belong to our study, they need hardly be excluded from it. The pedal-parts of each are not so exacting that they cannot be managed by the pianist himself, with or without the assistance of a second player.

One of the principal points of interest connected with this group of works is its relationship in style to Schumann's keyboard production as a whole. In many of his well-known earlier compositions such as *Carnaval*, *Études symphoniques*, the sonatas and *Faschingsschwank*, Schumann had shown a natural aptitude for working his musical material in canon and enlivening it with short canonic imitations. His most typical keyboard texture was largely homophonic. Even in the Six Studies for the pedal-piano, every one of which is a two-part accompanied canon, the style of the accompaniment of at least four of them brings these pieces into line with the composer's earlier works. Nos. 3–6 might easily take their places among the miniatures of *Kinderscenen* and *Bunte Blätter*.

The canonic writing, which in five of the Studies is confined to the upper and middle parts, is of several varieties. In the first, the canon occurs at the octave at the distance of half a bar. In the second, it runs at the unison and a whole bar apart: a species of canon which in this instance produces the unsatisfactory effect of making the piece sound as if it were composed entirely in pairs of repeated bars. The third Study differs from the others in having a brief introduction and a coda. The canon occurs at the fifth, two beats apart, while in the rhapsodic fourth Study it varies in interval and distance as the music proceeds.

Amid the crisp, feather-weight accompanying texture of the fifth Study, the canon (at the octave) stands out crystal clear to player and listener. But it is the elfin quality of the music itself rather than the contrapuntal skill that went to its making which has endeared this little piece to players. It is a triumph of artistry over intellectuality. Grieg's Canon in B flat minor (*Lyric Pieces*, Book II, op. 38, no. 8, 1883), likewise a miniature in ternary form, belongs to the same category. The canonic mechanism is very similar to that of the Schumann piece in question, but the chordal central section in the major mode, also in strict canon, offers a complete contrast to the accompanied melodies of the opening and closing sections.

The last of the Schumann Studies, an Adagio, is the only one of the six in which the pedal-part makes a contribution to the canonic interplay. It performs an essential role in the midget five-part fugato that comprises the central section. Elsewhere, it simply lends harmonic support to the upper parts while they proceed soberly in canon at the octave.

Throughout the set of Four Sketches for the Pedal Piano, op. 58, Schumann cut down the independence of the pedal-part to the very minimum. Only in the antiphonal no. 4 does it exercise an integral and artistically charming function, and only in a few bars of no. 3 is the canonic element strongly in evidence.

This opus is the least scholarly among the group of works that Schumann composed in 1845. The set of Six Fugues on the name BACH is the most recondite of his whole career. He asserted that none of his other works had cost him so much time in composing and polishing. Yet despite its seriousness in intention and its impressive contrapuntal technique, this forbidding-looking work springs from the same imaginative source as the ebullient little masterpiece *Carnaval*. It is based on a 'theme' of four notes and furnishes yet another example of the composer's faculty of realizing the infinite possibilities latent in apparently unpromising material; in a tiny motive with a melodic compass no wider than a minor third.

In only one of the fugues does the compressed thematic unit, which invariably forms the opening notes of the respective subjects of all six, show any alteration in its outline. This is in no. 4, where the A proceeds to C by falling a sixth instead of rising a third. Even so, the theme in its original close formation is later introduced into the texture 'per moto retrogado' (backwards) as a counter-subject to its second self. In each fugue the theme assumes new rhythmic guises and undergoes every conceivable permutation and combination in respect of contrapuntal treatment. It also shows its adaptability to fresh tonal surroundings. The basic tonality of the whole work is B flat major. When it is shifted to G minor in no. 3 and to F major in no. 5, the theme remains unchanged in notation but takes on an entirely new aspect by virtue of its altered harmonic relationship to the different keys.

A mere glance at the pages of this complete composition gives a fair idea of the great variety of figuration and the strong contrasts in expressive styles. The individual fugues range from the ponderous to the quicksilvery and culminate in a double-fugue of immense complexity shot through with passionate feeling.

* * * *

Pianists who know Schumann only from the brilliant and picturesque works of his 'first period' may hardly recognize him in this deeply learned and severe composition, which nevertheless repays their closest study and analysis. With the Four Fugues and the Seven Fughettas they find themselves on more familiar ground.

Schumann himself described the Fugues as 'characteristic pieces, but in stricter form'. In structure and contrapuntal technique these movements conform to current fugal standards. Recondite devices are not altogether banished, but a more definitely harmonic basis for the part-writing is clearly perceptible. Above all, the expressive style of the fugue-subjects is far more intimate than in the BACH Fugues. The first two, both in D minor, show marked differences in mood: the first, wistful; the second, eager and resolute. The third in F minor bears an unmistakable thematic likeness to Chopin's *Étude* in the same key. It is pervaded by a haunting melancholy which, together with a strong tinge of chromaticism, accentuates its affinity in style with this composer's works. The fourth Fugue in F major, with its undeniably cheerful subject, transparent part-writing, and sectional build, stands in complete contrast to the others. For a time, the subject assumes a slightly agitated air by having its longer beats first shortened and then syncopated. When it finally regains its habitual poise in the last few bars it sounds more buoyant than ever.

This same light-hearted mood prevails in the sixth of the Seven Pieces in Fughetta form (1853), 'allegro molto' in 12/16 time. There is not a single break in the semiquaver figuration, and the fugal entries, or segments of them, topple over one another in their breathless haste, leaving a wreckage of enchantingly crude discords in their wake. The other fughettas of this set are comparatively uneventful, but all are distinguished by the fierce concentration of their fugal style. The subject of each is practically never allowed to retire from extremely active service. In consequence, the pieces tend to sound monotonous; all the more so as the key-system of the whole work is narrow in range. The melodic lilt of the first and the fifth, however, and the headstrong determination of the fourth recall the untrammelled style typical of the composer's earlier productions.

*   *   *   *

Where Schumann spread the thematic metamorphosis of the BACH motto-theme over six individual fugues, Liszt concentrated it into one full-length composition, the Prelude and Fugue on the Theme BACH. He wrote it originally for organ in 1855 and arranged it for the piano in 1870. The exuberant passage-work, with its torrents of octave runs and handfuls of mighty chords, stands in indescribably sharp contrast to the stern linear counterpoint of Schumann's op. 60. In Liszt's hands the semitonal intervals which constitute the theme give rise to a kaleidoscopic web of sounds. The fugue-subject proceeds chromatically throughout its whole length, the key-signature changes eight times to allow the music to extend its harmonic boundaries to the furthest limits and there is hardly a page that is not strewn with a myriad accidentals. After the riotous opening Fantasy, the strict four-part exposition of the subject, 'pianissimo, misterioso', gives every indication of developing into a conventional fugue. But in a flash the contrapuntal texture dissolves into decorative figuration. The thematic particles are distributed over the keyboard to become ostinato basses, to be superimposed as chromatic embroidery upon diatonic foundations, to luxuriate in chordal finery and eventually to charge in the splendour of double octaves to a triumphant close. The virtuosic style of the piece predominates over the intellectual conception. Even so, this Fantasy and Fugue may claim consideration as a collateral descendant of Bach's Chromatic Fantasy and Fugue, which is itself permeated by a strong element of virtuosity.

* * * *

César Franck's two works in this category stand alone among large-scale piano compositions. Each consists of three separate movements that are closely inter-related by means of thematic connexions and each whole work is musically of the calibre of a sonata. In the Prelude, Chorale and Fugue (1884) the movements merge into one another without breaks. The constant interweaving of the principal themes strengthens the feeling of almost unbroken continuity, in which, however, the prevailing diatonicism of the Chorale and the acute chromaticism of the Prelude and Fugue stand in perpetually creative opposition. The process of dovetailing the thematic content is carried on ceaselessly throughout the whole work. The fugue-subject is already hinted at within a few bars of the opening of the Prelude. It is implicit, too, in the phrases which form the episodes between the statements of each line of the Chorale in the same manner as in a Bach chorale-prelude. It dominates the short section following the Chorale, and after it has run its full course in the Fugue itself, it is united with the Chorale in the resplendent passage-work of the final pages. Great diversity in the pianistic figuration and a strong sense of growth and of climax increase the effectiveness of a work in which the intellectual and the virtuosic elements are unusually closely integrated.

Throughout the Prelude, Aria and Finale (1887), the chain of thematic interconnexions is less continuous. The movements are separate entities and only in the Finale is the musical material of all three placed unmistakably side by side. Despite the homophonic style of the pianistic layout, the contrapuntal element is as strong as, if not stronger than, that of the Prelude, Chorale and Fugue. In every movement the melodic outline is transferred from one strand of the texture to another. The themes, which are mostly short and are very easily memorable, are frequently presented in double counterpoint, often with extremely decorative accompaniment. The technique of variation also plays an important part. Phrase after phrase is presented in new aspects and even whole sections reappear in unfamiliar guises.

In structure, each movement is markedly sectional. The Prelude is in older rondo form with a long anticipatory link between the second episode and the last appearance of the refrain. The Aria, set between a recitative-like introduction and an epilogue, comprises two panels, the second of which is a decorated version of the first. The Finale blends the rondo form of the Prelude with the panelled construction of the Aria. The principal theme from the Aria, soaring above a liquescent accompaniment, constitutes the central section. Lastly, the most distinctive subject-matter of the Prelude reappears majestically in augmentation to form the climax of the whole work.

This elaborately planned and harmonically enterprising piece is not cultivated by pianists to the same extent as its much-loved predecessor. Its comparative neglect may possibly be due to the tedium caused by the endless repetition and over-emphasis of short lengths of thematic material, as well as to the intricacies of the part-writing and the involved style of the formal construction.

*   *   *   *

Each of these two big works of Franck's is a compromise between a sonata and a fantasy.

A fantasy sometimes consists of several connected movements, as in Schubert's 'Wanderer' Fantasy; or of separate movements, as in Schumann's Fantasy in C and in Mendelssohn's Fantasy in F sharp minor. It may, on the other hand, constitute a free extemporization upon a given theme or themes: for instance, Liszt's Fantasy on two Swiss melodies and Balakirev's 'Islamey' Fantasy. At its very simplest it can be an almost symmetrical movement in binary form, such as Bach's Fantasy in C minor and Handel's Fantasy in C major.

The fantasy is a type rather than a form, and it is in this sense that the title is bestowed upon a number of shortish pieces which display little of the fantastic in their structural make-up however imaginative they may be in style. Such are Mendelssohn's Three Fantasies or Caprices, op. 16, and Brahms's Fantasies, op. 116, which comprise three Caprices and four Intermezzos. Some of these movements are approximately in simple ternary form; others show a mosaic-like pattern of great ingenuity and charm.

* * * *

Beethoven's one Fantasy for piano solo, op. 77 (1809) is a curious blend of improvisation and formality. After opening with a short phrase in G minor it roams through key after key in a succession of entirely unrelated paragraphs varying in length, style and tempo. Thereafter, it settles permanently in B major with a square-cut theme, Allegretto, which gives rise to nine florid variations and then returns, Adagio, to end the piece. The whole of the preludial section makes the effect of a rambling extemporization. In this respect the piece resembles Mozart's Fantasy in C major, K.394, which, like Beethoven's, ends in conventional style, but with a fugue instead of a set of variations.

* * * *

Schubert's 'Wanderer' Fantasy (1822), the most highly organized of all the fantasies of our study, differs profoundly from all his other piano compositions, both in the originality of its

K

design and in the extreme difficulty of the keyboard writing. As a whole work it possesses attributes of the sonata in its division into four movements. They are largely self-contained but they run continuously and are closely related. The first movement displays elements of both sonata and rondo forms. The second is a set of linked variations on a melody nearly identical with that of Schubert's song 'Der Wanderer' from which the Fantasy subsequently acquired its title. The third movement is a scherzo-and-trio and the Finale a fugue.

The unique character of the Fantasy is its organic unity. The whole work grows out of a single theme containing an all-pervading rhythmic figure which is announced in the very first bar $\left(\text{c} \; \tilde{\text{f}} \; \text{f} \tilde{\text{f}} \; \text{f} \text{f} | \text{f} \right)$. The sense of unity is further strengthened by other thematic connexions between the movements: for example, between the melody of the second episode (in E flat major) in the first movement and that of the trio section of the third movement. The principle of thematic metamorphosis underlies the entire composition. The main substance of each movement is derived from the same source but makes a completely fresh impression by its successive transformations in rhythm, key, tempo and expressive quality. The heavily-accented beats of the opening 'allegro con fuoco' in C major take on a more gentle, cantabile character in the first episode (in E major) of this movement. They lose all their fieriness as they announce the 'Wanderer' theme of the second movement in a hushed pianissimo, Adagio in C sharp minor, and again, as they dissolve into a luminous haze of demisemiquavers during the ensuing variations. Reborn as crotchets and quavers they dance in lilting triple rhythm through the presto Scherzo. Finally, resuming their original martial character, they stride furiously about the fugue.

*   *   *   *

The orchestral quality of Schubert's keyboard writing induced Liszt to arrange the Fantasy for piano and orchestra, in which quasi-concerto version it is now as well known to concert-goers as is the original form. It may have been Liszt's close acquaintance with a large-scale work based on a single theme that led to his adopting the principle of theme-transformation in some of his own symphonic poems. This species of composition owes its title to him, but in type and style it is deeply indebted to the 'Wanderer' Fantasy.

Liszt himself composed only one fantasy entirely upon original thematic material: the *Fantasia quasi una Sonata; après une lecture de Dante*, which we studied earlier in connexion with his Sonata in B minor. A few of the numerous fantasies he wrote upon other composers' works and upon national melodies will be referred to in the next chapter.

*   *   *   *

Mendelssohn's two full-sized Fantasies vary greatly in extent and shape. One, an improvisatory musing upon the Irish song 'The last rose of summer', op. 15, comprises a series of interlinking sections of passage-work, recitative and aria in widely differing tempi but all in the same tonality of E minor and major. The other, the much longer Fantasy in F sharp minor, op. 28 (1833), also known as *Sonate écossaise*, is divided into three separate movements. Their clear-cut structural outlines and unified key-system impart to the whole composition the character of a sonata. The alternately rhapsodic and narrative style of the opening movement do not wholly conceal its fundamentally binary form. The second movement, in the relative major, is a scherzo-and-trio in feeling despite its quadruple time-signature. The presto Finale is in regular sonata form with the traditional repeat of the exposition and a coda summing up the principal features of the movement. In point of expressive quality, this sonata-like Fantasy is differentiated from Mendelssohn's earlier Sonatas in E major and B flat major by the dark, romantic colouring which pervades the opening and closing movements and lends them great charm.

*   *   *   *

Despite the immense differences in length, scope, and style between Schubert's 'Wanderer' Fantasy and Chopin's Fantasy in F minor, op. 49 (1840–1), the two works alike convey a strong sense of unity, although by exactly opposite means. Schubert employed a minimum of thematic material and displayed it in a multiplicity of guises. Chopin assembled a number of distinctive but complementary musical ideas and arranged them in convincing succession with periodic restatements of well-defined paragraphs to ensure cohesion. Only the haunting opening phrases of the stately introduction are never heard again. Almost all the other themes in the main body of the piece reappear twice, sometimes in fresh keys but not always in the same order. One of them, the serpentine figure in triplets first announced immediately after the introduction, is later extended to serve as a linking passage between the more strongly melodic portions, most particularly before and after the tranquil episode in B major. It also underlies the coda and is one of the principal agents in maintaining the feeling of continuity that distinguishes a work in which the urgent flow of the musical thought determines the structural mould into which it is poured.

The Fantasy-Impromptu, which Chopin wrote six years before the Fantasy in F minor and which was published posthumously, is a trifle that belongs more correctly to the province of the miniature than to the realm of the imaginative fantasy. The large-scale Polonaise-Fantasy, op. 61 (1845–6), in which he experimented even more boldly in both form and texture, must await consideration with the composer's Polonaises in a later chapter.

*   *   *   *

Beethoven and Schubert each incorporated a set of variations into their respective Fantasies. Balakirev (1837–1910) went a step further by writing the whole of his *Islamey: Oriental Fantasy* (1869) as a series of continuously interwoven variations upon three separate themes. Each already contains much repetition of short figures. The ceaseless reiteration of the limited material throughout the longish piece would produce a hypnotic effect were it not for the infinity of its transformations within a pianistic layout that blazes and scintillates with chromatic brilliance. Two of the three themes, which are all Armenian and Caucasian in origin, are composed principally of tones and semitones, with only an occasional interval of a third or fourth. Running successively in unflagging semiquavers in 12/16 time with a periodic accent like a warning drum-beat, they form the vivid opening section which straightway evokes the exotic atmosphere that surrounds the whole piece. The third, more definitely melodic, theme steals in 'andantino espressivo' in 6/8 time. It soon quickens in pace until it is wholly assimilated into the resurgent semiquaver figuration of the two preceding themes and the three become more and more closely interlaced. Gradually the rhythmic tension tightens into a 2/4 'allegro vivo', the once languorous melody rings out in an exultant fortissimo and eventually sounds a last clarion call during the culminating 'presto furioso'.

Islamey is an amazing fusion of the primitive with the cultivated. The musical subject-matter is crude but the manner of its treatment reveals the utmost refinement of technical resource. The themes go through a process of fragmentation as they are hurled into the seething mass of chromaticisms which forms the coruscating texture. They are felt rather than heard, for when the melodic outlines become obscured, their rhythmic pulse beats on with inexorable regularity.

Balakirev's conception of the fantasy as an equal blend of unparalleled virtuosity and romantic impressionism was new in the history of the species. In point of pianistic style, however, *Islamey* is a concert-study. It is of the same calibre as Liszt's *Études d'exécution transcendante*, with which, but for its sub-title *Oriental Fantasy*, it might equally well have been bracketed for consideration under the heading of 'Studies' in a later chapter.

* * * *

Of the three different kinds of composition discussed in this chapter, two possess certain specific attributes. The rondo must perforce have a refrain and episodes, however loosely the piece as a whole is organized. The fugue, or the fugal movement, should at least begin with a formal exposition of the subject, even if it breaks off immediately afterwards into a less rigid style of contrapuntal writing. The fantasy, however, despite its long ancestry as a musical type, conforms to no definite rules, but shapes itself according to the composer's whim of the moment. For this reason it is inherently the most subjective, and consequently the most romantic of all the types of composition we have so far studied in these pages.

— 8 —

Romantic Music

*Nocturnes and other new types of Romantic pieces: Impromptus,
Scherzos, Rhapsodies, Ballades, and Novellettes. Descriptive
and Programme music. Romantic transcriptions.*

DURING the early decades of the century, when Beethoven,
Weber and Schubert were writing their sonatas, another composer was evolving a type of piano piece which was to secure
him lasting fame although his sonatas were destined to occupy
only a minor position in after years.

John Field (1782–1837), an Irish pianist who spent the
greater part of his musical career on the Continent, was the
first composer of the *nocturne*, or 'night piece'. The title he chose
for these romantic movements was not new in the history of
music. It had been used in the eighteenth century as an alternative name for an instrumental serenade or divertimento in
several movements. The novelty of Field's nocturnes consisted
in their being essentially piano music: single pieces with flowing
melodies and graceful arpeggio accompaniments whose effectiveness in performance depended to a great extent upon the
use of the sustaining pedal.

Some years before he embarked upon the composition of nocturnes Field had written three Sonatas which were first published in London (?1802) and subsequently in Paris in 1803 as
his Opus 1. They were dedicated to Clementi, to whom Field
was apprenticed as a pupil from the age of twelve and with
whom he eventually travelled to Russia, there to settle permanently.

The three Sonatas of op. 1: no. 1 in E flat major, no. 2 in A
major, and no. 3 in C minor, all of which are still available in
print, were succeeded in 1814 by a Sonata in B major which is

contemporary with the first of the nocturnes but is now no longer in circulation. Each of these four compositions consists of a pair of movements in the same key, strongly contrasted in expressive character. The first movement of each is in classical sonata form; the second movements of nos. 1, 2 and 4 are graceful or spirited rondos. That of no. 3 is in free scherzo-and-trio form with alternating sections in the major and minor. The Rondo of no. 1 in E flat, an irrepressibly gay, dance-like movement in 3/4 time, Allegro, has become well known apart from its context: first through having been published in a series of piano solos edited by Hans von Bülow, and latterly, by having been selected to form the first movement in a 'John Field' Suite arranged for orchestra by Hamilton Harty.

The musical style of Field's sonatas not unnaturally reveals the influence of Clementi. In the opening movement of the Sonata in A major, he even followed a formal precedent established by Clementi in some of his own sonatas. This was the recapitulating of the principal subject in the key of the sub-dominant; a procedure later adopted several times by Schubert, as we have already seen. In point of contrapuntal ingenuity and scrupulous workmanship the Field sonatas do not rival those by his master. Pianistically they are more delicate and imaginative, yet they contain surprisingly bold modulations, and passages invested with a fire and energy that lend them a Beethovenian tinge. The piano writing, with its occasionally intricate finger-work, vital left-hand parts and uncommon colour-effects, is rewarding to players, but the sonatas as whole works lack conviction in their structural outlines and tonal schemes. As examples of Field's production for the piano they stand far behind the nocturnes, which he composed and published at intervals between 1814 and 1835 and which were edited with a long and appreciative foreword by Liszt for republication in one volume in 1859.

Not all the eighteen pieces in this collection were written in the first place as piano solos. No. 6, Andante in F major, is an alternative version of the Larghetto in E major in Field's sixth Piano Concerto; no. 14 in G major is an excerpt from the first movement of the seventh Piano Concerto. The seventh Nocturne in A major and the twelfth, *Le Midi*, in E major, are movements from his Divertimenti for strings and piano. In pianistic and musical style, however, and in their independence of the string accompaniments, these compositions resemble the genuine nocturnes. Their inclusion in the Liszt collection is fully justified.

*   *   *   *

Field's Nocturnes were the prototypes of a new kind of piano piece which was subsequently cultivated by many nineteenth-century composers. They would possibly be better known and more frequently performed to-day had they not within a few years of their composition been surpassed in beauty and interest by Chopin's.

Chopin took the title and the general character of the composition from Field, but his own Nocturnes, composed between 1827 and 1846 reveal a depth of expression and an exquisite sensitivity in the piano writing that leave Field's far behind. Nevertheless, some features of Field's piano style foreshadow Chopin's. They include the wide-ranging figures of accompaniment in the left hand, the single-line ornamental passages in the right hand, the use of the very highest register of the piano and the immediate repetition of a phrase with the melody embellished almost beyond recognition. Only in Chopin's earliest nocturnes, however, is his indebtedness to Field as noticeable as it is in the Nocturne in E flat major, op. 9, no. 2, which bears a distinct resemblance to Field's Nocturne no. 1. Both pieces are in the same key and time (12/8) and both have the same kind of long-drawn melody over a flowing accompaniment of quavers. But Chopin's piano writing reveals a far more highly developed harmonic sense and a greater awareness of subtle keyboard effects.

In general, a comparison of the two sets of nocturnes shows that while Field's are for the most part distinguished by great continuity, they are inclined to be monotonous and to lack effective contrast. Even if the type of figuration varies and the key is changed during the course of a piece, the expressive mood remains fundamentally the same. The majority of Chopin's, however, even the early Nocturne in B major, no. 3, are strongly diversified by changes in either the figuration, key, mode, time-signature or tempo throughout a single movement. The third, a lilting Allegretto in 6/8 time, encloses an agitato section in the minor, 'alla breve', studded with syncopations and conflicting metres. In the seventh in C sharp minor, the serenity of the opening section is counteracted by the rhythmically vigorous 'più mosso' that eventually settles into the (enharmonic) major. The Nocturne in F sharp minor, no. 14, opens and closes with a stream of reposeful continuous melody in common time which is later thrown into strong relief by a slower but more firmly-accented interlude in triple time. The fourth Nocturne in F major furnishes the most extreme instance of a violent antithesis in expressive styles. Its turbulent passage-work 'con fuoco' in the minor mode is flanked by two supremely tranquil stretches of accompanied melody in the major.

In a few of Chopin's nocturnes the element of contrast is secured only by changes in the type of figuration. In the tenth, in A flat, the layout of twelve quaver chords in a bar in both hands during the interlude in compound time brings new life into a movement that consists primarily of a melody in simple time floating above a languorous accompaniment of triplet quavers. The G major Nocturne, no. 12, a rondo with both episodes thematically similar, is written throughout in 6/8 time, but there is an immense difference in rhythmic effect between the semiquaver arabesques of the refrain and the gently swing-ing theme in crotchets and quavers of the sostenuto portions. With the exception of the thirteenth Nocturne, in which a pair of contrasting themes in C minor and major undergo variation that intensifies their expressive qualities from the tranquil to the impassioned, most of the other nocturnes not referred to here remain in one mood throughout.

In one of Field's nocturnes, the poetic *Rêverie-Nocturne*, no. 13 in C major, the maintenance of a single mood is achieved by the continuous repetition of an eight-bar phrase alternately in the tonic and in nearly-related keys. The limited musical material

consists of a semi-staccato chordal progression in the left hand
and a melodic outline in the right that winds like a tendril
between the upper and lower notes of an octave:

The atmosphere of variegated sameness created by the tissue of
evanescent sounds over a monotone bass recalls that of Chopin's
Berceuse, which, as we noted in an earlier chapter, comprises a
long series of changing decorations above a repeated harmonic
pattern.

In point of structure, Field's *Rêverie-Nocturne* is a rondo, but
the episodes are simply translations of the refrain into fresh
keys. His *Nocturne caractéristique*, *Le Midi*, no. 12 in E major, a
more conventional rondo with episodes of contrasting material,
approaches the category of programme music. It ends with
twelve equidistant beats on the tonic, clearly marked in the
score as denoting the striking of the hour of noon. This romantic
effect is paralleled towards the end of Schumann's *Papillons* by
the six widely-spaced beats on the dominant which bear the
composer's direction 'The turret-clock strikes six' and which are
intended to indicate the approach of dawn.

Among nocturnes of a later date are two by Tchaikovsky. One
in C sharp minor, op. 19, no. 4 (1873), is a short piece in ternary
form with a varied reprise. The other, in F major, op. 10, no. 1
(1871), has points in common with Grieg's Nocturne in C
major, op. 54, no. 4 (1891), one of his *Lyric Pieces*. Both these

movements begin with accompanied melodies which merge into interludes of impressionistic tone-painting. Tchaikovsky's repeated chords, '*pp* e leggiero', recall the 12/8 section of Chopin's Nocturne in A flat, op. 32, no. 2, but Grieg's colour-effects with decorated dominant-ninth chords are unmistakably his own. They are of the type familiar in many of his piano works, from the Concerto to the smallest *Lyric Piece*.

*   *   *   *

The nocturne is among the earliest of several new kinds of pieces of medium length: *impromptus, novellettes, ballades, rhapsodies* and others with more specific titles such as *Berceuse, Barcarolle, Humoresque*, etc., that came into being in the nineteenth century. They were cultivated with enthusiasm by the romantic composers in preference to the older-established forms, such as the sonata, the variation and the fugue, with which they were unable to come to satisfactory terms. The very titles of these pieces denote the intention of composers to write subjective music unfettered by considerations of formal balance. But in point of structure some of the works to which the term 'romantic piano music' is loosely applied are based on classical precedent. For example, Brahms's Rhapsody in G minor is in straightforward sonata form. Schubert's Impromptu in B flat major, op. 142, no. 3, Schumann's Impromptus, op. 5, and Grieg's Ballade, op. 24, are sets of variations. Schumann's Novellettes include several in rondo form; many of Field's and some of Chopin's nocturnes are in well-balanced ternary form.

It is the style rather than the shape of these pieces that distinguishes them from movements conceived as abstract music. The Brahms Rhapsody in G minor follows the conventions of sonata form in its clear-cut division into three parts, in its modulatory central section based on material from the exposition and in the sonata-form key-relationship in the reprise. Yet it demonstrates from the very first bar that the composer was much less concerned with form in the abstract than he was with setting forth his musical ideas in boldly effective keyboard style, and with creating a particular atmosphere by maintaining one

type of figuration during the greater part of the piece. Schubert's
two Impromptus in A flat (op. 90, no. 4, and op. 142, no. 2) are
formally the equivalents of a scherzo-and-trio and a minuet-
and-trio respectively, but the eloquent cantabile melodies and
the quivering or impassioned broken chords throughout both
these pieces differentiate them in intensity of expression and in
pianistic style from movements of the same shape in the composer's sonatas.

As a general rule, the structure of romantic music is flexible.
Sometimes it combines the characteristics of several forms. At
others, it develops on entirely fresh lines in the process of giving
musical significance to the emotional content, especially when
the piece in question has a literary basis and the music is intended to portray a story, a scene, or a state of mind: in other
words, when it is programme music.

The various generic titles used for romantic piano music have
no very exact connotations. Pieces with the same title by the
same composer often evince strikingly different conceptions of
the basic idea. Six out of Schubert's eight impromptus make the
very opposite impression from that of being genuine improvisa-
tions, and the whole group comprises a variety of formal types.
One, as we have already seen, is a set of variations, and two are
in minuet-(scherzo-)-and-trio form. Two others, in E flat and
G flat, op. 90, nos. 2 and 3, are in ternary form with a coda, and
the Impromptu in F minor, op. 142, no. 1, is a blend of rondo
and sonata forms. The remaining two show definitely improvisatory characteristics. The first in C minor, op. 90, no. 1,
comprises rambling continuous variations on two alternating
themes. The last, in F minor, op. 142, no. 4, is made up of a
succession of units, short and long, of vividly rhapsodic music
with a Hungarian tinge. Schumann's short Impromptu in F
major, no. 9 of the *Albumblätter*, op. 124, and Dvořák's longer
and more rhapsodic Impromptu in G minor, op. 52, no. 1, both
sound genuinely extempore. They consist mainly of short
phrases or sections many times repeated and they sound as
though the respective composers were simply toying with the
musical ideas. Another Impromptu by Dvořák, which has only

recently been published (1949), is composed with the utmost precision, even though it begins in one key and ends in another (G major and E major). It is a model of symmetrical ternary form, but the evasive tonality and persistent syncopation lend this tiny movement a bewitchingly subtle character.

Two of Chopin's Impromptus, no. 1 in A flat major (1837), and no. 3 in G flat major (1842), are likewise in straightforward ternary form. The pianistic style of the outer sections of these three pieces recalls some of the composer's *Études* and the central episodes are suavely melodic in the manner of the Nocturnes. Only the second Impromptu in F sharp major (1839) displays unconventional attributes in design and tonality. The march-like interlude in D major is linked to the reprise by means of a tentative opening phrase in F instead of F *sharp* major, and the principal theme ultimately dissolves into a fine chain of demisemiquaver runs. But even these 'impromptu' features appear to be the outcome of close thinking rather than of extemporization at the keyboard. Tovey cites this Impromptu as an example of Chopin's capacity when writing in 'larger than lyric forms', to produce 'something essentially classical in more or less free form'. He goes on to speak of Chopin's first two Scherzos as being 'rare cases where a classical form will lend itself to a "romantic" idea'.

*   *   *   *

The *scherzo* as a musical form dates back to the seventeenth century, but as a piece of instrumental music it was a development of the minuet and remained for some time within the sphere of the classical sonata and symphony. Chopin was the first to raise it to the rank of a full-sized piece of 'romantic piano music'. His four Scherzos were composed between 1831 and 1842. All are marked presto and are constructed with the greatest freedom upon a sonata-form basis. They reveal their derivation from the earlier type of scherzo only by the retention of the triple time-signature and the inclusion of self-contained trios (interludes) in three of the pieces. The interlude in the first Scherzo in B minor is based on the melody of a Polish Christmas cradle-song. The rocking accompaniment and slower tempo that it inspires form an effective contrast to the coruscating passages of the presto sections. In the second Scherzo in B flat minor, the interlude, placed between the exposition and the development-section, is in A major. The gap between these two distantly-related keys is bridged by the ending of the exposition on the chord of D flat and the opening of the interlude with a phrase in which the enharmonic C sharp is the most prominent melody-note. The character of this interlude is restrained. The melodies are short, and as they are closely confined within the texture, they make a less immediate effect than does the eagle-winged tune in D flat major that dominates the first and last portions of the movement. A spacious melody of the same kind but in the minor mode forms the core of the fourth Scherzo in E major. Its long phrases and leisurely progress distinguish it sharply from the brief, scintillating thematic units that surround it on all sides.

The third Scherzo in C sharp minor differs from all the others in style and shape owing to its less melodic character as well as to the absence of a central cantabile episode. The thematic material is essentially instrumental in type. Rumbling bass-notes and terrific thunderclaps of chords form the introduction to an unyieldingly stark theme in double octaves. The dignified chordal contrasting subject is continually interrupted by showers of quavers descending upon it leggierissimo from the heights of the keyboard. The whole movement is closely integrated. The music never strays very far from the original tonality, minor or major; the form is symmetrical without being rigid and the coda sums up the thematic and pianistic features of a work that is the very embodiment of dynamic energy.

*　　*　　*　　*

Mendelssohn interpreted the term scherzo (joke) much more literally than did Chopin. His two works of this kind were both composed in 1836. The tiny Scherzo in B minor consisting of feather-weight detached chords and notes, and the 'scherzo a capriccio' in F sharp minor, a longer movement in binary form, are charming fairy pieces entirely lacking in the daemonic forcefulness that characterizes Chopin's powerful works in this category. Brahms's one and only Scherzo in E flat minor, op. 4 (1851), his first published composition, demonstrates an altogether different conception of the form. It is a revival of the earlier type of scherzo with two trios and is inevitably sectional in build. Yet its generally ample proportions and the skilful overlapping of themes where the second trio leads back to the scherzo by way of a linking passage lend it a certain feeling of continuity. The piano writing is vivid and effective, but is much less assured than that in Brahms's later pieces of similar length: the three Rhapsodies.

*   *   *   *

Technically, the title *rhapsody* applied to a piece of instrumental music denotes that it is a composition of 'emotional character and irregular form'. In actual fact, two, at least, of Brahms's rhapsodies belie the second part of this definition. The G minor Rhapsody, op. 79, no. 2, 'molto passionato', as we noted earlier, is in strict first-movement form. Its companion in B minor, op. 79, no. 1, is ternary in its main outlines, but each of the two outer sections is itself in first-movement form and the whole piece is lengthened by a coda. Though the music is rhapsodic in pianistic style, the arrangement of the subject-matter is carefully planned. Two themes dominate the movement: the opening phrase containing a little figure in triplet semiquavers that lends itself to development later in various parts of the texture, and the 'second subject', whose characteristic feature is the interval of a rising fourth. This latter theme, which is in the minor mode, assumes a less plaintive aspect on being transposed into the major and expanded to form the interlude, but it reverts to the minor for the coda, where its sombre character is emphasized by the depth of pitch to which it is confined. Only in the last four bars does it send up a faint echo to the treble surface.

The two Rhapsodies, both composed in 1879, were followed in 1893 by another which is less well known. This third Rhapsody in E flat major, op. 119, no. 4, 'allegro risoluto', is shorter, more open-heartedly melodic, and freer in form than the others. It is built up arch-wise. The three sections of musical material rise towards the interlude in A flat major which forms the key-stone and then descend in reverse order of appearance, varied either in key, mode or figuration. For instance, when the open-ing theme recurs after the interlude it is transposed from E flat to C major, it is placed much lower on the keyboard and its robust chords are reduced to an awed pianissimo. During the coda its salient features, disguised in the minor mode, are only just recognizable within the triplet figuration. Rhythmically, this Rhapsody is the most interesting of the three. Some of the principal phrases are irregular in length and accentuation. The theme in E flat major runs in five-bar periods with the strong accent sometimes falling on the weak beat; the buoyant eight-bar melody of the grazioso interlude in A flat major is given a subtle and wayward twist by being divided into phrases of three and five bars respectively instead of the conventional four and four.

*   *   *   *

Liszt's numerous Hungarian Rhapsodies, which are as irre-gular in shape as Brahms's are symmetrical, come within a different category. In the first place, they are not entirely ori-ginal compositions, but are based upon the kind of gipsy music with which Liszt was familiar through having heard it per-formed in his native land. In many instances it was not genuine gipsy music such as has been collected during the present cen-tury, chiefly by the two Hungarian composers Bela Bartók and Zoltán Kodály. It was simply music which gipsies heard in the towns and which they re-interpreted by performing it in their own picturesque style. Liszt in his turn submitted this alternately barbaric, melancholy and wildly exultant musical material to the most graphic pianistic treatment imaginable.

As performing pieces, the Hungarian Rhapsodies have a fascination all their own. They display every facet of Liszt's colossal keyboard technique and exploit the resources of the piano to the very utmost. The pieces vary in extent from two or

L

three pages to over twenty, but all are composed in sections differing in length, speed and expressive style. A few bear titles: no. 5, *Héroïde-élégiaque*, one of the least impetuous, in quasi-rondo form; no. 9, the long *Carnaval de Pesth* with a separate Finale mounting to a frenzied climax, and no. 15, the *Rakoczy March*, which is based on a tune already well known as a march for the Hungarian army.

With the exception of the Third and the Fifth, which are short, restrained and comparatively easy to play, the Hungarian Rhapsodies bristle with technical difficulties for the performer. Yet the pianist who reads them through, simply for the sake of becoming familiar with their contents and not with a view to studying them for performance, will find himself greatly enriched in pianistic experience by having examined Liszt's methods of cajoling the keyboard into producing a limitless range of astounding colour-effects.

Certain basic characteristics persist throughout the Hungarian Rhapsodies. The pieces generally include at least one languorous or melancholy theme and others of quicker, more specifically rhythmic type. The melodies, which often contain repetitions of a short phrase or of a single figure and which tend to be strongly accented or syncopated, undergo variations of many kinds. They are placed in every part of the texture in turn, sometimes divided between the two hands and flung to and fro across a wide compass. Often they are broken up into small segments and decorated with mercurial figuration or percussive ornaments, or their barest outlines are incorporated in lambent passage-work so that the tunes seem to be dissolved into a fine spray of sounds.

Distinctive features of the piano writing which may be found to a greater or lesser degree in all the fifteen Hungarian Rhapsodies published in standard editions are cadenza-like passages in single or double notes; quick repetitions of notes, octaves or tiny rhythmic figures; phrases of odd bar-lengths; melodies combined with accompanying trills in the same hand; passages in which the two hands are closely interlocked while they play in staccato thirds, sixths or octaves; ornaments that impart an incisive accent to melody-notes or chords and the use of very low pitch, either for drum-like tremolandos, as in no. 14, or for a heavy chordal theme, as in the Finale of the *Carnaval de Pesth*. Among the more specialized effects are imitations of the sounds produced by the Hungarian cimbalom, an instrument of the dulcimer type whose strings the player strikes with hammers. Typical examples occur during the whole of the opening section of the Eleventh Rhapsody, 'quasi zimbalo', in the 'allegretto a la zingarese' of the Fourteenth and again in the glissandos of nos. 10, 14, and 15.

The Hungarian Rhapsodies, which date from the 1840s, have one feature in common with the Brahms Rhapsodies: every one of them is written in quadruple time. Liszt's *Rhapsodie espagnole* (1863) differs from all these pieces by being based largely on themes in triple time. The themes in question are the *Folies d'Espagne*, andante in 3/4 time, and the *Jota aragonese* in 3/8, both of them well-known melodies which have been used by other composers. They were submitted by Liszt to fantastic decoration of the type that he used in the Hungarian Rhapsodies. The cimbalom effects, however, are transformed into the simulated beating of castanets.

*　　　*　　　*　　　*

The 'emotional character and irregular form' which are typical of many rhapsodies are also distinguishing marks of the *ballade*, but a more dominating trait of the latter is its narrative style. As a general rule the music is invested with spaciousness and continuity; it unfolds, rather than proceeds in ordered sequence. Themes or thematic fragments once heard are re-introduced periodically, as if to recall to the listener's memory the salient points of the tale that is being told. The nature of the tale itself may or may not be indicated by the composer. The origin of Brahms's 'Edward' Ballade is revealed by the sub-title, but Chopin's Ballades, which are generally considered to have been suggested by the epics of the Polish patriot Adam Mickiewicz, bear no descriptive titles. Neither do Liszt's two works in this category.

The ballade as a single movement for the piano was Chopin's creation. It was an outcome of his need to evolve a structural framework within which to develop musical ideas that transcend the bounds of orthodox forms. His four Ballades sometimes display the tensions of sonata form or the alternations of refrain and episodes familiar in the rondo, but each is entirely individual in design and expressive character. He composed them at longish intervals between 1831 and 1842, and apart from the fact that all are written in compound duple time, they bear little resemblance to one another except in greatness of conception.

The first Ballade in G minor is the most strongly influenced by sonata form. The two main subjects, the plaintive theme in G minor and the radiantly expansive melody in E flat major, stand in mutual relationship as first and second subjects. They undergo development in the central section of the piece but escape formal recapitulation. Instead, the melody in E flat is ultimately restated in its original key, enhanced in expressive power by fuller chords and a more rapidly flowing accompaniment. The G minor theme follows, desolate as ever, to merge into a furiously energetic coda, 'alla breve'. The whole dramatic movement in 6/4 time is held together by brilliant passages which exemplify Chopin's art of weaving significant inner melodies into the pianistic texture and of making effective use of the heights and depths of the keyboard. The solemn Introduction, lento in common time, consisting of a phrase in subdued plain octaves starting out of the basic key, prepares the listener for the heroic style of the music. The downward-swooping octave passage brings the movement to an appropriately violent end.

The later Ballades are less sombre in character. All are in 6/8 time and in quicker tempo than the first. The second in F major, the composition of which long occupied Chopin's thoughts, was completed in 1839 and dedicated to Schumann, to whom he had played the first draft in 1836. It stands apart from the others by being cast in a unique structural mould. The piece opens with a pair of strongly-contrasted sections: a contemplative, song-like

Andantino in lilting rhythm and a volcanic 'presto con fuoco'. The two sections are straightway restated, the musical material undergoing contraction, expansion or development in sonata style, but the mutual contrast in expression remaining unchanged. This twofold presentation of the musical subject-matter is followed without a pause by a final section of agitated passage-work which is suddenly halted by a terrific sforzato, whereupon the Ballade fades out pianissimo in a haunting phrase in A minor from the Andantino. A distinctive flavour is imparted to the piece by the unpredictable changes in tonality which occur throughout its length. The opening panel in F major shows a tendency, later more pronounced, to slip in and out of A minor and the music subsequently passes through many keys. Even after the key of A minor seems to have been definitely established, a series of chromaticisms perpetuates the tonal ambiguity until within a few bars of the concluding phrase.

The third Ballade in A flat major (1840-1), which belongs to the same period as Chopin's Fantasy in F minor, is distinguished from the latter by its slighter dimensions and by the close concentration of the thematic material. The Fantasy abounds in a variety of musical ideas; the Ballade is evolved from a very few. The six-note fragment of a rising scale in the first bar of the Ballade and the two-note rhythmic figure with which it is clinched form the nucleus of the musical substance. From this slender material, and from the descending-scale motive in the third bar, Chopin created a movement which never slackens in interest as the music presses on inevitably towards the magnificent climax.

Thematic metamorphosis is an essential feature of the composition. The rising-scale theme, after several restrained appearances in the centre of the keyboard, finally soars in octaves high in the treble to form the culminating point. Three units of the contrasting subject are detached to play their parts, singly or combined, in the development of the material.

The graceful falling-octave motive (a) in quavers is quickened into continuous figuration in animated semiquavers that leap to and fro above the phrase in descending notes in the minor (c):

The opening phrase (b) reappears in a succession of keys, its former accompaniment of dancing chords transformed into restless broken octaves and chromatic scales:

The alternations of whole sections of smoothly-flowing and persistently syncopated music ensure the Ballade unflagging rhythmic vitality. The rounding off of the movement with an allusion to the regularly-accented theme from the central section seems to resolve all the preceding rhythmic conflicts.

The fourth Ballade in F minor (1842) has two points in common with the first in G minor. Both works are based chiefly on two acutely contrasted subjects, and in both, the first subject is made up of short fragments many times repeated, while the second comprises a melody whose wide intervals and swaying rhythm endow it with an unforgettable, ear-haunting quality. In other respects the two Ballades differ profoundly. The F minor is far more highly organized in structure. It combines attributes distinctive of sonata form with those of the rondo and the variation. Indeed, the principal subject in F minor assumes the character of a rondo refrain; it is presented three times in the same key, varied at each re-appearance. The second subject undergoes variation of a more fundamental kind. After first being announced in simple chords in B flat major, it re-emerges in D flat major with the left-hand part running eagerly in passages of triplet semiquavers. The melody, released from the bondage of its plain chordal substructure, rides majestically at a higher pitch, making an impression of unlimited, unassailable freedom. This section constitutes the emotional climax of the movement. Thereafter, the threads of the thematic argument are gathered up and woven into the fabric of a coda whose intricate passage-work is the logical outcome of the contrapuntal writing that distinguishes the whole piece.

*   *   *   *

The Chopin Ballades, with their vitally interesting subject-matter, their brilliant and sympathetic piano writing, hold a place in the affections of pianists which Liszt's examples of the type have never attained. Of his two Ballades, only the second approaches Chopin's in grandeur of conception. The first in D flat major (1845-8) is of slighter dimensions than those by Chopin and is less dignified in style. Fundamentally in ternary form, it has an introduction to which allusion is made later and a coda derived from the central section. The principal theme, an 'andantino con sentimento' in waltz rhythm, is varied at every successive appearance. It becomes progressively more ornate and the 'tempo di marcia' theme gradually loses its original sparse crispness in a welter of heavy chords.

The narrative quality which distinguishes Chopin's Ballades is almost entirely lacking in this first Ballade of Liszt's, but it may clearly be perceived in the second Ballade in B minor (1853), a far longer piece which is free in form, powerful and cumulative in effect. The thirty-four-bar introduction in B minor with mysteriously surging chromatic scales low in the bass followed by placid chordal phrases is immediately repeated without alteration in B *flat* minor. It makes the impression that the narrator of the Ballade is intent upon securing the close attention of his audience before beginning to tell them the story which eventually starts in animated fashion at 'allegro deciso', and which, after running an adventurous course, reaches a quiet ending in B major with the chordal phrase of the introduction. As in the first Ballade, the thematic material undergoes extensive variation, but it is much less exuberant and its expressive character is intensified rather than trivialized. Surprising modulations and harsh dissonances deepen the sense of mystery which surrounds many sections of this dark, romantic piece.

In comparison with Chopin's and Liszt's Ballades, those by Brahms are less elaborate in style and technique and are straightforward though by no means conventional in form. Moreover, they are short, and as their key-system is closely unified, the four Ballades that constitute op. 10 (1854) are often played as a whole group. The first in D minor hovers on the borders of programme music. It is headed 'After the Scots ballad "Edward"' (in Herder's German translation). The music of the principal phrases actually follows the metre of the poem, and the piece as a whole gives dramatic expression to the bloodthirsty sentiments of the narrative. Like Brahms's Rhapsody in E flat, this Ballade displays the characteristics of 'arch' form. The two opening themes, Andante and 'poco più moto', rise towards the arch, an Allegro episode in D major. They descend in reverse order, their design and expressive character modified in accordance with the spirit of the narrative. The literary content of this ballad evidently exerted a strong attraction over Brahms. Many years later, in 1877, he set the words to music as a duet for contralto and tenor. The piano writing of this new version reveals the composer's entirely fresh conception of the poem.

None of the other Ballades of op. 10 has an avowed poetic background, but the second and fourth make the impression of being narratives in intention. The second Ballade in D major is full of mysterious implications, especially in the middle section in B major (6/4), which comprises a series of phrases in furtive staccato crotchets in both hands revolving on an axis of sustained longer notes. The fourth Ballade in B major, the longest and most sectional and the only one in triple time, is the most consistently lyrical. It is melodic throughout, but the type of melody and the style of accompaniment change with the changing sections. The cantabile theme that floats easily on the surface of the 'andante con moto' gives place in the ensuing Lento to one of reflective character that threads its way with difficulty through a dense fabric of murmuring quavers. Later, another theme moves stealthily in five-bar phrases of quiet, low-pitched chords. Although it is free in structure, the piece shows some of the attributes of rondo form, but the recurrent refrain is gradually reduced in importance. At its first appearance after the Lento interlude it is shortened and the accompaniment is thinned out. Lastly, eight bars before the end, only a single wraith-like phrase, twice repeated, reminds the listener of the once radiant cantabile.

The third Ballade in B minor, sub-titled *Intermezzo*, the slightest in dimensions, is composed in simple ternary form. It hardly narrates a tale but it creates a fairy atmosphere by means of its transparent texture and unusual harmonic progressions. The opening section of cascading semiquaver runs and strongly syncopated light chords conjures up a vision of sprites at play. The music of the interlude, which sounds from the heights of the keyboard in serene phrases of chords in root position, is so ethereal in character as to suggest a distant chorus of birds.

When it fades away the sprites resume their pranks, but in a hushed pianissimo as though the tranquillizing spell cast by the far-away bird-song were still unbroken. The rare cadence, mediant to tonic, at the very end, imparts a final touch of fantasy.

Brahms's remaining Ballade in G minor, which he composed in 1893 as the third of the six *Klavierstücke*, op. 118, is more strenuous than its imaginative predecessors. It is an 'allegro energico' of detached chords with a contrasting episode in B major which, although it is marked 'pianissimo, una corda', also makes an impression of unflagging energy. It contains not a single breathing-space, except where the flow of eight quavers to the bar is temporarily broken by an incursion of a chordal phrase from the opening section. A typically Brahmsian touch in this Ballade is the overlapping of some of the phrases and the division of others into uneven bar-lengths.

*   *   *   *

Schumann did not compose ballades. Their nearest equivalent in his production for the piano is the set of eight *Novellettes*, op. 21 (1838) which he described as depicting 'longish connected tales of adventure'. He gave some of them titles, which, however, he suppressed before publication. His conception of the ballade, first exemplified in the tenth movement of his *Davidsbündler* (1832) to which he prefixed the performing-direction 'In the ballad style', is passionate and urgent in the extreme. The tiny dance movement races breathlessly along in two conflicting rhythms: compound duple in the right hand and simple triple in the left, with the beats, strong and weak, heavily accented. It prefigures the vigorous, rhythmically intricate style of portions of the Novellettes, such as the Intermezzo 'presto con fuoco' of no. 3.

We noted earlier that some of the pieces are composed in rondo form. Others are in ternary form. Schumann treated both these formal types with equal freedom, except in the conventional miniature Novellette in B minor which, although he wrote it at the same period, he did not publish until many years later among the *Bunte Blätter*, op. 99 (1851). Whether he used much or little subject-matter in the individual Novellettes of op. 21 he generally arranged the paragraphs in unwonted sequence and restated them in fresh keys. By these means he enhanced the interest of their mutual key-relationships and secured variety as well as continuity. For instance, in the centre of the first Novellette, the refrain, which is first heard in F major, recurs in D flat major; the Trio, also originally presented in F major, reappears in A major. When the opening section of the fourth Novellette, 'tempo di ballo', makes its final appearance, only its rhythmic foundation emerges intact; melody and harmony are both transformed. The fifth, 'pomposo e brioso', is dominated by two short figures. They recur jointly or severally in every part of the texture at intervals throughout the piece; now to form linking passages, then to set a fugato in motion and eventually to fade out like distant drum-beats at the very end. The sixth Novellette, 'vivace assai con molto spirito', is composed of a multiplicity of themes which recur in unpredictable order and run through a succession of tonalities involving no fewer than nine changes of key-signature. The tension never slackens for a moment.

Unconventional in form as are most of the Novellettes, none is so irregular or so complicated as the eighth. It begins in F sharp minor as a scherzo with two trios respectively in D flat and D major. The restatement of the scherzo after the second trio is omitted and is replaced by a short interlude entitled 'Continuazione'. The piece eventually develops into another scherzo, now in D major, with two more trios in A and B flat major. This pair of large-scale movements is unified by the theme marked 'Voice from the distance'. It first steals in quietly in minims before the end of the D major trio in the first main section of the Novellette and is developed in a leisurely manner, though in shorter notes, during the ensuing interlude. It finally returns in minim octaves at the point where the key-signature changes to one flat, about a hundred bars before the end of the whole movement.

These are only the main outlines of a piece of music in which the imaginative dovetailing of themes and the fitting together of numerous component parts are points that well repay close study.

The piano writing of the Novellettes represents Schumann's individual style from the exuberant to the intricate. The glowing broken-chord figuration and the lyrical accompanied melody of the second; the dance-rhythms of the fourth; the persistent metric pattern in the G minor section of the fifth and in the outer sections of the miniature Novellette in B minor; the canonic imitations in the first and the seventh and the mysterious utterances in close chord-formation in the B flat major interlude of the fifth are a few of the many features that all students of this composer's work will recognize as typically Schumannesque.

*   *   *   *

Of the many pieces so far mentioned in this chapter, only two have been found to be qualified for inclusion under the heading of 'programme music': Field's *Le Midi* Nocturne and Brahms's 'Edward' Ballade. The title of this type of nineteenth-century romantic music was invented by Liszt, but music of this kind came into existence centuries earlier.

Programme or *descriptive* music has existed ever since composers could find the means of portraying non-musical ideas in terms of instrumental music. The Elizabethan virginalists wrote this type of music; for example, William Byrd's *Battle Piece*, which is composed in several sections, each with a descriptive title. The seventeenth-century German composer Johann Kuhnau composed a series of vividly descriptive *Bible Sonatas* for the keyboard (published in 1700) to each of which he prefixed long accounts of the events depicted in the music as well as annotating the music itself. The French clavecinistes wrote numerous miniature portrait-studies and nature-sketches, among which Couperin's *Les tricoteuses* (The knitters) and (*Les petits moulins à vent* (The little windmills), Rameau's *La Poule* (The hen) and *Les Tourbillons* (The whirlwinds) and Daquin's *Le Coucou* are well-known examples. J. S. Bach composed a *Capriccio on the departure of a beloved brother* (1704) in the form of a suite. Each movement bears a title indicating the various stages of the 'departure' and the whole ends with a fugue '*all' imitazione della cornetta di Postiglione*'. Clementi's *Didone abbandonata* Sonata and Beethoven's 'Lebewohl' Sonata come more or less within the same category. So too, does Weber's 'Programme' Sonata, though only indirectly, for when he published it he did not actually print the story it is intended to illustrate. His *Invitation to the dance*, with its specific descriptive title is, however, a genuine piece of programme music which requires no analytical notes, as the music exactly corresponds to the very obvious 'programme'.

* * * *

Among the composers of piano music during the Romantic period it was Schumann and Liszt, both of whom had strong literary interests and were themselves writers, who developed programme and descriptive music to a much higher state of expressiveness than hitherto. Schumann most particularly in the smaller forms, and Liszt, in both larger and smaller forms. Mendelssohn, who was a gifted painter in water-colour, concentrated his finest powers of musical scene-painting upon his orchestral works, and Schubert his, upon the piano accompaniments of his songs. Chopin wrote only two pieces with descriptive titles which may be interpreted as implying that he had definite pictures in his mind while composing them: the *Berceuse* and the *Barcarolle*.

The *Berceuse*, whose static harmonic and rhythmic scheme and ever-changing melodic line we noted when studying variations, conveys the sense of utter peacefulness implicit in the title. The *Barcarolle*, which is composed in unbroken swaying rhythm but is structurally and pianistically far more complex than the *Berceuse*, creates the atmosphere of a boating scene in which the lapping of the waters, the shimmering heat, and the luxuriant beauty of the summer sky find their perfect musical counterpart. Despite its picturesque style the *Barcarolle* is as clear in form as are most of Chopin's large-scale pieces, even though they are generally unorthodox in the arrangement of their constituent parts. Basically, it is in ternary form with an introduction and coda, but in the repeat of the opening section some of the original material is omitted and the gap is filled by a longish paragraph from the interlude. The feeling of continuity already established by the uniform rhythm is further enhanced by the periodic references to themes already heard. The little flickering semi-quaver figure in sixths that adorns the opening pages returns to prelude the final cadenza. The interval of a rising fourth in the bass which opens the interlude in F sharp minor rings out fortis-simo in double octaves in the very last bar.

*   *   *   *

In character, the *Barcarolle* is impressionistic rather than des-criptive, as are some of Liszt's pieces of this type and length. Their formal outlines are less distinct, especially when they portray a subject that has no definite beginning or end: a storm, the play of fountains, or the effect of a landscape upon a human soul. Representative examples are included in the three books of the *Années de Pèlerinage* (Years of pilgrimage) (1836-77). *Orage* (Storm) rages without intermission in octaves and heavily-accented chords, *Les jeux d'eaux à la Villa d'Este* scintillates in pellucid arpeggios and tremolandos, and neither piece comes to a decisive climax. *Vallée d'Obermann*, which is prefaced by Liszt with two quotations from de Senancourt's novel *Obermann* and one from Byron's *Childe Harold*, extends for over two hundred bars. During its course the limited musical material is presented in a myriad pianistic guises. It makes the impression of a desperate struggle against the forces of nature.

Liszt's two *Legends*: *St. Francis of Assisi preaching to the birds* and *St. Francis of Paula walking on the waves* are essentially program-matic. Their form and style are inevitably conditioned by the events they set out to illustrate, and the pieces are extremely graphic in their respective simulation of the twittering of a multitude of birds and the surging of angry waves. Theoretically, they can hardly be enjoyed to the full by anyone unfamiliar with the details of the legends. Nevertheless, the music itself and the style of the piano writing are sufficiently interesting and attractive to make their own appeal to listeners and players.

Similar in type are the longest items of Liszt's *Harmonies poétiques et religieuses* (1845-52), the title of which the composer borrowed from Lamartine, whose poems were the inspiration of three of the pieces in question. *Invocation* (no. 1) and *Bénédiction de Dieu dans la solitude* (no. 3) are both prefaced with verses from the relevant poems, whose sentiments they interpret in music alternately contemplative and passionate which makes the very most of the singing-tone and the warm resonance of the piano. *Pensée des Morts* (no. 4) works up to a tremendous climax of heavy chords metrically spaced to simulate the intoning of the *De profundis*, the words of which are printed above the chords. *Funérailles* (no. 7), composed in memory of three Hungarian friends of Liszt's who were killed in the Petöfi rising of 1849, needs no written programme, for the characteristic dotted rhythm of the funeral march, the grief-stricken melody and the deep, throbbing, drum-like bass-notes are sufficiently graphic to paint the tragic scene of this, the most powerful of all the four intensely expressive movements.

*   *   *   *

Shorter pieces of descriptive music by Liszt, Schumann, Grieg and other composers will be considered in the chapter on miniatures. Here, we are concerned only with longer works, among which we may include Grieg's principal composition of this type, *Scenes from Folk life*, op. 19 (1872).

When studying Grieg's Sonata we noticed that two of the movements displayed characteristics of Norwegian folk-music. The *Scenes from Folk life* are even more strongly nationalist in style. None of the themes is a genuine folk-tune, but the whole of the musical material is permeated by Norwegian folk-idiom. Some of the piano writing, too, deliberately imitates the sounds of the native instrument, the Hardanger fiddle, which has a set of sympathetically-vibrating strings in addition to the usual equipment and is capable of producing resonant chords. The work consists of three movements which are thematically inter-related and should be played as a whole group. The second movement in E major, which is by far the most original and effective, has inevitably become detached from its context and has acquired world-wide fame. This is 'The Bridal Procession passes by', a piece of sensitive piano writing that is as satisfying in design as it is realistic in giving expression to the title. The approach of the procession, its resplendent passing at close quarters and its gradual withdrawal into the remote distance are denoted by the dynamic markings and by the relative density of the texture. The stateliness and dignity of the occasion are expressed in the steadily marching rhythm, while the festive spirit is implicit in the decorative figuration. The first and third movements, 'On the mountains' and 'Carnival scene', both in A minor and each with a trio section in the major, are structurally similar to many of Grieg's *Lyric Pieces*, but in their rhythmic vitality they are closely related to his Norwegian Dances.

The idealizing of folk-music and national music, if not an exclusively romantic trait, was of absorbing interest to some nineteenth-century composers, notably Liszt, Smetana, Dvořák and Grieg. Liszt's Hungarian Rhapsodies, which represent one branch of this form of musical activity, we have already examined. Less virtuosic examples are his three *Glanes de Woronince* (Gleanings from Woronince) based on Polish and Ukrainian airs and the *Fantasie romantique sur deux mélodies suisses*, the melodies of which he also used in his well-known *Le mal du pays* (Home-sickness) in the *Années de Pèlerinage*. Grieg wrote two *Improvisata on Norwegian folk-tunes*, op. 29, but they are of minor interest compared with his other works based on folk-music which we shall study, together with nationalist compositions of other types and countries, in later chapters on dance forms and piano duets.

*   *   *   *

Another type of romantic piano music which came into prominence during the nineteenth century requires consideration before we leave this whole subject: the transcription or 'piano arrangement'.

The art of translating music from one medium to another: from the voice to an instrument, or from a body of instruments to the keyboard, was already flourishing in the sixteenth century. It has subsequently been cultivated with varying degrees of intensity. Among the earliest examples relevant to our study are the two 'Lachrymae Pavanes' in the Fitzwilliam Virginal Book, transcribed respectively by William Byrd and Giles Farnaby from the song 'Lachrymae' ('Flow, my tears') by their contemporary, John Dowland. At a later period, Bach arranged some of Vivaldi's Violin Concertos for solo harpsichord as well as freely transcribing pieces of various kinds by other composers.

Composers often re-arranged their own works. Sometimes, perhaps, simply as a recreation between periods of intensive work on original compositions; at other times, because opportunities may have arisen for hearing their works performed on instruments different from those for which the music was originally conceived. Rameau adapted five pieces of his chamber music, *Pièces en concert*, for harpsichord solo, and he interchanged movements of his harpsichord suites with instrumental excerpts from his operas. Handel transferred his compositions from one medium to another. For instance, he made use of his Lesson in D minor as the presto Finale of the Third Suite for harpsichord, as the last movements of the Organ Concerto in D minor, op. 7 and of the Oboe Concerto op. 3, no. 6, and as a portion of the Overture to the opera *Pastor Fido*. Beethoven re-wrote his Violin Concerto as a Piano Concerto. Schumann, as we saw earlier, constructed the slow movements of two of his piano sonatas out of songs he had composed long before; Brahms re-wrote for piano solo the Waltzes, op. 39 that he had originally written as piano duets, and Grieg transcribed at least a dozen of his songs for piano solo. Liszt turned several of his own vocal works into piano pieces. The *Petrarch Sonnets* in the *Années de Pèlerinage* and the three *Liebesträume* all originated in songs for voice and piano. Three of the ten movements of his *Harmonies poétiques et religieuses* ('Ave Maria', 'Pater noster', and 'Hymne de l'enfant à son réveil') are reductions of his own choral works. The Prelude and Fugue on the name BACH, which we studied in the previous chapter, is one of a few organ compositions he transferred to the piano.

M   *   *   *   *

The typically romantic transcription was the outcome of the romantic composer's faculty of make-believe; of his conception of the cantabile tone of the piano as equivalent to the human voice, the strings or the wind instruments; and of the piano's percussive qualities and pedal-effects as capable of evoking other orchestral colours. Liszt, the romantic *par excellence*, practised the art of transcription with an enthusiasm that knew no bounds. Never was a composer more assiduous in arranging his own works and those by other composers. The catalogue of his activities in this direction runs into several pages of print and includes the names of well over a score of composers whose works inspired him to these tireless feats of re-creation. He considered that 'with the immense development of its harmonic powers the piano seeks to appropriate more and more all orchestral compositions. In the compass of its seven octaves it can, with few exceptions, reproduce all features, all combinations, all figurations of the most learned and deepest creations in sound. . . .'

It was in this spirit of enterprise that he embarked upon writing pianistically resplendent fantasies on the operatic music of all the well-known composers from Mozart to Wagner and Verdi, and that he made piano arrangements of orchestral, chamber and vocal works by greater and lesser composers. In so doing, he was not actuated solely by the desire to demonstrate the limitless variety of tone-colours that could be produced on the modern grand piano. He was genuinely anxious to secure recognition for compositions of all kinds which he considered were too little appreciated in their original forms. Among these were Bach's Preludes and Fugues for organ, the Beethoven symphonies, symphonic poems by Berlioz, overtures by Weber, songs by Schubert, Schumann, Mendelssohn, Chopin, Rossini, and others, piano solos and duets by Schubert.

At the present day, when compositions of every type and period are much more readily available to the general public in their original versions, the need for this kind of 'second-hand' music has passed and the taste for it has declined. Even so, Liszt's prodigies of transcription are deeply interesting as

literature for the piano. They afford musicians unrivalled opportunities for observing both his supreme mastery of the keyboard
and his insight into the musical qualities of the works he transcribed. To the performer, they are a challenge to imaginative
interpretation and a stimulus to studying the originals and the
re-creations side by side.

Among the numberless transcriptions still extant only a few
representative examples can be referred to or described here.
They will include works in several categories, chosen to exemplify some of Liszt's many methods of treating the given
material. The literal arrangement of orchestral and instrumental
works; the imaginative transcription of songs; the free composition based on or incorporating Italian vocal arias, the transformation of intimate piano music into concert-pieces, and the
paraphrasing of operatic music.

*   *   *   *

The literal arrangements are represented at their finest by the
Beethoven Symphonies. Liszt made them at intervals between
1837 and 1864 and published them complete in 1865 with the
avowed intention of 'contributing to the knowledge of the great
masters and to the formation of a sense of beauty'. He carried
out his task with the utmost faithfulness. The very look of the
printed pages of these arrangements conjures up in the mind's
ear the sounds of the symphonies in their original version.
Details of the scoring are marked in so that the player can
follow the part-writing and can bear in mind the timbres of the
instruments which he is called upon to simulate as best he can
by gradating his touch.

These splendid re-creations are unfortunately no longer
current; they are accessible only in the volumes of the Collected
Edition of Liszt's works. For practical purposes they have been
superseded by easily available reductions for piano made for
study purposes by excellent musicians who would never claim
to be considered poets of the keyboard. To show the distance
that separates Liszt's realistic interpretation of a romantic
orchestral effect from a prosaic rendering by one of his succes-

sors, two versions of a single phrase from the 'Storm' movement
of the 'Pastoral' Symphony may be quoted:

It will be seen that Liszt's reverberating spread chords deep in
the bass depict thunderclaps far more graphically than do the
comparatively tame tremolandos placed higher up the keyboard.

In Bach's Fantasy and Fugue in G minor for organ Liszt's
amplification of single-line runs with sixths, octaves or tenths is
no empty decoration, but an attempt to reproduce on the piano
the greater resonance of the organ. In the Fugue, the incorporating of the pedal-part within the pianistic texture is so contrived
that it makes the effect of exercising its original function. The
upper parts, re-arranged to lie easily under the pianist's hands,
maintain the fugal argument unbroken (see next page).

*   *   *   *

Between these straightforward arrangements of orchestral and
instrumental works and the free adaptations of solo vocal and
operatic music there is an infinity of difference. In the latter
types of composition Liszt employed all the resources of keyboard virtuosity at his command, but his feeling for the expressive character of the music was in many cases so acute that his
elaborations intensify, rather than distort it. Singers and accom-
panists, strongly though they may disapprove in principle of
Liszt's attempts to rival their unique art of ensemble, can but

admire his imaginative skill in interpreting upon one instrument the fundamentals of music designed so sympathetically for two performers.

The art of variation played a large part in Liszt's transcriptions, especially in strophic songs, where he generally devised a fresh and more decorative type of figuration for each successive verse. Schubert's 'Hark, hark the lark' and 'Ave Maria' (1838) are typical examples. Some of the finest of the song-transcriptions are at the same time literal and impressionistic. They preserve the outline of the vocal part and the essentials of the piano accompaniment, while evoking the distinctive tone-colour and the rise and fall of the voice by variations in the pitch of the melody and by gradations in the volume of sound of the accompanying passage-work. An example of this kind of treatment may be found in Schubert's 'Das Wirtshaus' (The wayside inn) (1839). The voice part, written on a third stave, is placed first in the tenor, then in the contralto register in the centre of the texture, and gradually rises to the surface. The subdued quaver and crotchet chords of the original are broken up into quivering demisemiquavers by the right hand; the left hand adds support with deep bass-notes or trills, occasionally crossing over the right hand to add little flashes of brilliant colour high up in the treble.

This transcription preserves the structure of the original. In some of the other Schubert song-transcriptions Liszt added or subtracted portions varying in extent from the repeat of a whole verse to a few bars. In 'Du bist die Ruh' (Thou art repose) he cut out the introductory bars and started off with the first verse arranged expressively for left-hand solo. But his insertion later of a repeat of one verse in elaborate chordal figuration extending across four octaves weakens the ensuing climax and disturbs the tranquil atmosphere of the whole.

Liszt's additions to some of the songs, however, can hardly be considered out of keeping with the character of the original. The little melismata (decorative passages)

at climactic points and the precipitate four-bar arpeggio passage just before the end of 'Die Post' (1839) are features which emphasize the agitated mood of the song. The extension of 'Auf dem Wasser zu singen' (To be sung on the water) (1838) by the repetition of a verse elaborated in style to form a postlude enhances rather than diminishes the effectiveness of a transcription which faithfully integrates the ebullient voice-part and the exquisitely sparkling figuration of the original. Similarly, the doubling in length of Schumann's 'Frühlingsnacht' (Spring night) (1872) by a repeat of the whole composition with more intricate and brilliant piano writing seems to give fuller scope to the expression of the emotional exaltation inherent in the song.

*　　　*　　　*　　　*

In the Six Polish Songs which he selected from Chopin's Seventeen Polish songs, op. 74 and published complete in 1860, Liszt employed other methods of transcription. By arranging the songs in a succession of related keys and contrasted moods and by joining two (nos. 3 and 4) together by a modulatory link, he built up a sequence of pieces which can effectively be played as a whole. The individual transcriptions vary in type. The first, 'The maiden's wish', which opens with a lightly-decorated version of the original prelude, continues with a set of three variations on the melody. None of them resembles any of the variations included by Liszt in his original piano composition *Mélodies polonaises* (no. 2 of *Glanes de Woronince*) based on the same theme. The second piece of the Chopin song-sequence, 'Spring', approximates the most closely to the original. As Chopin himself incorporated the vocal melody within the accompaniment, Liszt found little scope for making alterations beyond occasionally thickening the right-hand part with octaves. In no. 3, 'The Ring', he varied the accompaniment of the second verse, adding coloratura-like passages at climaxes; in no. 4, 'Bacchanal', he increased the feeling of excitement by inserting glissandos and by adding a long final section based on motives from the song.

For the fifth song, 'My darling', he used a much more elaborate technique. He transformed the simple song in E flat major with an extremely sparse chordal accompaniment into an expressive, poetic Nocturne in G flat major in which the left-hand part runs in legato arpeggios and the right hand embellishes the melody with trills, *fioriture* (flourishes) and decorative cadenzas in single or double notes. The piano writing of this piece sounds far more typical of Chopin than does the simple accompaniment which the composer himself designed for the original. In the final piece, 'The Bridegroom', Liszt turned

Chopin's spare harmonic pattern into brilliant passage-work in the style of the 'Revolutionary' Study in C minor, op. 10, no. 12.

He ended the piece with the last thirteen bars of the original spun out in expressive fashion to nearly three times their length by means of augmentation.

*   *   *   *

Liszt was strongly attracted to the vocal music of Italian composers. He both transcribed it and made it the basis of some of his own compositions. The 'Canzonetta del Salvator Rosa' (1849), no. 3 of the Second Book (Italy) of the *Années de Pèlerinage*, is the most straightforward of the four pieces of this type which he included in the last-named collection of original compositions. (The correctness of the attribution of the canzonetta, 'Vado ben spesso' to Salvator Rosa has been questioned in recent times and the name of G. B. Bononcini put forward as the most likely composer.) Liszt presented the martial tune of the canzonetta without superfluous pianistic decoration, but with a strong feeling for the swinging rhythm, which he maintained unbroken between the verses by effective interchanges of scraps of melody between the two hands.

In directness of musical statement the Canzonetta offers a striking contrast to the three virtuosic pieces of *Venezia e Napoli* (1859) which form the Supplement to the Second Book of the *Années de Pèlerinage*. They abound in pianistic embellishments. In the first, 'Gondoliera', the canzone by the Cavaliere Peruchini is set within a decorative filigree of rapid notes, 'pianissimo e leggierissimo', and the whole is interspersed with cadenzas. Throughout the second piece, 'Canzone', the melody of the aria 'Nessun maggior dolore' (No greater sorrow) from Rossini's *Otello* proceeds slowly above and below a harmonic foundation of mysterious tremolandos. The last piece, 'Tarantella', which opens with a whirlwind of passages alternately in 6/8 and 2/4 time, develops into a cumulatively brilliant series of variations upon a 'canzona napolitana' by G. L. Cottrau and ends in a blaze of chromatic chords.

The florid piano writing of these movements accords with the warm-blooded character of the tunes. The transcriptions of twelve songs by Rossini which Liszt published in 1837 were made in the same spirit but with less virtuosity. None of the individual items is so ornate in style or so difficult to play as the Tarantella just mentioned, and some are distinguished by extreme simplicity. These twelve charming pieces in a variety of moods which were once widely played are now almost forgotten, both as songs and as piano solos. The music of only one is well known to music-lovers to-day: no. 9, 'La Danza'. It recovered some of its former popularity when it was pressed into the service of dancing to form part of the musical background to the Rossini ballet, *La Boutique fantasque* in 1919, and it is still sometimes sung in its original form.

*   *   *   *

Liszt named the Rossini song-transcriptions *Soirées musicales*. Many years later he applied a similar title to another kind of transcription: the *Soirées de Vienne*; *Valses-caprices d'après Fr. Schubert*.

Liszt was not only a great admirer of the Schubert songs, over fifty of which he transcribed for piano solo. He had early shown a partiality for this composer's piano music, in the first place by transcribing several movements from his duets both as piano solos and as orchestral pieces. They comprise sections of the *Divertissement à la hongroise* (1838-9) and three Marches from op. 40 and op. 121 (1846). In 1851 he transformed the 'Wanderer' Fantasy into a symphonic piece for piano and orchestra, as we noted earlier in these pages. In 1852-3 he published the nine *Soirées de Vienne*: paraphrases of some of Schubert's short pieces in dance forms which we shall study in their original versions in a later chapter.

The ninth *Valse-caprice* is a set of six variations on the waltz known as the *Sehnsuchtswalzer* (Le désir) which Schubert composed in 1816 and which Schumann used as the basis of the opening movement of *Carnaval* in 1835. Each of the other eight *Valses-caprices* consists of a free arrangement of two or more dances which are formed into a coherent whole movement by means of introductory and linking passages derived from the thematic material and by the repetition of individual sections, either in their own keys or transposed. A brief description of the make-up of one of these pieces will give an idea of Liszt's mosaic-like method of constructing them.

No. I, 'allegretto malinconico' in A flat major, is founded on three dances: a German dance, op. 33, no. 15, phrases from which Liszt used for the prelude, the postlude, and the modulatory links as well as presenting the dance once in its entirety; and two Waltzes, op. 9, no. 22 and op. 67, no. 14. The first Waltz forms the two sections flanking the initial statement of the second Waltz which, after having appeared in B major, recurs twice, transposed into A flat major. A glance at the original dances reveals how effectively Liszt utilized their fluctuations between the major and minor to impart variety and contrast to the paraphrase as a whole. An examination of the manifold styles of piano writing which characterize Schubert's complete production of dance music shows that Liszt's work of transformation in the *Soirées de Vienne* was carried out in a manner which only occasionally does violence to the simplicity and the subtle beauty of the basic material.

*   *   *   *

The *operatic* or *dramatic fantasy* was Liszt's invention. He was only eighteen when he produced the first of the long series of works of this kind which he wrote over a period of more than fifty years and which he named indifferently *Grande fantaisie*, *Grande paraphrase*, *Paraphrase de concert* and *Réminiscences*. As the listener's appreciation of this type of composition depends almost entirely upon his familiarity with the operas thus paraphrased, and as many of these operas are now seldom if ever heard, few of the fantasies have survived to be printed in modern editions. One of the most important and the most easily obtainable is the *Réminiscences* of Mozart's *Don Giovanni* (1841). It magnificently represents the finest qualities of these genuinely creative works, which not only embody significant portions of the music, but which convey a general impression of the character of the drama itself.

The musical extracts that Liszt chose as the foundation of his *Réminiscences de Don Juan* symbolize the supernatural and the worldly elements present in the opera. The fantasy, which consists chiefly of two long, contrasting sections respectively typifying the Don's amorous proclivities and his devil-may-care conviviality, begins and ends on a serious note. The longish introduction is founded on the two solemn phrases, successively in common and triple time, which are sung by the statue in Act II; a fateful theme consisting largely of repeated notes which is heard again towards the end of the next section. This section comprises the whole of the duet, 'Là ci darem la mano', preluded by a few bars derived from a little ornamental figure in the accompaniment (bar 29) and followed by two elaborate variations. The drinking-song, 'Finchè han dal vino' forms the basis of the presto final section. It is rounded off by a brief cadential passage, andante, containing an allusion to the solemn phrase of warning uttered to the unrepentant Don.

It is not possible here to analyse details of Liszt's subtle treat-

ment of the basic material. One point, however, may be referred
to as typical: the transformation of a three-bar chromatic
progression in the predominantly diatonic aria 'Finchè han dal
vino' into a twenty-seven-bar passage during which the chroma-

ticisms are carried to their furthest conclusion. The first few
bars are quoted for the purpose of identification.

*   *   *   *

In the creation of yet another specialized type of transcription
Liszt was inspired by the same model as was Schumann: by
Paganini's *Caprices* for solo violin. The piano pieces that came
into being as the result of the two composers' having been capti-
vated by Paganini's indescribably virtuosic playing of his own
works belong to the sphere of the piano study. They will be
discussed under that heading in the next chapter. So, also, will
Brahms's few transcriptions which, although of a very different
type, are on the whole of greater interest technically than
musically. His version for piano of the Gavotte in A from
Gluck's opera *Paris and Helen* is a more genuinely romantic
transcription in the sense that the technical considerations are
subordinated to the artistic. The solid piano writing in thirds
and sixths in the major section and the gossamer lightness of the
staccato arpeggios in the minor section realistically interpret
the contrasts in the orchestral colouring and help to re-create
the poetic atmosphere of the original.

— 9 —

Studies, and Pieces for Beginners

Origin and early history of Studies; pioneers of concert-studies: Clementi, Czerny, Moscheles, Cramer. The Étude: Mendelssohn, Chopin, Schumann, Liszt, Brahms, Grieg. Pieces for beginners: from Clementi to César Franck.

THE origin of the study may be ascribed to the teacher's need to provide his pupils with materials suitable for developing their technical abilities and their powers of interpretation. In modern times the writing of studies and 'educational' music has grown into a separate branch of composition, but in earlier times it was not so. Musicians who took pupils composed studies for them as a matter of course. As a consequence, many simple pieces came to be written by the great composers of all periods.

Among the earliest of those which have been preserved are two little collections of pieces, mostly in dance forms, composed by J. S. Bach for his second wife, Anna Magdalena, and his eldest son, Wilhelm Friedemann. Earlier still is a set of Toccatas by Alessandro Scarlatti (1659-1725). It is of special interest to pianists, not only as the work of a man who won undying fame as an opera composer and who was the father of one of the greatest of all harpsichordists, Domenico Scarlatti, but also because it throws light upon early systems of fingering. The Toccatas are accompanied by a short preface containing a drawing of two outspread hands with each finger marked by a distinctive sign. This was Scarlatti's method of elucidating the system of fingering which he indicated in the score and which he recommended the 'studious pupil' to follow in order to 'place his hands in the most advantageous position for producing good tone'. A tiny five-finger exercise preceding a *Menuet en rondeau* in Jean Philippe Rameau's *Pièces de clavecin* (1724) is another reminder of a composer's concern for technical efficiency in the playing of his works. Yet another is the supplement of Eight Preludes that François Couperin included in his textbook *L'Art de toucher le clavecin* (The art of playing the harpsichord) (1716) as exercises for loosening the player's fingers before performing the composer's *Ordres* (Suites).

Many of the more advanced 'educational' pieces by great composers have proved to be of lasting value, not only as 'studies' but as music. Some of the works which were written in the first place as studies have become indispensable in the concert-room. Bach's six Partitas, the Italian Concerto, the French Overture, and the 'Goldberg' Variations were published, together with several compositions for organ, in a series of four volumes which he named *Clavier Übung* (Keyboard Practice). Domenico Scarlatti's Sonatas were originally issued as 'Exercises'; the title the composer himself gave to a set of thirty, the only ones out of a total of nearly six hundred that he ever troubled to publish. Handel's Suites, which he wrote for his royal pupils, were published as *Lessons*.

Apart from their great importance as music, all these pieces demonstrate the types of keyboard technique current in the first half of the eighteenth century, the period of the harpsichord. Mendelssohn's, Chopin's, Schumann's, and Liszt's *Études* are the epitome of nineteenth-century piano technique. At the same time, they are pieces that are played and listened to with enjoyment on account of their musical expressiveness. They are concert-studies: a new kind of composition, designed as much to display the performer's mastery of certain aspects of technique as to instruct him in the acquisition thereof.

*   *   *   *

The early pioneers of this kind of piano study were Clementi, Czerny, Moscheles, and Cramer. They were themselves fine performers, much sought-after teachers, and composers of other kinds of music: sonatas, concertos, fantasies, etc. At the present day they are remembered almost exclusively for their many volumes of piano studies, which are still in use for didactic, but not for artistic purposes. There can hardly be a pianist living who has not learned some of his art of dexterity from one or other of these 'classics' of piano studies. The composers have inevitably come to be regarded primarily as pedagogues, but in their own time they were notable personalities in the musical world and were intimately connected with the great musicians of the period. Clementi, the 'Father of the Piano' and the composer of about sixty sonatas, was on one occasion a close rival of Mozart's in a contest of extemporization before the Emperor Joseph II at Vienna. He was also a publisher, in which capacity he was responsible for launching some of Beethoven's large-scale works.

Clementi's principal contribution to educational music, the *Gradus ad Parnassum*, is of greater interest musically than any series of studies composed by his contemporaries. It comprises a hundred pieces ranging from brilliant technical studies to movements in sonata form, fugues, canons, capriccios, and scherzos. They are interspersed with a few impressionistic pieces with titles: *Scena patetica* (no. 39), *Bizzarria* (no. 95), and the *Stravaganze* (no. 94) which we considered earlier in connexion with variations. Many of the pieces are arranged into groups of several movements resembling various types of sonata.

The contents of the three volumes of the *Gradus* sum up Clementi's whole art of composing for the piano, and in addition, give a pre-view of some of the pianistic styles of later years. At the time the collection was published, between 1817 and 1826, the principal romantic composers were still in their boyhood. Yet the pianist of to-day who plays through the complete work discovers intimations of the distinctive styles that these composers were later to develop. Mendelssohn's is anticipated in no. 91, a 'song without words' in which a tenor solo is performed by the left hand; Schumann's, in no. 95, an essay in conflicting rhythms; Chopin's, in no. 34, a study based on a repeated figure necessitating quick changing of fingers on the same note, and in no. 60, which displays the blending of a cantabile melody with an accompaniment of double notes in one hand. Liszt's is forestalled in no. 94, an *étude* comprising the florid decoration of an eloquent left-hand melody, and cadenza-like passages. Composers of a later period are also brought to mind: Brahms, by no. 85, a presto 'Hungarian dance'; Debussy, by no. 24, in which the broken-chord figuration shot through with chromaticisms looks forward to that of the impressionistic *Jardins sous la pluie* (1903); and Scriabin, by nos. 56 and 83, two movements of the romantic type which this composer cultivated in his early Twenty-four Preludes, op. 11 (1895). In the individual studies just named and in many others of their kind throughout the *Gradus*, Clementi at the age of seventy is revealed as an amazingly forward-looking musician and a bold inventor of new styles of piano writing.

Czerny, who as a boy was a pupil of Beethoven's, was later promoted to being his amanuensis and the teacher of his nephew Karl. In due course he numbered among his own pupils the greatest of all nineteenth-century piano virtuosi, Franz Liszt, who later dedicated to him his *Grandes Études* (1839). It is not wholly impossible that Liszt derived his passion for making transcriptions from Czerny, who himself transcribed for piano solo a vast number of classical compositions, the most important of which are all Beethoven's symphonies and overtures, Haydn's oratorios, and six of Mozart's symphonies.

Czerny was a born teacher. His several text-books on playing and composing, written in dignified but impassioned style, reveal his burning zeal for his art. His fertility as a composer is almost beyond belief. The opus-numbers of his published works run to well over nine hundred, but his enduring legacy to the pianist comprises only a few books of studies. Many of them are purely mechanical in style but are magnificently adapted to the purpose for which they were designed. Among the twenty or so of these collections still in print, the *School of the Legato and Staccato*, op. 355 includes among its fifty studies a few that show an unfamiliar, imaginative side of the composer's genius.

Cramer studied the piano with Clementi, and eventually, through the medium of his own Eighty-four Studies, became closely associated with Beethoven. The last-named composer, who could not find time to write the piano-method he once projected (though he did make time to contribute five *Bagatelles* (op. 119, nos. 7-11) to Friedrich Starke's *Piano School*), thought very highly of Cramer's Eighty-four Studies. So highly, indeed, that he selected the twenty-one which he considered the most suitable for players of his own compositions and annotated them in accordance with his individual views on interpretation. These twenty-one pieces, now known as the Beethoven-Cramer Studies, were first edited and published by J. W. Shedlock in 1893 with all Beethoven's invaluable and inimitable comments. They have secured for Cramer a place in the affections of pianists that he might not otherwise have attained.

Moscheles taught the fifteen-year-old Mendelssohn. When his famous pupil became the principal of the newly-founded Leipzig Conservatorium, he appointed his former master as chief professor of the piano, a post he held for many years after Mendelssohn's death. Schumann had a great admiration for Moscheles, whose 'Alexander' Variations he played as a youth and whose Twenty-four Studies, op. 70 undoubtedly influenced the keyboard style of some of his early compositions: the 'Abegg' Variations, the Impromptus, and the Toccata. Schumann acknowledged his indebtedness to Moscheles by dedicating to him his Sonata in F minor, op. 14 (*Concert sans orchestre*). He also expressed his opinion in writing that the Twenty-four Studies entitled Moscheles to be considered 'one of the leading composers of piano music' at the time.

The Studies are still in existence, but to many music-lovers at the present day the name of Moscheles is perhaps best known in connexion with the *Études* he persuaded Mendelssohn, Liszt, and Chopin to write for the *Méthode des Méthodes* which he was compiling with the Belgian musician J. Fétis for publication during 1842.

*   *   *   *

These *Études*, Mendelssohn's in F minor (1836), Liszt's *Étude de Perfectionnement* (1840) and Chopin's *Trois nouvelles Études*

N

(1839), show at a glance the three composers' different conceptions of the species. Mendelssohn's is a 'presto agitato' in
common time, with a soaring melody over a ceaseless accompaniment of broken chords in semiquavers divided equally
between the two hands. This *Étude*, and the first two of the three
which, together with three Preludes, form his op. 104 (1836),
are all examples of the facile, moto perpetuo type of study that
reflect the composer's own fluent style as a pianist. The third
Étude of op. 104 in A minor, likewise a moto perpetuo, is both
musically and pianistically much more interesting. The right
hand's pattern in quavers clashes with the left hand's foundation of broken chords in semiquavers. The series of discordant
intervals thus produced on the main beats imparts to the whole
a sinister undertone:

As a writer of studies, Mendelssohn followed the line of least
resistance. He produced charming pieces that give the player
practically nothing new, interesting or intricate to widen his
pianistic horizon. Liszt's single *Étude de Perfectionnement*, 'presto
impetuoso', which ranges high and low over the keyboard,
tests more of the player's resources in technique than do all
Mendelssohn's four studies put together, and every one of
Chopin's is designed to give performers an opportunity of over-
coming some particular kind of technical difficulty.

*   *   *   *

Of the *Trois nouvelles Études* that Chopin wrote for Moscheles, two are studies in conflicting rhythms. In the first in F minor, an Andantino in common time, the curving melody in the right hand runs in triplet crotchets against a left-hand accompaniment in groups of four quavers. In the second, the well-known Allegretto in A flat major in duple time, the right hand maintains a continuous pulsation of chords in triplet quavers. The left-hand part, proceeding steadily in duplets, occasionally attains an independent melodic significance that emphasizes the prevailing rhythmic disparity. The third *Étude* in D flat, another Allegretto, in triple time, is rhythmically straightforward. Technically it is more exacting than the others, since it calls for the simultaneous blending of two kinds of touch in one hand throughout the whole piece. The right-hand part comprises a double line of notes, the upper being marked to be played legato and the lower, staccato. The left hand has its own difficulties in leaping wide distances. At the culminating point, the figuration is intensified in an exciting passage composed of a series of stretches of ninths in the right hand combined with leaps that increase in width up to nearly two octaves in the left. The *Trois nouvelles Études*, the last that Chopin wrote, are 'studies' in the truest sense of the word. As performing pieces, their expressive musical qualities engage the listener's attention far more closely than do the technical problems.

These particular technical problems, however, pale into insignificance beside those treated in the studies which Chopin began to compose ten years earlier in 1829. It was then that, as a youth of nineteen, he heard Paganini play in Warsaw. The violinist's feats of virtuosity made a profound impression upon him and inspired him to try to achieve parallel effects on the keyboard. The first-fruits of this stimulating experience were the Twelve Studies, op. 10 (1829-31). The second set of Twelve Studies, op. 25 followed between 1832 and 1836, after Chopin had settled in Paris.

* * * *

Throughout the Twenty-four Studies the composer maintained an even balance between satisfying inner structure, surface brilliance, and poetic atmosphere. In every study he treated a detail of performing-technique from both the functional and the artistic standpoints, the result in every case being a piece of music that has given untold delight to players and listeners for more than a hundred years. In respect of form and style the studies are of several different kinds. Some are organic; they grow out of one figure or theme and are largely continuous. Such are no. 5, the 'Black Key' Study; no. 11 in E flat major, a long succession of arpeggiated chords in both hands; no. 13 in A flat, consisting of a cantabile theme constantly renewed above a shimmering haze of uniform broken-chord accompaniment; no. 21 in G flat major, known as the 'Butterfly' Study, and no. 24 in C minor, a raging torrent of arpeggios.

A few of the studies are architectural in character; they are clearly divided into balancing sections. They include no. 3 in E major, in which a placid accompanied melody gives way for a time to agitated passage-work; nos. 17 in E minor and 22 in B minor, each with a central interlude in the tonic major differing in rhythm from that of the outer sections; and no. 19 in C sharp minor, which is ternary in conception but nearly continuous in effect. Of all the Twenty-four it is the least like a concert-study, but is nevertheless a magnificent study for the interpretation and phrasing of melodic lines concurrently in both hands. This study, no. 3 in E major, and no. 6 in E flat minor are the only ones in even moderately slow tempo. All the others are quick; they require extreme brilliance in performance.

Some of the more obvious problems of technique, the playing of thirds, sixths, and octaves, are dealt with in exhaustive and thrilling fashion in nos. 18 in G sharp minor, 20 in D flat major, and 22 in B minor respectively. Arpeggio-playing ranging over the span of the octave in both hands is exemplified in no. 24 in C minor, and over the span of the tenth in one hand only, in no. 1 in C major. Figuration in opposing rhythms forms the basis of no. 14 in F minor, where triplets of quavers in the right hand are pitted against triplets of crotchets in the left. Again, in no. 10, a 'vivace assai' in 12/8 time, the twelve quavers in a bar in both hands are arranged in mutually differing schemes of accentuation. No. 15 in F major and no. 16 in A minor are studies in persistent syncopation, in each of which the principal melody-note or chord falls on the weaker half of the beat. Studies in which the figuration is derived from a rhythmically distinctive opening unit include no. 15 in F major, and to a lesser degree, no. 17 in E minor.

The independence of the left hand is cultivated in no. 9 in F minor. The perpetual legato accompaniment in semiquavers below a semi-staccato melody in the right hand not only involves the left hand in wide stretches but obliges it to interpret a melodic 'inner voice' of its own. The supreme 'left-hand study', however, is no. 12 in C minor, known as the 'Revolutionary'. It has counterparts in the 'right-hand studies', nos. 23 in A minor and no. 8 in F major. In each case the virtuosic passages in semiquavers are merely the accompaniment to a chordal theme in the other hand, but they assume overwhelming importance owing to their sheer technical brilliance. In no. 4 in C sharp minor, the passage-work is divided fairly evenly between the two hands.

In these four last-named studies, chromaticisms play a prominent part in the passage-writing. The chromatic scale as an entity is treated in the most thorough and original fashion in no. 2 in A minor, where it is combined with light chords in one hand. This layout necessitates the use of the weaker fingers of the right hand as well as the unorthodox crossing of the third finger over the fourth and fifth ascending, and of the fourth and fifth under the third descending. Another study concerned with a specialized problem of fingering is no. 7 in C major. The lower strand of the two-fold right-hand part is arranged in pairs of repeated notes, the two notes of which are played alternately by the first finger and thumb. The upper strand is as jagged in outline as the lower strand is smooth.

The character of the piano writing throughout the Twenty-four Studies is predominantly decorative, but it also shows many traces of Chopin's skill in designing a more contrapuntal kind of texture. They may be found most particularly in the four-part writing of the sprightly no. 15 in F major; in the contrapuntal harmony of the opening and closing sections of no. 3 in E major and in the ardent melodic duologue of the nocturne-like no. 19 in C sharp minor.

*　　*　　*　　*

The influence of Paganini, as a performer, upon Chopin as a writer of studies was highly stimulating, but it was neither so direct nor so decisive as was the impact of Paganini, the performer of his own compositions, upon Schumann and Liszt. The two composers, who as young men in Frankfurt and Paris respectively heard him play his *Caprices* for violin solo, were fired with the idea of re-interpreting these dazzlingly brilliant pieces in terms of the keyboard. In carrying out this exacting self-imposed task, one of them modified his own style of composition. The other influenced the whole style of piano writing for many years to come.

Schumann, who had at that time composed little of note beyond his 'Abegg' Variations and *Papillons*, added many cubits to his stature as a musician. In translating to the keyboard a kind of music that needed considerable amplification in order to make its full effect in the new medium, he gained valuable experience in expressing his own musical ideas in vivid pianistic style. It was to stand him in good stead all his life.

Before Schumann's two sets of Paganini transcriptions appeared in 1832 and 1833, Liszt, who had early shown a marked predilection for writing fantasies on themes from works by other composers, had already written a *Grande Fantaisie de bravour sur la Clochette* (1831-2) basing it upon the 'Campanella' theme from Paganini's Violin Concerto in B minor. A few years later he re-wrote twelve of his own early piano studies in the light of Paganini's virtuosic style and issued them in 1839 as *Grandes Études* with a dedication to Czerny. At about the same time, he set to work to transcribe six of Paganini's *Caprices*, which he published in 1840 as *Études d'exécution transcendante d'après Paganini* and dedicated to Clara Schumann. (Actually, only five are from the *Caprices*; the sixth (no. 3) is another version of the 'Campanella' theme).

With these two publications, both of which he revised
extensively and reissued respectively as *Études d'exécution transcendante* and *Grandes Études de Paganini* in 1851, Liszt revolu-
tionized the art of playing the piano. Chopin's Studies had set
a new standard for concert-performers, but despite their great
technical difficulty many of them can also be played with enjoyment by pianists of average ability who perform only in private.
Liszt's Studies cannot be adequately performed in public except
by pianists of the very highest attainments. For the less expert
they are appallingly difficult to play. The very look of them on
the printed page may well strike terror to all but the boldest
sight-readers. Schumann's 'Paganini' Studies, however, are
much less exacting to play than the majority of Chopin's
Twenty-four or all Liszt's Studies. In addition, they are
musically extraordinarily interesting as examples of a composer's ingenuity in spreading over the whole keyboard material
originally limited to the treble clef.

*   *   *   *

In the six *Studies after Caprices by Paganini*, op. 3 (1832) Schumann aimed at making the transcriptions as literal as possible.
He added such basses as he considered correct, supplied harmonies and complementary melodic parts whenever he thought
suitable and distributed the violin part throughout the texture,
constantly changing its pitch to lend it variety in tone-colour.
Thus he succeeded in making the studies sound like pieces of
original piano music rather than arrangements.

Schumann had once thought of writing a Piano-School. Now,
instead, he wrote a longish preface to his op. 3 and included a
set of excercises that he had composed with a view to smoothing
out the technical difficulties relevant to each Study. He stated
that, although his interest in the music itself had incited him to
make the transcriptions, it was also his intention to 'give solo
players an opportunity of removing a reproach often cast at
them. Namely, that they made too little use of other instruments
and their peculiarities for the improvement and enrichment of
their own'. The following example from the sixth Study shows

his gift for turning a single-line passage from Paganini's six-teenth Caprice into a stretch of interesting piano writing that preserves both the letter and the spirit of the original:

This sixth Study, while remaining basically true to its model, is the most enterprising item of op. 3 in respect of its qualities as piano music.

In the second set of six, which Schumann entitled *Études de Concert d'après des Caprices de Paganini*, op. 10, he treated some of the given material with greater freedom than previously, altering the structure of the Caprices when he considered the musical result to be justified. The piano writing of this whole set is far more elaborate than that of op. 3. Much of it points forward to the assured pianistic style of the *Études symphoniques*, op. 13 which Schumann was to compose a year later. The following bars from the fourth *Étude* (Paganini's fourth Caprice) show a typically Schumannesque piece of contrapuntal figura-tion foreshadowing that of the fifth variation of the *Études symphoniques* and of the thumbnail sketch 'Paganini' in *Carnaval*. In each of these two pieces the accentuation falls persistently on the weak division of the beat (see example on next page).

It is not possible in these pages to exemplify any more of Schumann's apt transformations of characteristic violin passages into their nearest pianistic equivalents. Musicians who wish to go deeper into this fascinating subject can do so without diffi-culty by comparing Schumann's versions with Paganini's easily

available *Twenty-four Caprices*, op. 1. For the purpose of identification, a table showing the relationship between the numbering
of both Schumann's and Liszt's transcriptions and that of
Paganini's *Caprices* is given at the end of this book.

Schumann's most important studies, the *Études symphoniques*,
were discussed in the chapter on Variations. Another well-
known but much less significant example of his study-writing is
the Toccata in C major, op. 7, a bravura concert-study in
sonata form. He wrote it a year before the 'Abegg' Variations,
op. 1, as an *Étude fantastique* in D major, but subsequently altered
both the key and the title. The Toccata affords yet another
example of his fondness for 'varying' his own compositions such
as we noted much earlier in connexion with his remodelling of
songs as sonata movements.

Only two of Liszt's *Grandes Études de Paganini* are based on
Caprices that Schumann had already transcribed. A comparison
between them shows the difference in the musical outlook of the
two composers. Schumann gave the preference to the musical
qualities of the pieces; Liszt, to their essentially pianistic presentation. In his capacity as a superlatively fine executant he had
a closer affinity with the phenomenally brilliant violinist than
had the introspective Schumann, whose performing technique
was extremely limited. Liszt's fifth *Étude* in E major, known as
La Chasse, and Schumann's op. 3, no. 2, which are both based
on Paganini's ninth Caprice, reveal the respective composers'

sensitivity to the finer points of keyboard style. Schumann supplied a prosaic left-hand accompaniment to Paganini's light passages in double-stopping. Liszt left them as they are to make their own magical effect, but divided them between the two hands to reproduce their distinctive accentuation. Schumann either doubled the volatile runs heavily at the distance of two octaves below, or turned them into passages of sixths. Liszt, throwing caution to the winds, secured a more arresting if unconventional effect with successions of double glissandos. But Schumann's lightly arpeggiated chords catch the style of Paganini's bowing effects in treble-stopping far more accurately than does Liszt's melodic line which is placed in the resonant lower-middle compass of the keyboard with chords above and below.

Liszt's version of Paganini's sixth Caprice in G minor retains the never-ceasing tremolandos in various parts of the texture. In Schumann's op. 10, no. 2 they are transformed into groups of repeated chords in triplets with an added melodic counterpoint. During the middle section, the chordal figuration is dissolved into its constituent notes. Schumann's version thus avoids monotony of sound and fatigue in performance, but Liszt's is more romantic in tone-colour. The hypnotic effect of the demi-semiquaver tremolandos is offset by an introduction and a postlude of rushing scales and arpeggios which Liszt, with true artistic acumen, detached from Paganini's fifth Caprice in A minor and transposed into G minor for this purpose.

The remaining four of Liszt's 'Paganini' Studies display the virtuoso in his element, re-interpreting the sometimes exiguous violin figuration in terms of luxuriant piano music. In the second in E flat major, Paganini's improvisatory opening bars take on an elaborate character similar to that of the introduction to Liszt's much later Concert-study in A flat, *Il Lamento*; the violinist's scale passages are converted into miniature cadenzas in thirds, sixths and light chords. The third Study in B minor, based on the 'Campanella' theme, out-distances all the others in the width of the stretches and leaps, the persistent intricacy of the decorative passages and the unparalleled use made of the highest octave of the piano. The fourth in E major is written on only one stave throughout and looks deceptively easy. Yet it requires the utmost precision in fingering if the player's frequently crossing and overlapping hands are not to impede each other's freedom of action.

For the sixth and last Study, Liszt chose Paganini's twenty-fourth Caprice, itself a set of variations upon the theme that Brahms subsequently used as the basis of his two sets of 'Paganini' Variations. In seven of the variations the violin part runs in single lines or octaves. When transferring this sparse material to the piano, Liszt was never at a loss in finding effective means of amplifying it. In the first variation he added the theme itself in the left hand as a contrapuntal foundation below Paganini's high-pitched arpeggios. In the third, he superimposed it upon the bass. In the second variation he scattered the groups of four semiquavers at random over the lower regions of the keyboard and in the fifth he devised an antiphonal interplay between the two hands to correspond to the violinist's alternations of high and low pitch. Paganini's double- or treble-stoppings he translated into their nearest effective equivalents. He let the scales in thirds or tenths in the sixth variation blossom into passages in enhanced octaves running in contrary motion to scales in thirds. In the eighth he released the treble-stopped chords from their captivity of slurs and ties to prance in light staccato. In the final variation he obliterated the crisp broken chords and nimble arpeggios of the original in a whirlwind of passage-writing, beneath which he finally re-introduced the distinctive unit of Paganini's theme to thunder out its indomitable six-note battle-cry.

*   *   *   *

This tendency of Liszt's to restate a theme or figure, either note-for-note or in a succession of hardly-concealed disguises, is a distinguishing feature of most of his studies. He seldom developed his material rhythmically in the Beethovenian manner, nor did he let it grow organically from the initial figure as did Chopin in the majority of his studies. Chopin, as we have already seen, often created an entire study out of a single well-defined thematic unit which he steered through a whole circle of keys, never letting it deviate from the figuration he had designed for one specific technical purpose. Liszt took a fragment of melody and submitted it to endless restatement with changing styles of accompanying passages that require several kinds of touch and technique within a page or two. His concert-studies are essentially concert-*pieces*. The fact that many of them have titles and are composed in the style of programme or descriptive music suggests that Liszt was more deeply interested in their artistic than in their educative value. The *Étude de Perfectionnement* that he wrote for Moscheles was renamed *Ab irato* (In a rage) in accordance with its expressive style when he re-wrote it ten years later. The tone-pictures *Waldesrauschen* and *Gnomenreigen* were his fanciful response to a request for studies for inclusion in Lebert and Stark's Piano-Method.

Gnomenreigen (Dance of the gnomes), which sparkles gaily in free rondo form, comprises alternating panels of two strongly contrasted types of figuration. *Waldesrauschen* (Forest murmurs) is one long accompanied melody which passes from the left hand to the right. It is worked in canon for a time and is only occasionally interrupted by rhetorical cadenzas. In its predominantly melodic character it recalls *Un sospiro* (A sigh), the third of Liszt's Three Concert-Studies (1849), each of which is virtually a set of free continuous variations upon a strongly marked theme. The theme of the first Study in A flat (*Il Lamento*) consists of two phrases. The second of these does not come into its own until the middle section, but even there, it cannot escape being punctuated by the distinctive descending figure of the principal phrase. The second Study, *La Leggierezza* (Lightness), is the very apotheosis of chromaticism; it contains not a single bar without accidentals. Although it begins and ends nominally in F minor, the flexible principal theme adapts itself so easily to harmonization in either the major or the minor that the modality of the whole remains enchantingly indeterminate.

*   *   *   *

Persistently chromatic figuration is also an essential feature of the majority of Liszt's *Études d'exécution transcendante*. This collection of twelve studies, musically the most interesting of all the composer's works in the category under discussion, comprises the final, definitive version of his *Grandes Études* mentioned earlier in this chapter. They represent many aspects of Liszt's style, not only as a study-writer but as a composer of tone-poems. The first, *Preludio*, is nothing but a flourish of chords and arpeggios covering the whole compass of the keyboard. The second, 'molto vivace, a capriccio' in A minor, consists of a rhythmic figure of repeated notes in quavers and a whirling accompaniment of detached semiquavers which eventually unite in a coda of heavy staccato chords. These two items and the much longer no. 10 in F minor, 'allegro agitato molto' are studies according to the generally accepted meaning of the term. Each is written in a more or less uniform pattern of notes and none bears a descriptive title, although the Study in F minor, which is headed *** has come to be known as 'Appassionata'.

The other nine studies make the impression that the composer's chief aim was the creation of poetic atmosphere to give appropriate musical significance to their respective titles. *Feu follets* (Jack o' Lantern), no. 5, is lambent with flickering chromaticisms; *Wilde Jagd* (Furious chase), no. 8, is an intricate mesh of cross-beat rhythms. *Chasse neige* (Snow plough), no. 12, makes its way to and fro through a blizzard of swirling demi-semiquavers. *Mazeppa* (the Cossack patriot), no. 4, *Vision*, no. 6 and *Eroica*, no. 7 present their bold themes in progressively more ornate varieties of figuration and are virtually sets of continuous variations. *Paysage* (Landscape), no. 3, *Ricordanza* (Recollection), no. 9, and *Harmonies du soir* (Evening Harmonies), no. 11 are immeasurably quieter and more melodic in character. They avoid the fiercest technical difficulties, the speed and the violence of the others but they offer perplexities of their own in the form of prolonged passages involving stretches of ninths and tenths in either or both hands. The restful *Paysage* is perhaps the only one that can be played by an average pianist with hardly a thought of insuperable problems in performing-technique, but with unalloyed enjoyment of the musical content: the blending of two complementary themes into an indivisible whole.

*   *   *   *

Brahms's contribution to the piano study was very different from that of the preceding generation of composers. The post-humous influence of Paganini's virtuoso style upon his own is manifest in the two colossal sets of 'Paganini' Variations, which he himself styled 'Studies', but which the musical world considers as being among the finest sets of variations ever written.

In writing less intellectual studies Brahms followed Liszt's example as a transcriber. His Five Studies are arrangements or amplifications of well-known pieces by other composers which he made with a view to their use for advanced technical pur-poses rather than for concert performance. He transformed the flowing right-hand part of Chopin's Study in F minor, op. 25, no. 2 into a succession of much less mobile sixths and thirds. He reconstituted the 'moto perpetuo' of Weber's Sonata in C major by transferring almost the whole of the brilliant right-hand part to the left hand and leaving the right hand little to do beyond supplying the relevant harmonic basis above, instead of below the thematic substance. In other words, he turned this whole movement upside down for the benefit of the player's left hand. He employed the Presto of Bach's first Sonata in G minor for violin solo as the foundation of a pair of studies in two-part playing. In the first, he placed the given material at its correct pitch in the right-hand part and wrote a counterpoint below for the left hand; in the second, he gave it to the left hand an octave lower and wrote a fresh counterpoint above for the right hand. Lastly, he arranged Bach's Chaconne in D minor for solo violin as a study for the left hand alone. It is an almost note-for-note transcription, an octave below the original pitch, which not only gives the pianist experience in executing many different kinds of passage-work with the left hand, but affords him a magnificent opportunity of becoming closely acquainted with one of the masterpieces of violin literature.

The Fifty-one Exercises (Übungen) that Brahms wrote for the purpose of developing the individual style of technique requisite for performing his own works, are completely devoid of musical qualities. They are simply mechanical finger-exercises of the most utilitarian kind. Nevertheless, they cover every type of fingering and touch likely to be found in Brahms's piano compositions and they are invaluable to all pianists, whether or no they specialize in playing the composer's works.

Some of the exercises pay special attention to the combining of two varieties of touch in one hand (nos. 4, 9, 22, 32, and 43), or to the execution of two, three or even four different metrical patterns jointly by the two hands (nos. 1 and 18). Others are designed to promote independence of the fingers by tethering one or more of them to a long-sustained note or notes while the others perform all manner of convolutions in shorter notes (nos. 10-19, 23, 28, 39, 43 and 45). The supreme examples of this kind of digital acrobatics are nos. 46, a and b. In these, the free fingers have to cross and recross the perpetually static thumb. Other ingenuities in fingering, such as the changing of the fourth and fifth fingers at the top of one chord to the second finger or thumb at the bottom of the next without any audible break in sound are exemplified in nos. 43, a and b. The passing of the fourth finger over the fifth during ascending passages is the subject of no. 44, b, and the sliding of fingers from black notes to white, of nos. 25, a, b and c. These Fifty-one Exercises, the 'Paganini' Variations and the Five Studies comprise a 'Brahms Piano-Method' in everything but name.

*   *   *   *

Grieg made only a single addition to this branch of composition in the form of a Study in F minor which he included as no. 5 of his *Moods*, op. 73 (1905). It bears the sub-title 'Hommage à Chopin' and imitates the style of that composer's studies so closely as to leave hardly a trace of Grieg's own, generally undisguisable, idiom.

*   *   *   *

Side by side with the intensive production of concert-studies to satisfy advanced performers' requirements for musical material with which to perfect their technique and to win triumphs in the concert-room, a whole literature of simple small-scale music came into being to meet the humbler needs of beginners and young players. Many composers took part in its making and the music thus produced is of many types and styles. Here, we must confine our attention to that written by the better-known composers and still in use at the present day.

This simple music also serves purposes other than those for which it was originally intended: the training of young fingers and the accustoming of young minds to musical forms. It affords musicians an opportunity of studying the respective composers' work in miniature, and of observing its relationship in style to their large-scale production. Moreover, some of it possesses the same magic quality as do certain kinds of fairy tales which, though written primarily for children, also exert an irresistible fascination over adult minds.

One of the most conventional types of 'teaching piece' is the *sonatina*, many examples of which were written during the nineteenth century. As the title denotes, it is a small-scale sonata, usually light in texture and easy to play. The sonatinas written by the composers of our prescribed period include twelve by Clementi and three each by Beethoven and Schumann.

Clementi's and Beethoven's classical sonatinas, the most enduring of their species, were composed during the 1790s. Beethoven's three, in C major, G major and F major—not to be confused with the three small-scale 'Bonn' Sonatas which he wrote at the age of thirteen—are each in two movements. Only one of all the six movements is in sonata form: the Allegro of the C major Sonatina. Four of the others are in simple binary form and the second movement of the F major is a rondo. The two little movements of the Sonatina in G major, Moderato and 'Romance,' as well as the rondo of the F major Sonatina are written in the same ingenuous style as the earliest pieces in the composer's Bagatelles which we shall study as a whole collection in the next chapter. Simple as are the Sonatinas as a group, they are typically Beethovenian both in their direct manner of stating the subject-matter and in the expansive method of treating it, most especially in the first Sonatina, the longest and the most sonata-like of the three.

These slender compositions found successors in three of Beethoven's Thirty-two sonatas, which, although they are not actually entitled sonatinas, pertain to that small-scale class. They are the pair of two-movement Sonatas in G minor and G major, op. 49, nos. 1 and 2 (1796) and the Sonata in G major, op. 79 (1809) which was originally published as *Sonate facile*.

Clementi's twelve sonatinas, all in major keys, are more diversified in structure and in the style of the piano writing than Beethoven's. The first five (op. 36, nos. 1-5) are each in three movements; the remainder (op. 36, no. 6, op. 37, nos. 1-3 and op. 38, nos. 1-3) are in two movements only. In every one of the twelve sonatinas the first movement is in sonata form, but the central movements and finales vary in design and style. They include rondos, pieces in ternary form, a minuet-and-trio (op. 37, no. 2), a 'tempo di minuetto' (op. 38, no. 1), a picturesque little *Air suisse* (op. 36, no. 5) based on a repetitive six-bar phrase that simulates yodelling, and a longish sonata-form Presto (op. 37, no. 1) whose buoyancy of spirit and nimble piano writing recall the mercurial finales of some of the Haydn sonatas. Entirely opposite in expressive character are the meditative slow movement, 'un poco adagio', of op. 36, no. 3 consisting of sixteen bars in sparse two-part writing, and the central Allegretto of op. 36, no. 2, throughout whose length the uniform dotted rhythm seems to denote the measured steps of a dance.

*   *   *   *

Intermediate in period and in style between these classical sonatinas and Schumann's more expansive Sonatas for Young People (1853) are Mendelssohn's Six Children's Pieces, op. 72. They were written when the composer was in England in 1842 and are also known as 'Christmas Pieces'. The second and fourth, a pair of melodically expressive Andantes in E flat major and D major, are similar in character to the best-known type of the

o

Songs without Words. The first is a brisk Allegro in G major
with a jaunty tune that insists on being accented on the weakest
part of the bar. The other three pieces are typically Mendelssohnian scherzos sparkling with fun. No. 3, a compact little
Allegretto in G major, is based on a short rhythmic theme.
Although frequently repeated, it undergoes so many changes in
melodic or harmonic details that it never loses its original freshness. No. 5 in G minor is a rondo in which both episodes are
composed of the same crisply staccato material presented in
different keys. The vivacious no. 6 in F major, the longest of all
and the most enterprising in construction and in pianistic style,
is distinguished by the extreme independence of the treble and
bass parts. It is a battle of wits between the two hands, which
every now and again reverse their positions with the aid of
double counterpoint. These tactics prove most effective at the
beginning of the recapitulation (bar 40). The opening phrase of
the piece is turned upside down and the melody on thus being
translated to a more sonorous pitch gains in forcefulness of
expression. But although the left hand secures this temporary
advantage over the right hand, the contest ends with a narrow
victory for the latter, who celebrates it with a tiny mocking
arpeggio.

*   *   *   *

Schumann did not name his compositions in this category
'sonatinas', but 'Sonatas for Young People', as distinguished
from the three 'Grand Sonatas' he composed in his prime. The
three Sonatas of his op. 118, which were written for, and dedicated to his three eldest daughters respectively, are genuinely
romantic in type and expression and are progressively more
elaborate in keyboard style. They are all composed in four
movements, the last two of which bear descriptive titles. In this
respect they combine attributes of the sonata and the suite.
Indeed, the first in G major, the simplest in style and the easiest
to play, was originally planned by Schumann as 'Kinderscenen'
(Scenes of childhood). Unlike the two others it includes no
movement in sonata form but is made up of a tuneful Allegro,

a Theme and Variations, a 'Doll's Slumber Song', and a final 'Rondoletto'.

The opening and closing movements of the second and third Sonatas in D major and C major respectively are in sonata form; the others are less conventional. The second movement of no. 2 is a strict but lively two-part accompanied canon at the octave, and the third, 'Evening Song', a piece of continuous melodic writing. The Finale, 'Children's Party', is appropriately a babble of semiquaver figuration. The movements of the third Sonata depict strongly contrasted moods. The first, 'alla marcia', is robust, and the 'andante espressivo' which follows is pensive after the manner of Schumann's most reflective piano pieces, and is almost as intricate in texture. From the aspect of interpretation it is the most difficult movement among the twelve. The third movement, a quick Bohemian Dance with strong accents and many repetitions of two-bar phrases, establishes a slightly exotic atmosphere which is, however, completely dispelled by the artless 'allegretto con tenerezza' of 'A Child's Dream' which forms the Finale. Into this movement in 6/8 time Schumann inserted quotations in 2/4 time from the Allegro of the first Sonata, as if to symbolize the affinity in spirit existing between the children to whom he dedicated them.

The piano writing of Schumann's second and third Sonatas indicates the fairly high standard of performing-technique already attained by the youthful players for whom they were composed. Some of the forty-three items in the *Album for the Young*, op. 68 (1848) are more genuinely suitable for the beginner. The first eighteen are specified as 'for the young', and the remaining twenty-five, 'for more advanced players'. Moreover, all the pieces are short. All but a few bear descriptive titles to endear them to struggling players, and many possess the 'fairy-tale' quality which we shall rediscover in Tchaikovsky's *Album for the Young* (1878). Such are Schumann's 'The Stranger', no. 29, 'First Sorrow,' no. 16, 'Winter Time', nos. 38-39, 'The Horseman', no. 23, 'Santa Claus', no. 12, 'The Poor Orphan Child', no. 6, and 'Sheherazade', no. 32, to name a few.

Yet even in the simplest pieces Schumann could not forbear

to introduce contrapuntal devices. In 'The Wild Rider', no. 8, the opening phrase in A minor in the right hand is straightway presented in F major in the left, below instead of above the original chordal accompaniment. In 'Little Folk-song', no. 9, the melody of the doloroso section is later concealed within the left-hand part of the final phrase. Canonic imitations occur between the upper and lower parts of 'First Sorrow', no. 16 and of 'Theme', no. 34. No. 27 is a 'Song in Canon', throughout which the canon is treated so skilfully that it never attracts undue attention, and no. 40 is a 'Little Prelude' enlivened by double counterpoint, and a (three-part) Fugue. In 'Northern Song: greeting to G*', no. 41, Schumann used the four-note theme

denoting the name of the Danish composer, Gade, as the basis of miniature 'variations' in which he placed the theme alternately in the treble and the bass. He also 'varied' no. 4, 'Chorale' in G major, by re-writing it as 'Figured Chorale' in F major, no. 42, with a flowing accompaniment instead of the plain chords of the original. Among the movements most typical of the composer's introspective style are 'Theme', no. 34 and 'Winter time, I', no. 38. Each is made up of a series of short repetitions of a little figure which is nearly as plaintive in character as is that of the ever-questioning *Warum* (Why), no. 3 of the *Fantasiestücke* op. 12.

*   *   *   *

Schumann wrote the whole of the *Album for the Young* in sixteen days as a recreation after the exhausting process of composing his opera *Genoveva*. Thirty years later Tchaikovsky wrote the twenty-four pieces of his *Album for the Young*, op. 39 under similar circumstances, as a relaxation after he had composed his opera *Eugène Onegin*. That the *Album* begins and ends on a serious note, with 'Morning Prayer' and 'In Church', may be the outcome of his having been engaged at the same time upon the writing of a musical setting of the Liturgy. The other pieces in the *Album* are predominantly gay in mood, except the two which depict the illness and funeral of a doll (nos. 6 and 7). The titles and character of several items denote a more international outlook than Schumann's. The 'Mazurka', no. 10, 'Polka', no. 14, 'Italian Air', no. 15, 'Old French Song', no. 16, 'German Song', no. 17, and 'Neapolitan Dance-tune', no. 18, all conjure up the salient features of their respective national styles, and the tune of 'The Organ-grinder', no. 23, is one that Tchaikovsky heard performed by a street-singer in Florence. The distinctively Russian items include 'Peasant's Song', no. 12, in which the alternate tonic and dominant chords represent the sounds of a harmonica; 'Folksong: Russian dance', no. 13, which is written in the lively style of a *trepak*, and 'Russian Song', no. 11, throughout which the grouping of the tune into units of six beats, each containing a recurrent three-note figure, lends it an agreeably primitive character.

The imaginative 'fairy-tale' pieces are more graphically descriptive. 'Winter Morning', no. 2, creates a sensation of intense, numbing cold with its detached pairs of quiet slurred chords. 'The Witch', no. 20, portrays Baba Yaga chasing her quarry in determined staccato up and down the keyboard, muttering terrifying sforzando imprecations. 'Nursery Tale', no. 19, narrates a not unduly alarming story but passes through a period of acute suspense, while a bell tolls relentlessly on middle C and the left hand writhes, agonized, in short spells of ascending chromatic thirds. 'Song of the Lark', no. 22, filled with ecstatic trilling above a restful chordal foundation, evokes the enchantment of spring in wide open spaces, and 'Soldiers' March', no. 5, depicts in ever-precise, light staccato texture the approaching and receding steps of a regiment of midget soldiers.

A remarkable feature of these little pieces is that they are undeniably poetic in effect despite the extreme squareness of their rhythmic schemes. Every one of them runs in strips of four or eight bars; a method of construction that also underlies two others. 'The Little Horseman', no. 3, gallops through seventy-two bars of never-ceasing quavers without once drawing rein. 'The New Doll', no. 9, awakens admiration and delight which are expressed in a melody that never exceeds the eight-bar limit but breaks up in sheer rapture into one-bar units while the waltz-like accompaniment beats on imperturbably.

Rhythmic subtleties are not entirely lacking. The twelve-bar opening phrase of the incense-shrouded 'In Church' falls naturally into sub-divisions of five, three and four bars; the square rhythm of 'Mazurka' is modified by the insertion of a six-bar phrase prolonged by a pause, and the unyielding symmetry of 'Sweet Memories', no. 21, is twice softened by the overlapping of two melodic lines in canonic imitation. In 'Song of the Lark', which begins off the main beat, the fitting of the duple-rhythmed melody into bars in triple time causes metrical displacements that increase the prevailing sense of urgency. At the climax, two four-bar phrases coalesce as the lark ascends, scattering its song to the winds, and then descends in a fine chain of twittering sounds.

*   *   *   *

Tchaikovsky wrote the *Album for the Young* (1878) long before composing the Symphonies in E minor (1888) and B minor ('Pathétique') (1893) and the 'Nutcracker' Suite (1892), but the thumbnail sketches for piano have many points in common with the full-length orchestral works which can hardly escape the notice of musicians already familiar with them.

A relationship of the same kind exists between some of César Franck's short pieces for the keyboard and his best-known orchestral, chamber, and piano compositions. In this instance, however, the miniatures were written both before and after the large-scale works.

The little pieces in question were composed originally for the harmonium in response to a request made by a former pupil for advice on his work as a village organist and for musical examples in connexion therewith. Franck wrote a number of movements for this purpose between 1858 and 1865 and a further series of

fifty-nine within a year of his death in 1890. From these two
collections, sixteen items were selected for publication as piano
music, together with two rather longer pieces originally composed for the piano. Although none of the individual pieces is
artistically of any great value to the practising pianist, the
volume forms an instructive preparation to the study of Franck's
longer piano works. It possesses greater fascination as an anthology of distinguishing traits of the composer's general musical
style.

Of the sixteen little movements, nos. 9, 12, 13, 14 and 16 may
be considered as displaying the greatest number of typically
Franckian 'fingerprints'. These include the tying of a melody-
note from a weaker to a stronger beat, such as occurs in the
slow movement and the Finale of the Symphony in D minor:

(1886-8), and the pivoting of a melody upon one note, as in
the oft-repeated theme in the first movement:

The opening of a phrase with short figures before it becomes
more continuous, a trait exemplified in the main themes of the
Symphonic Variations (1885) and in the fugue-subject of the
Prelude, Chorale and Fugue; and the use of falling intervals
of a fourth, fifth or sixth in the melodic outline, a characteristic
of the themes of the Prelude, Aria and Finale. Other representative features throughout the volume are sudden changes from
major to minor, the choice of keys with many sharps or flats
and the working of thematic material in a series of chromatic
sequences.

Franck's partiality for writing in canon is exhibited in nos. 7 and 17. The former, a little piece in E major, written throughout in canon at the octave, bears a distinct thematic likeness to the last movement of his well-known Sonata for violin and piano (1886).

Of the two pieces composed originally for the piano (nos. 1 and 10), the artless *Les plaintes d'une poupée* (The doll's complaint) (1865) in sparse two-part writing, may be accounted a genuine 'piece for beginners'. The other, *Danse lente*, which is more advanced in pianistic style, was composed in the same year as the Symphonic Variations (1885) and is itself in variation form of the very simplest kind. Musically, it is a miniature; a type of composition we shall study in the following chapter.

— 10 —

Miniatures

Early history and types of miniature. The Bagatelle, Moment musical, Album Leaf, Prelude, Intermezzo, Capriccio, Humoresque, Eclogue, Romance, Song without Words, Characteristic piece, Fantasy piece. Miniature pieces of descriptive, impressionistic, and programme music. Suites.

THE little educational pieces we examined in the previous chapter constitute only a small proportion of the immense number of miniatures which were written by all the composers of the period from Beethoven to Grieg and which go to form one of the largest categories of nineteenth-century piano music.

This type of small-scale composition had flourished from early times, long before large-scale forms had been evolved. The many different kinds of short pieces by the Elizabethan virginal composers, and the delicate character-sketches, descriptive pieces and nature-studies by the late seventeenth-century and early eighteenth-century clavecinistes were its ancestors. After the sonata and allied forms had become established during the later eighteenth century the composition of short pieces had declined. In the opening years of the nineteenth century it was revived. Beethoven, who had written two Bagatelles in 1797, began his long series of these little movements in 1802; Tomašek's *Eclogues* and *Dithyrambs* started to appear in 1810 and Schubert's *Moments musicaux* in 1823. But it was the romantic composers, whose genius lay in the direction of expressing the essentials of a poem or a painting and of creating a definite atmosphere within the space of a few bars or a page of music, who were largely responsible for restoring the miniature to favour. With their respective Songs without Words, Characteristic Pieces, Preludes, and Consolations, Mendelssohn, Schumann, Chopin, and Liszt set an example to composers which has been followed without interruption down to the present day.

The whole collection of this small-scale music is distinguished by great diversity in the type of the individual pieces, or sets of pieces. Notwithstanding their tiny size, they exemplify nearly every kind of musical form and texture current during the century. They range from the strictly classical to the unrestrainedly romantic. In point of expressive style they display the same tendencies as do the large-scale compositions of the same period. They are either abstract, descriptive, impressionistic, or even improvisatory, but the great majority are symmetrical in design however fantastic they may be in mood. They blend classical balance with romantic feeling in their own inimitable way, and although they can be arranged into groups according to their nomenclature, the strong family likeness that exists between them makes any rigid classification impossible. A *Moment musical* by Schubert does not differ fundamentally in character from an Intermezzo by Brahms or a Romance by Schumann; neither does an 'Album Leaf' by Tchaikovsky from a Bagatelle by Beethoven, a Prelude by Chopin, or a 'Poetic tone-picture' by Grieg.

As far as their formal structure is concerned the miniatures might well have been included in the chapters dealing with their respective large-scale relatives. But the small dimensions which invest them with their distinctive and intimate aura entitle them to consideration as a category apart. In the present chapter they will be sorted as far as possible into two main classes: those with generic, non-committal titles, and those whose specific descriptive titles bring them within the sphere of programme music. The two classes inevitably overlap now and then, for pieces of both kinds were sometimes included within a single series. Schumann's *Album Leaves*, several of Grieg's books of *Lyric Pieces* and Borodin's *Petite Suite* are compositions of this heterogeneous type.

Among the earliest miniatures published after 1800 are two improvisatory Preludes by Beethoven which he composed in 1789 at the age of nineteen but did not publish until 1803. Each

of these pieces passes through the whole cycle of the sharp and
flat keys in the major mode beginning and ending in C. The
second, although little more than half the length of the first,
goes through the modulatory procedure twice over. The music
sometimes remains in the same tonality for only one bar during
this rapid transit from key to key. These two Preludes, and
another in F minor composed even earlier, are curiosities, of
interest to the historian rather than to the performer. On the
other hand, Beethoven's principal contribution to the category
of miniatures, the series of Bagatelles which he wrote at intervals
during the space of about twenty-five years, is a treasured pos-
session of pianists of all grades. Not only does it number among
its twenty-six items several which are suitable in calibre for
inclusion in recital programmes. As a whole collection it may be
considered a microcosm of Beethoven's art as a composer for the
piano. It represents many phases of his creative career from the
time he composed the Piano Concerto, no. 1 in C major in 1797
down to the year in which he wrote the 'Diabelli' Variations
and completed the Ninth Symphony (1823). The series is
divided into four groups: the two early Bagatelles, the seven of
op. 33 (1802), the eleven of op. 119 (1820-2) and the six of op.
126 (1823).

The use of the title 'Bagatelle' (a trifle) for a single piece dates
back at least as far as to François Couperin, who included a
short *rondeau* entitled *Les Bagatelles* in his second book of compositions for the clavecin published in 1716. Beethoven was the
first to apply the title to a whole series of pieces of various kinds.

* * * *

The Beethoven Bagatelles vary in length from sixteen or
twenty bars to three or four pages. In emotional intensity they
are comparable with movements from the composer's longer
works. One of the most mature, op. 126, no. 3 in E flat, well
known in recent years from its inclusion in the *Myra Hess Album*,
is as serene in mood as the 'adagio sostenuto' of the 'Hammerklavier' Sonata. It even resembles this movement in the re-
distribution of the melody among the weaker parts of the beat:

At the other extreme is the Presto in B minor and major, op. 126, no. 4. Relentless in its furious energy and unflagging rhythm, it makes the impression of being an offshoot of the Scherzo of the Ninth Symphony. Rhythmic interest is also paramount in the Scherzo-and-Trio in C major, op. 33, no. 2 and in the explosive Presto in A flat, op. 33, no. 7.

The latter, which consists largely of chords and arpeggios and is purely instrumental in type, is one of several that exemplify Beethoven's technique of variation. Others that do so more expansively are predominantly melodic in interest; their cantabile melodies lend themselves readily to decoration when they are restated. In the Bagatelles in A major and D major, op. 33, nos. 4 and 6, the variation of the main theme is straightforward and conventional. In others it is more subtle. The reprise of op. 119, no. 1 in G major is treated so freely, with the melody divided between the two hands, that it is not easily recognizable. In no. 5 of the same opus, the reprise is merely a contracted, etherealized version of the opening statement. Similarity in rhythm is the only link between the first and last phrases of the Bagatelle in B flat, op. 119, no. 11, and the tiny coda made of fresh material increases the feeling that the piece is simply an extemporization.

Still more irregular is the curious Bagatelle in E flat, op. 126, no. 6. The principal thematic material, after having first been presented in the key of E flat major, is repeated by inference rather than by direct restatement, in the key of A flat. The mysterious character of this 'andante amabile con moto' is emphasized by the phrase of tonic and dominant harmonies marked presto which opens and closes the movement with headlong violence and is responsible for the general title Presto. Strongly individual in type are the Bagatelles in G major, op. 119, no. 6 and in G minor, op. 126, no. 2, each an improvisation unified by a characteristic metrical figure. Op. 119, no. 7 in C major, which opens in leisurely fashion in crotchets and quavers, gathers momentum until it ends feverishly in a spin of high demisemi-quavers over a long, low trill.

Five Bagatelles of op. 119, nos. 2, 5, 8, 9 and 10, resemble some of Chopin's shorter preludes in being composed through-out in one style of figuration. Two of them display characteri-stics of Beethoven's expressive style which stand in mutual opposition. No. 2, 'andante con moto' in C major, is a supremely delicate and witty colloquy between an imperturbable cantabile melody and a rippling accompaniment. No. 8, 'moderato cantabile', also in C major, is one of the shortest and most inti-mate in expression. It contains a sudden, unprepared modula-tion from the major chord on G to a plain octave B flat; a harmonic progression comparable in its magical effect to the unforgettable transition from the major chord of D to that on B during the opening sentence of the composer's Fourth Piano Concerto in G major.

*   *   *   *

Among the few other composers of Bagatelles was Smetana, who at the age of twenty wrote a set of seven Bagatelles and Impromptus (1844) as one of his earliest compositions. In size and scope the individual pieces are not unlike Beethoven's, but in character they are different. Each bears a descriptive title and the style of the piano writing is mainly impressionistic.

*　　*　　*　　*

Of the small number of short pieces written by Schubert, apart from his many dances which will be discussed in the next chapter, the six *Moments musicaux* composed between *c.* 1823 and 1827 are the most important and the best known. Despite the fanciful title, which Schubert was the first to employ and which has been little used by later composers, the *Moments musicaux* are as abstract in style as are a few much less well-known pieces to which he gave no names beyond their tempo-indications. The second *Moment musical*, a deeply expressive Andante in A flat major, is in free rondo form. The third in F minor is composed in a series of strips, all except one of which begin with a few bars over a pedal-bass. This animated little movement, one of the best known of the set, was first published as 'Air russe' in Vienna in 1823 in an *Album musical* containing pieces by various composers including Rossini, and was reprinted in a London almanac in 1831 as 'Russian Air'. The sixth *Moment musical* in A flat major, a minuet-and-trio of the type familiar in the composer's Sonata in E flat, but harmonically more sensuous, appeared in the next year's issue of the *Album musical* under the inappropriate title of 'Les Plaintes d'un Troubadour'. No. 4 in C sharp minor, a moto perpetuo of semiquavers except in the interlude and coda, and no. 5 in F minor, an 'allegro vivace' in lively rhythmic patterns, are remarkable among Schubert's piano solos in being little melodic in character. The first *Moment musical* in C major, however, contains a typically Schubertian song-melody in the interlude. The outer sections are filled with transient modulations and alternations between the major and the minor modes such as distinguish many of his compositions.

*　　*　　*　　*

A tiny piece by Schubert, an 'Album Leaf' in G major composed in 1825, belongs to a species of movements of indefinite type that were written by several nineteenth-century composers including Wagner. The title originated in the custom of writing such pieces for inclusion in the albums of patrons or friends, but gradually lost its meaning and came to be used for any piece of slight dimensions or ephemeral character. Schubert's 'Album Leaf', with its lilting rhythm and two balancing phrases, is a ländler in all but name, similar in style to the dozens of his compositions bearing that title. Beethoven's one example of the species, *Albumblatt für Elise* (1810) is a simple rondo in flowing triple time with light openwork texture. The haunting refrain runs in short curves of melody and accompaniment which are so often repeated that the music seems to be perpetually ebbing and flowing. Mendelssohn's *Album Leaf*, op. 117 (1845), subtitled 'Song without Words', is a long stretch of accompanied melody in E minor and major. One by Smetana, in B flat minor (1848), consists of the continuous working of a melodic phrase in which the interval of a falling sixth is a recurrent and prominent feature.

Schumann's conception of the species was quite different. He composed five little pieces at intervals between 1836 and 1841 which he subsequently named *Album Leaves* and included as a single unit in the heterogeneous collection of fourteen pieces entitled *Bunte Blätter*, op. 99 that he published in 1851. He used the title again to cover twenty, mostly unrelated items, all with names, which he had composed between 1832 and 1845 and which he gathered together for publication as *Albumblätter*, op. 124 in 1854. Some of these little movements, nos. 4, 11, 15, and 17, which embody the ASCH motto of *Carnaval*, had been discarded from that work before its publication in 1837. But Schumann never lightly destroyed any of his compositions, however slight; he generally found some other use for them. We saw earlier, for instance, how he drew upon his youthful songs when in need of material for the slow movements of his piano sonatas.

Of Wagner's three separate *Album Leaves*, the last in E flat major (1875), which as piano music is ungrateful to the player on account of its widely-spaced texture, is nevertheless of great interest as a miniature example of the composer's musical style. It consists largely of the working of a leitmotive containing a *grupetto* (turn), and a rising-scale figure which is strongly reminiscent of the principal theme of the *Siegfried Idyll*.

Grieg, who compiled his collections of *Lyric Pieces* in haphazard fashion with little regard for the mutual relationship of the individual items, included a single, short 'Album Leaf' in E minor among the descriptive and nationalist pieces in the First Book of the *Lyric Pieces*, op. 12 (1867). Three years earlier, however, he had composed the first of the *Four Album Leaves* which he was to publish as a separate work (op. 28) after he had composed the last two of the set in 1878.

The four pieces are uneven in quality. The first and third (1876) are of the same light-weight salon type as the 'Album Leaf' in E minor just mentioned. But while the first in A flat lacks any distinctively Norwegian touch such as characterizes the majority of Grieg's compositions, the third in A major, essentially a waltz, includes a central section in the minor in which the native idiom is discernible in the bare fifths of the bass and the downward-dropping flattened seventh in the melodic line. The wistful type of the melody and the dotted rhythm of several bars recall the unforgettable refrain of 'Solveig's song'. The second and the fourth 'Album Leaves' also contain interludes in refreshingly Norwegian style. That of no. 2 in C major (1874) is a meditative cadenza embodying Grieg's much-loved chord of the dominant ninth, and that of no. 4 in C sharp minor, an evocation of a peasant dance in D flat major, 'pianissimo, una corda', is also composed largely upon a pedal bass with a salient recurrent rhythmic figure (♩ ♫. ♫ in 2/4). Each affords a striking contrast to the surrounding paragraphs which are filled with chromaticisms of an almost Wagnerian intensity. Another 'Album Leaf' by Grieg, published in the Fourth Book of the *Lyric Pieces*, op. 47 in 1888, is pianistically more interesting than its predecessors but is equally sectional in construction.

Tchaikovsky's 'Album Leaf' in D major, 'allegretto semplice', op. 19, no. 3 (1873) differs entirely from those by Grieg in being composed in a single span without a contrasting interlude. Like some of Grieg's, however, it has a nationalist tinge. The opening phrase, which comprises the fourfold repetition of a metrical unit and which recurs regularly throughout the piece, calls to mind the characteristic Russian rhythms of the brisker dance movements in the 'Nutcracker' Suite. Mussorgsky's Album Leaf: *Meditation* (1880), a plaintive Andante that falls into clear-cut sections in the minor and the major, likewise makes a total impression of continuity. The uniform left-hand part runs without a break in flowing or beating quavers until within a few bars of the end.

*   *   *   *

The titles *prelude* and *intermezzo*, which were originally applied to movements placed either before or midway between other movements of a suite, acquired fresh meanings during the nineteenth century. They were then applied to shortish pieces that were neither introductory nor intermediate in their functions. Chopin's Preludes and Brahms's Intermezzos form series of pieces from among which individual members are often played singly or in groups according to their respective length and character. They gain much, however, by being played as wholes. Chopin's Twenty-four Preludes, op. 28, in all the major and minor keys, follow one another in an effective succession of contrasting moods, as do Brahms's Intermezzos, which are arranged in groups of varying number, sometimes with Capriccios or other pieces. Schumann's Intermezzos, op. 4 are not only homogeneous in style as well as nearly related in key. A few of

P

them are definitely marked to follow one another without any
break.

*   *   *   *

The Chopin Preludes, which were composed between 1836
and 1839, resemble the Beethoven Bagatelles in epitomizing the
creative style of their composer. Slight as are most of them in
size, they manifest the greatness in conception that distinguishes
Chopin's large-scale works. They are, so to speak, reflections in
miniature of his studies and nocturnes. Some of them exploit a
single pianistic idea, others are romantically expressive tone-
poems, and others, still, are dramatic in feeling. The majority
are interesting melodically, even when the melody is closely
interwoven with the accompanying texture. In no. 1 in C major
it is relegated to an inner voice but gains in intensity of expression by throwing up an echo into the voice an octave above.
Throughout the whole of no. 8 in F sharp minor it is imprisoned
between clouds of decorative notes in the treble and wide-spread
chords in the bass, and in no. 19 in E flat major, it dances
vertiginously above a trellised accompaniment of never-ceasing
quaver triplets.

Among the other study-like preludes based on a single
pianistic idea are nos. 3 in G major and 23 in F major. They
have features in common, as their decorative passage-work,
respectively in the left hand and the right hand, is infinitely
more interesting than the melody which it accompanies. The
perpetually flowing figuration of both no. 5 in D major and
no. 11 in B major disguises the fundamentally simple harmonic
progressions. The cascading semiquavers in the treble of no. 10
in C sharp minor lend wings to the prosaic supporting harmonies.

Midway between these preludes of the study type and those
of the nocturne type stand a few which are instrumental but not
melodic in style. Among them are no. 12 in G sharp minor,
whose severe chordal basis is enriched by successions of pungent
accented passing-notes, and the turbulent nos. 14 in E flat
minor, 18 in F minor and 22 in G minor. Each of the three last-

named displays a fresh conception of figuration in octaves, single or double. The layout of plain octaves in triplet quavers 'alla breve' of no. 14 recalls that of the Finale of the 'Funeral March' Sonata, which this Prelude exactly resembles in figuration and in darkness of mood. No. 16 in B flat minor, 'presto con fuoco' runs its headlong course largely in scale-wise passages, while no. 24 in D minor, 'allegro appassionato', is both melodically and harmonically an exposition of the arpeggio or the broken chord.

Most of the other preludes come within the category of tone-poems. Their musical content is supremely beautiful and its presentation in terms of the piano reveals the same flawless workmanship that characterizes Chopin's much larger compositions. Many of these preludes consist principally of long accompanied melodies, but in most instances it is the accompaniment that lends the pieces their chief distinction. The inconspicuous melodic phrases of no. 2 in A minor are superimposed upon an enigmatic, murmuring left-hand part composed of two disparate strands that consistently obscure the harmonic plan until they are cut short just before the ending. In nos. 4 in E minor and 6 in B minor, the gently beating accompanying chords enhance the innate melancholy of the themes; the so-called 'Raindrop' Prelude (no. 15 in D flat major) owes its soothing effect chiefly to the tranquil monotony of the incessant quaver beats below or above the plaintive melodic line. The deep, serpentine bass-part of no. 13 in F sharp minor suffuses the opening and closing sections with a heart-warming glow. The short interlude of this Prelude, as well as the whole of the impassioned no. 17 in A flat major, and the B flat major, no. 21, (a forerunner of Liszt's equally dreamlike *Paysage*), are compact of chordal texture which is rich in contrapuntal harmony.

The remaining three preludes of op. 28 stand apart from the others; not only by reason of their extreme brevity. No. 9 in E major is unique in having melodies of equal importance in both the treble and the bass. No. 7 in A major is the only one which reminds the listener that Chopin was a composer of dance music, and no. 20 in C minor, the shortest of all, is alone among the preludes in consisting of plain chords without a vestige of pianistic decoration.

The single Prelude in C sharp minor, op. 45, which was composed a little later than the Twenty-four, shares the nocturne-like character and even the serpentine figuration of no. 13 in F sharp major. It differs in design from all the others by having a brief introduction and coda and by being interspersed with a cadenza of iridescent chromatic harmonies.

*   *   *   *

Mendelssohn used the title 'prelude' in its original, literal sense for the six Preludes belonging to the Fugues of op. 35. In its newer sense he applied it to the three Preludes written at about the same time and published with three Studies as op. 104 after his death. These three Preludes do not serve a preludial purpose to the Studies, either in key or in mood, and they are in no way distinguishable from them in style. As specimens of the prelude as a single piece they may be compared with those of Chopin's preludes which, as we have just seen, resemble studies. But with this difference: that Chopin's require a skilled and experienced performer, whereas Mendelssohn's can be played effectively by any pianist with nimble fingers. They are well-written prose; Chopin's are sheer poetry.

*   *   *   *

An example of the *intermezzo* as a genuinely intermediate whole movement exists in Schumann's *Faschingsschwank aus Wien*, where a passionate Intermezzo in E flat minor separates the lively Scherzino in B flat major from the tumultuous Finale in the same key. As subsidiary interludes within larger movements, intermezzos occur in the third movement of the Piano Sonata in F sharp minor, and in nos. 2 and 3 of the Novellettes, where they form contrasting sections. Two such intermezzos are included in the third and longest of his Three Romances, op. 28 and in the second item of *Kreisleriana*, op. 16.

Each of them functions as an episode in the rondo-form construction.

When Schumann wrote his Intermezzos, op. 4 (1832), six

pieces in ternary form, he used the title 'Alternativo' for the contrasting interludes in the first, third, fifth and sixth. In the second he wrote the words 'Meine Ruh' ist hin' over the song-like theme of the central section, thus indicating a romantic conception of the music. For the fourth Intermezzo he simply transformed another of his early songs, 'Der Hirtenknabe' (The shepherd boy) into a piano solo. This whole set of pianistically interesting compositions, which are seldom played, is romantic in the free organization and the improvisatory style of the individual pieces. Schumann originally named them *Pièces fantastiques* and described them as 'extended *Papillons*'.

*   *   *   *

Brahms's eighteen Intermezzos have several points in common with Schumann's. They are predominantly in ternary form and in the minor mode, and they are more often serious than light-hearted in character. One of them, like Schumann's no. 2, has an avowed poetic basis. This is the well-known Intermezzo in E flat major, op. 117, no. 1. It is headed, like Brahms's 'Edward' Ballade, by a quotation from Herder's collection of folk poetry; in this instance, the opening lines of a Scots cradle-song, 'Lady Anne Bothwell's Lament', to which the music of the first four lines is made to fit.

Brahms was already in middle life when he wrote the first set of these pieces (op. 76) in 1878, the year in which he composed his Violin Concerto. The succeeding four sets, opp. 116-119, were written much later, between 1891 and 1893, and are contemporary with two of his most mature chamber works, the Clarinet Trio and the Clarinet Quintet. They represent his style at its most fully developed.

The Intermezzos and Capriccios of the eight *Klavierstücke*, op. 76, Brahms's first pieces for piano solo since the 'Paganini' Variations, are separated from that tremendous work by an interval of fifteen years. They display a very different kind of piano writing from that of his 'first-period' compositions. All the calculated virtuosity of the Variations is absent from these short 'middle-period' pieces and their successors. While they retain a strongly intellectual element, they are sometimes lyrical in expression.

As there is so little essential divergence between the musical styles of the intermezzos and the capriccios—which are included only in the first two sets—these two species can be considered side by side without differentiation. Not every one of the twenty-five can be discussed as a separate entity. A few representative pieces must serve to exemplify the outstanding characteristics of the works as a whole group.

One of the chief distinctions of the piano writing is that it is almost entirely devoid of unessential ornamentation. The Intermezzo in A minor, op. 116, no. 2 is among the very few in which the texture is enlivened by a purely decorative pattern: by broken octaves that add delicate overtones to the treble part during the 'non troppo presto' section. The dark-coloured Intermezzo in B flat minor, op. 117, no. 2 owes its velvety mysteriousness primarily to the heavily-pedalled broken-chord formations of which it is largely composed. But even in this context, the apparently decorative passage-work really serves as strong a harmonic purpose as it does in the 'più mosso ed espressivo' of op. 117, no. 3 in C sharp minor. There, the simple chord progressions are thinned out and distributed up and down the keyboard. Other examples of this procedure occur in the A minor (6/8) portion of the Capriccio in D minor, op. 116, no. 7, throughout which the melody and its accompaniment change places from one hand to another every alternate bar. Again, in the central paragraph of the Intermezzo in F minor, op. 118, no. 4, the imitation of the right-hand part by the left hand a beat later and an octave lower leads to cross-hand figuration and occasional harmonic clashes.

Rhythmically, few of the pieces are straightforward. The well-known Capriccio in B minor, op. 76, no. 2 and the passionate G minor, op. 116, no. 3 are among those in which the accentuation is mainly direct. In the majority of the others it is irregular. The Capriccio in C sharp minor, op. 76, no. 5, 'agitato ma non troppo presto' is written in 6/8 time, but the treble line runs for long stretches in implied 3/4 time against the clear 6/8 of the lower parts. When the time-signature is changed to 2/4 in the central portion, the melody is persistently witheld from sounding on the strongest beat of the bar, and during the closing bars in 6/8 time, three metric figures run concurrently to build up the final climax. A much later and far more mellow example of this kind of irregularity is furnished by the Intermezzo in C major, op. 119, no. 3, which in expressive style fully lives up to the performing-direction 'grazioso e giocoso'. Although it is written in 6/8 time, it contains many bars in which accentuation according to compound duple or simple triple time is inferred rather than stated and must be decided by the player.

Rhythmic displacements of this kind inevitably cause harmonic complications. Together with the lavish use of suspensions and accented passing-notes, they are in part responsible for the musical obscurity of some of the pieces. The overlapping arpeggios of the Intermezzo in B flat minor; the inter-penetrating broken chords all through the 'più mosso ed espressivo' of the C sharp minor, op. 117, no. 3; the suspensions in the B minor, op. 119, no. 1 and the colliding fragments of diminished-seventh chords in the A minor, op. 118, no. 1 are all liable to sound confusing to the listener, even though their meaning may be perfectly clear to the player.

Another kind of obscurity is sometimes due to ellipsis or understatement in the harmonic scheme. The cryptic utterance in the opening phrases of the Intermezzo in E major, op. 116, no. 4 is hardly clarified as the piece proceeds. The texture of its successor is exiguous in the extreme; some of the harmonies are implied simply by two notes placed far apart on the keyboard. The intermediate notes exist only in the imagination. This feather-light little piece in lilting 6/8 rhythm, 'andante con grazia ed intimissimo sentimento', is the very opposite of the Intermezzo in E major, op. 116, no. 6, whose rich chordal texture in steady 3/4 time leaves no doubt whatsoever as to its harmonic intentions.

In few of the pieces is the melodic outline as continuous as it is in the opening and closing sections of the cantabile Intermezzo in E flat major, op. 117, no. 1 and throughout the supremely tranquil Intermezzo in A major, op. 118, no. 2. Elsewhere, the melodic interest is concentrated mainly into the central interlude and revived in the coda, as in the Intermezzos in B minor and E minor, op. 119, nos. 1 and 2. In some, however, the element of melody is strongest in the expressive inner voices. In the sprightly Intermezzo in C major, op. 119, no. 3, already mentioned, it is entrusted principally to the thumb and first finger of the player's right hand in the middle of the texture. In the Intermezzo in E flat major, op. 117, no. 1 it moves to and fro between a protecting outer covering of octaves. The sinewy opening theme in plain octaves of the Intermezzo in C sharp minor, op. 117, no. 3 takes on a new and graceful aspect when it is shrouded in richer texture at its subsequent appearances. It is a motive rather than a melody, as are the main themes of the brusque Intermezzos in A minor, op. 118, no. 1, 'allegro non assai, ma molto appassionato' and in E flat minor, 'andante, largo e mesto', op. 118, no. 6. The stealthy serpentine theme and furious outbursts in staccato chords in the latter make it the most dramatic in effect of the whole collection.

As piano music the twenty-five pieces are not technically very difficult to play. Their attractions lie beneath, rather than on the surface, but the outward severity of the music is often only a disguise thrown over fundamentally genial ideas. Closer acquaintance reveals many beauties in the planning and the workmanship of this whole variegated series of miniatures.

* * * *

In their terse, intellectual style Brahms's Capriccios stand alone among their kind. They are different in type from those by his predecessors, Weber and Mendelssohn, which are more extensive and more purely instrumental in keyboard style; more, indeed, in the character of the eighteenth-century *capriccio* which sometimes resembled a fantasy. Weber's *Momento capriccioso*, 'prestissimo staccato' (1808) is a miniature simply by virtue of the gossamer lightness of the piano writing. Mendelssohn's five *Caprices*: the early F sharp minor, op. 5 (1825), the

three of op. 33 (1833-4) and one in E, op. 118 (1837) are long
pieces of the same structural and instrumental type as movements in his sonatas. They stand right outside the category of
the *caprice* defined as a 'short piece in a humorous or whimsical
manner', of which Tchaikovsky's Capriccio in B flat, op. 19,
no. 5, with its tuneful 'allegretto semplice' and frisky 'allegro
vivacissimo' is a more typical example.

*   *   *   *

Closely allied in spirit to this kind of short movement are the
scherzo and the *humoresque*, miniature relatives of those by Chopin,
Brahms and Schumann which we studied among the romantic
pieces in Chapter 8. Schumann's Scherzo in B flat major,
op. 32, no. 1 (1838) and a Scherzo in G minor (1841), one of
the *Bunte Blätter*, op. 99, are respectively playful and impetuous
in character and are composed in the same vein as his *Faschingsschwank*. The tiny Scherzino in F (1832), no. 4 of the *Albumblätter*, op. 124, originated as a sketch for *Papillons* and bears a
thematic likeness to the last movement.

All these little pieces are made up of contrasting sections, as
are Grieg's Scherzo in E minor, no. 5 of the Fifth Book of *Lyric
Pieces*, op. 54 (1891) and the Scherzo-Impromptu from *Moods*,
op. 73 (1905). They differ from Schumann's in each being based
on a main theme which changes in character during the course
of the piece. In the Scherzo in E minor the scale-wise left-hand
part in crotchets and quavers in the minor becomes the right-
hand part in minims and crotchets in the interlude in the major.
The wayward subject of the Scherzo-Impromptu is worked
again and again in different keys, is slowed down to half its
original note-values and tightened up into a stretto coda.

Grieg's four *Humoresques*, op. 6 (1865), which were written
soon after he had begun to draw inspiration from the folk-music
of his native land, are dances in all but their generic title. The
first in D major and the second in G sharp minor are headed
respectively 'tempo di valse' and 'tempo di minuetto ed energico'. The third in C major, an 'allegretto con grazia' and the
fourth, 'allegro alla burla' in G minor are equally irresistible as

music for dancing. All four are tinged with the Norwegian idiom, and the style of the piano writing blends elegance with rustic sturdiness. The *Humoresques* are among the earliest of Grieg's compositions to display facets of the strongly individual style which was still only nascent in the Four Piano Pieces, op. 1 that he wrote as a young student at Leipzig in 1862, and in the six little-known *Poetic Tone-pictures*, op. 3 (1863); a set of artless miniatures that reveal the composer's youthful allegiance to the musical ideals of Schumann.

*   *   *   *

The implication of the title *humoresque*, which denotes 'capricious' rather than 'humorous', is fully borne out in Tchaikovsky's *Humoresque*, op. 10, no. 2 (1871). Though rhythmically extremely precise, it is capricious in its tonal scheme. It begins in E minor but plunges into G major where it stays during the remainder of the opening (and closing) section. The note D sharp, which is a prominent feature of the opening bars and an intruder in the coda, forms an enharmonic link with the interlude in E flat major in which the chromaticisms stand out in contrast to the surrounding diatonic paragraphs.

Dvořák's eight *Humoresques*, op. 101 (1894), like those by Grieg and Tchaikovsky, are made up of short themes which are many times repeated, either note-for-note, sequentially or in distantly-related keys. Every one of Dvořák's Humoresques is written in 2/4 time, but the pieces vary in tempo from vivace to 'poco lento' and they are arranged in an effective sequence of major and minor keys. The melodies are narrow in span, seldom going beyond the confines of an octave in compass. Those of the world-famous Humoresque in G flat major are exceptional in this respect, but even they do not overstep the bounds of a tenth.

The frequent repetition of the short-range tunes and of the strongly-marked rhythmic patterns of their accompaniment is one of the most striking characteristics of the whole series. An extreme instance occurs in the fifth Humoresque in A minor, vivace, in which a short phrase that opens with four heavily-accented crotchet beats on the same note is stated no fewer than thirty-two times and in five keys. The persistent reiteration is even intensified in effect by the stark simplicity of the harmonic scheme.

In most of the other humoresques the constant fluctuation of the music between the major and the minor modes, the subtle harmonies and the startling modulations go far to counteract the prevailing repetitive style. The sixth Humoresque in B major starts out of its basic key with a poignantly beautiful harmonic progression

which is restated in remote keys as one of the motto themes of the outer sections. Chromatic alterations are a feature of some of the cadences throughout the eight pieces. The last two bars of the principal phrase of the fourth Humoresque in F major hover precariously between the major and the minor:

The closing bars of no. 3 in A flat major and of no. 8 in B flat minor are filled to overflowing with accidentals. The two chromaticized cadences in the outer sections of the eighth in B flat minor stand out prominently against the intensely diatonic background.

The melodic charm and rhythmic animation of the Dvořák Humoresques are greatly enhanced by the interesting piano writing. The texture often comprises two or more concurrent melodic lines, and it is sometimes enlivened by the transference of themes from the outer to the inner parts. In the central section (in E major) of the third Humoresque, the treble and alto parts of a four-bar phrase reverse their positions in the ensuing bars. The eighth in B flat minor opens with the melody first in the left hand and then in the right; the maggiore interlude is compact of ingenious free canonic imitations and of phrases in double counterpoint. The theme first announced in bar 17 of the sixth Humoresque in B major becomes an expressive inner voice beneath a new melody a few bars later.

The piano writing of the seventh Humoresque in G flat major is not of this contrapuntally vital kind. The piece makes its effect by the memorable quality both of the melody and of the rhythmic pattern in the outer sections, and by the completely contrasted style of the interlude in the minor. The popularity of this one movement and the neglect by pianists of the remaining seven may possibly be due to the homogeneity in the pianistic style and expressive character of the former as compared with the fragmentariness and diversity in the make-up of all the latter.

*   *   *   *

Kindred in spirit to the humoresque but simpler and more rustic in pianistic style is the *eclogue*, a type of miniature evolved by the Czech composer Václav Tomašek (1774-1850). He published his first set of six movements bearing this title in 1810, and several other sets later. Of all these compositions, only one collection of ten Eclogues is now easily available. The pieces are in ternary form with a *da capo* repeat, and all are strongly pastoral in style, whether they are robust or delicate in expressive character. Easy to play, rhythmically clear-cut, melodious and naïve in spirit, they form a delightful addition to the literature of the nineteenth-century miniature. They show the influence of Czech folk-music in the composer's preference for passages in thirds and sixths (nos. 1, 3 and 6), and for sudden changes from major to minor (no. 7). Their simplicity in style is sometimes accentuated by the bare fifths or heavy chords in the left-hand part (nos. 1 and 9). Only one of these eclogues is in triple time: no. 5 in E flat major, in which the trio section in simple two-part writing has the easy, graceful lilt of a ländler by Schubert, and even gives a hint of that composer's subtle art of modulation.

An Eclogue in A flat major composed by Liszt in 1836 and published in the Swiss volume (II) of his *Années de Pèlerinage*, and one by Dvořák in G minor, op. 52, no. 4 (1880) resemble those by Tomašek both in the constant repetition of short melodic phrases and decorative figures and in the use of sustained or repeated pedal-basses. The piano writing in these two pieces is more advanced in style than Tomašek's and contains sensuously beautiful passages. Dvořák's is additionally interesting by virtue of containing material originally used in the third of *Four Eclogues* which he composed at the same period but which remained in manuscript until 1949 when they were published in Prague. A comparison of the piano writing of the four opening bars of this third Eclogue in G major with those of the 'poco tranquillo e molto espressivo' sections of op. 52, no. 4 shows Dvořák's treatment of the same material in very different, but equally effective styles; the one rustic and the other, suave.

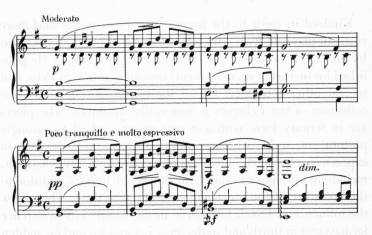

Liszt's Eclogue is distinguished from all the others of its species in being preceded by a written explanation of its contents: a lengthy extract, entitled 'De l'expression romantique, et du ranz des vaches', from de Senancour's novel *Obermann*. That the composer should have felt it necessary to prefix to this short movement a leisurely description of alpine sights and sounds which takes at least as long to read as does the piece to play, shows how strongly he conceived the music as the expression of non-musical ideas.

*   *   *   *

Among the other kinds of miniatures which bear generic titles denoting a romantic conception of the music but which are not actually programmatic, even if they are sometimes impressionistic in style, are the *romance* and the *song without words*. To some extent they are allied in character. The romance can be as preponderantly vocal in style as the typical 'song without words', and both may be purely instrumental in texture. Either may be spirited or deeply emotional in point of expression.

The three Romances of Schumann's op. 28 (1839) display all these mutually contrasting characteristics. The second and best-known in F sharp major consists largely of a cantabile melody which is placed in the expressive middle register of the keyboard to be played by the thumb of each hand while the fingers execute the murmuring accompaniment. The third Romance in B major, a lively rondo in the narrative style of the composer's Novellettes, is vocally tuneful only in the intermezzos. The first Romance in B flat minor, like the composer's Romance in D minor, op. 32, no. 3, is more instrumental in style. Throughout both these pieces a soaring melody runs unbroken above a never-ceasing accompaniment in semiquavers divided between the two hands.

Tchaikovsky's Romance in F minor, op. 5 (1868) consists of two different kinds of musical material: an 'andante cantabile' composed of a languorous curving melody which alternates with an 'allegro energico' made up of short figures. The distinctive rhythmic pattern maintained in each section by the left hand lends the whole piece the character of a dance rather than of a song. Brahms's short Romance in F major, op. 118, no. 5, which we studied in the chapter on Variations, is melodious only in its outer sections. During the interlude it is purely instrumental in style.

*   *   *   *

The title *Song without Words* was invented by Mendelssohn for a kind of short piece, generally in strophic (verse) form, in which the melody, the accompaniment and the prevailing mood of a song are expressed in terms of a piano solo. The forty-eight pieces bearing this title, which Mendelssohn composed between 1830 and 1845, make up a collection containing several that have become so universally popular in transcriptions for other instruments that their origin as piano music is almost forgotten. Among the others, many that are musically more valuable are little known, even to practising pianists.

A study of the collection as a whole shows that the pieces are mainly of four different types.

The 'solo song', throughout which the melody flows almost continuously above an accompaniment in uniform figuration, is exemplified by the so-called 'Spring Song' (no. 30) and 'Spinning-Song' (no. 34), and by nos. 1, 2, 7, 13, 15, 19, 25, 36, 37, 40, and 42.

The 'two-part song' displays its distinctive attributes in no. 18 in A flat, 'Duetto', the most realistic example of the type, and in the three poetic 'Venetian Boat-Songs' (nos. 6, 12, and 29). In nos. 14 and 20, however, the second voice is only of subsidiary interest.

The 'chordal song' is implicit in nos. 4, 9, 16, 23, 28, 35, and 41, all of which consist of paragraphs in four- or five-part harmony placed between an introduction and a coda in contrasting decorative style. No. 23, 'Folk-song', also contains spirited interludes in the same broken-chord pattern as the opening and closing passages, and no. 48 is chordal from beginning to end.

The fourth type comprises the more definitely instrumental 'song without words', in which the melodic content is not necessarily vocal in character and is in any case less interesting than the accompanying texture. Of this kind are several bearing the performing-direction 'agitato'. They are nos. 5, 10, 17, 21, 38, 43, and 46; no. 26, 'allegro con fuoco' and no. 39, presto. Every one of them is virtually a moto perpetuo in effect. Nos. 8, 45, and 47 are fairy studies in quick staccato. No. 24, with its furious accompaniment vibrating in a whirl of chromatic seconds, is pianistically one of the most original.

This grouping according to type is only approximate. Many of the 'Songs without Words' already referred to blend the features of two or more types. Of the others, nos. 11 and 31 are intermediate in style between the 'solo song' and the 'instrumental piece'. The strong contrasts in colour-effects and the extensive compass of nos. 3 and 27, known respectively as 'Hunting Song' and 'Funeral March', suggest an orchestral rather than a vocal origin for these two miniature tone-poems. The composite character of no. 22 in F major, adagio, defies exact classification.

Mendelssohn's *Songs without Words* enjoyed enormous popularity for many years after their original publication but subsequently fell into disfavour with progressive musicians. By now, they have acquired a 'period' charm which endears them to players and listeners who like to be reminded of the days when the singing-tone of the piano was rated high above its percussive qualities. Tchaikovsky's two *Chants sans paroles*, op. 40, no. 6 in A minor and the better-known op. 2, no. 3 in F major, are predominantly 'solo songs', but in each, a second voice sings for a time in imitative canon with the soloist.

*   *   *   *

The 'song without words' is by its very nature subjective. Sometimes it intentionally creates a poetic atmosphere, as in Mendelssohn's 'Venetian Boat-Songs'. The *characteristic piece* sets out to portray specific moods to which the respective title gives the clue. It is a kind of piece which is romantic in conception and is sometimes even descriptive or programmatic in type.

Each of Mendelssohn's Seven Characteristic Pieces, op. 7 carries a written indication of the mood it depicts, but the music of nearly all of them is classical in form and style. No. 1, 'Gently and with feeling' and no. 6, 'Yearningly' might well be 'songs without words' of the more reflective type. No. 3, 'Energetic and fiery', and no. 5, 'Serious, with increasing animation', are fugues, as we noted in Chapter 7. No. 2, 'With robust movement' is in the style of a free two-part invention, and no. 4, 'Quick and sprightly', resembles a toccata. No. 7 in E major, 'Light and insubstantial', 'sempre staccato e pianissimo', with a texture as ethereal as thistledown, is in miniature sonata form and is rounded off by a coda of legatissimo broken chords in the minor that mount to the very top of the keyboard and vanish into thin air. This fairy movement, the most immediately attractive of the seven, is often played as a single item. It would be even more effective if it were heard in its proper context. The whole set could well be performed complete, for the seven pieces are arranged in a sequence of nearly-related keys and are mutually well contrasted in expression.

Smetana conceived the 'characteristic piece' as both subjective and descriptive music. In the group of six entitled *Rêves* (Dreams) which he wrote in 1874, each piece bears the title of a mood: 'Lost happiness', 'Consolation'; or of a scene: 'At the castle', 'In the salon' (an elaborate waltz), 'Bohemian peasant festival', and 'Pastoral scene in Bohemia'. The piano writing throughout is vivid in the Lisztian manner, the melodic lines being overlaid with a wealth of decorative passages.

*   *   *   *

Schumann wrote of his Four Fugues, op. 72, that they were 'Characteristic pieces in the severe style', and similarly, of his *Gesänge der Frühe* (Morning songs), op. 133, that he conceived them as 'characteristic pieces depicting the approach and waxing of the morning, but more as expression of feeling than painting'. He did not, however, add the qualifying epithet 'characteristic pieces' to the title-page of either of these two sets of pieces as he did to the eighteen miniatures of *Davidsbündler*, op. 6, which are among the most romantic of all his short pieces.

The *Davidsbund* or David League, to which the title of this opus refers, was a society of imaginary personages invented by Schumann for the purpose of combating the activities of the Philistines, musical and otherwise, and of upholding the poetic against the prosaic. Two of the principal characters, Florestan and Eusebius, who respectively typify the passionate and the dreamy sides of Schumann's temperament, made their first appearance in print in the article which he wrote on Chopin's 'Là ci darem' Variations in 1831, to which reference was made here in Chapter 6. When Schumann founded his own musical journal, the *Neue Zeitschrift für Musik* in 1834, he contributed a long series of critical articles under their signatures, as well as under others that concealed his identity. In 1835 Florestan and Eusebius took their places as the subjects of portrait-sketches in *Carnaval*; the following year they figured as the composers of the Sonata in F sharp minor and in 1837, of the *Davidsbündler* just mentioned. Schumann appended to each piece the initial of whichever of these imaginary characters seemed the more appropriate to the temper of the music. He prefaced the work with an 'old saying' in verse and added descriptive comments to a few of the movements. The second, revised edition was published under his own name in 1851.

The first edition of this work was published under the title *Davidsbündler-tänze*, but hardly any of the movements is a dance in the conventional sense. The whole collection portrays a variety of moods, from the pensive to the uproarious, in music during the course of which stimulating cross-rhythms and syncopations alternate with passages of tranquil radiance. Despite the fact that *Davidsbündler* opens and closes in different keys, the eighteen movements were evidently meant to be played in unbroken succession. The continuity of the musical thought is emphasized by the reappearance of the second movement within the framework of the seventeenth, and the latter, which is headed 'As if from the distance', seems to recollect in tranquillity all the emotional vicissitudes of the preceding pages.

Davidsbündler has points in common with *Carnaval* over and above its similar construction as a series of vivid musical impressions. The two compositions are centred round the same group of fictitious personages, and they are thematically interconnected. No. 3 of *Davidsbündler* embodies a direct quotation from *Promenade*, the last movement but one of *Carnaval*. It also makes an allusion to the *Grossvatertanz*, which occurs in the Finale of the same work (*'Marche des Davidsbündler contre les Philistins'*). Although *Carnaval* bears a later opus number, it was composed two years before *Davidsbündler*, in 1835.

* * * *

Four other sets of Schumann's miniatures, each with an inclusive title, were composed in response to an extra-musical stimulus. They are the *Morning Songs* (1853) just mentioned, *Kreisleriana*, op. 16, (1838), *Nachtstücke* (Night pieces), op. 23 (1839), and Four Marches, op. 76 (1849). The first of these works, which comprises five movements, each based on a theme that is subjected to free variations, was inspired by Friedrich Hölderlin's *Diotima* poems. The musical style is involved and the whole work is much less compelling than *Kreisleriana*, a supremely homogeneous work which represents Schumann at the height of his powers as a composer of intimate, imaginative piano music.

The eight pieces of *Kreisleriana*, which are all in nearly-related keys, are filled with unforgettable melodies and vital rhythms. Their structure is straightforward and generally easy to follow, although the musical atmosphere is sometimes darkly mysterious. In the slow portions of nos. 4 and 6 the music seems to ask questions that can never hope to find an answer. On the other hand, the tumultuous energy of nos. 1, 3, 5, 7, and 8 sweeps all musical ambiguities out of the way. In no. 2, 'moderato con molto espressione', a rondo with two clear-cut episodes, the sharply-contrasted sections are blended into an indescribably satisfying whole movement composed in Schumann's most deeply expressive and picturesque style. The title of the work is taken from E.T.A. Hoffmann's book of the same name, the hero of which, Kapellmeister Johannes Kreisler is thought to have been suggested by the eccentric personality of the German musician Ludwig Bohner. Schumann had actually heard Böhner improvise in Leipzig in 1834, and had once toyed with the idea of sketching this strange character in words. But the inimitable portrait he eventually painted in musical sounds is a treasure that no interpretative musician would lightly exchange for a literary portrayal, even from Schumann's whimsical pen.

Night Pieces was conceived as a *Funeral Fantasy*, for while Schumann was composing the four items he was haunted by disturbing visions of funerals and mourners. The titles he originally intended bestowing on the pieces, 'Funeral March', 'Strange Company', 'Nocturnal Carousal' and 'Round, with solo voices', were never printed. Had they been, the music might possibly receive as much attention from performers as do the composer's other sets of pieces with imaginative individual titles. The opening movement marches with a splendid swing; the strongly rhythmical refrain gains in power at every one of its repetitions, and the piece works up to an impressive climax before it dies away in heart-broken sighs. The second and fourth movements, also in free rondo form with many repetitions of the principal themes, and the third, which is a scherzo with two trios, all resemble the Novellettes in their discursive style.

The composition of the Four Marches was stimulated by the Dresden rising in 1849 which caused Schumann to take flight from the city during the fighting. The Marches give vigorous and colourful expression to his feelings as an ardent republican. One of them actually makes a fugitive reference to the Marseillaise, to which he had already alluded less guardedly in *Faschingsschwank*. The music is martial in style but its sharp outlines are softened by the frequent division of the beats into triplet quavers. No. 3, 'Camp scene', is less strongly rhythmic than the others. It is a 'characteristic piece', similar in type to some of the movements of the *Forest scenes* composed the same year.

These four sets of compositions stand only on the threshold of programme music, and *Papillons* hardly even so near. The Finale of the latter contains an indication of a poetic basis, but the work as a whole belongs to no very exact category. It will be more appropriately discussed in the next chapter among the dance forms with which it has an artistic affinity. *Carnaval*, which likewise combines the attributes of programme music and dance music, has already been discussed under the heading of variations.

*   *   *   *

There is no mistaking the programmatic intentions of *Fanta-siestücke* (Fantasy pieces), op. 12 (1837), *Kinderscenen* (Scenes of childhood), op. 15 (1839) and *Waldscenen* (Forest scenes), op. 82 (1849). Schumann admitted that he often added the titles to pieces only after he had composed them, simply as a guide to performers on points of interpretation. As the titles he habitually chose correspond so perfectly with the musical content of the pieces, the two have long since become indissolubly connected in the minds of interpreters.

That Schumann planned these three compositions as indivisible wholes may be gathered from his having designed the last movement of each to sum up or round off the work. In *Fantasy pieces*, the Finale is entitled *Ende vom Lied* (The end of the song); in *Scenes of childhood*, it is *Der Dichter spricht* (The poet speaks), and in *Forest scenes*, simply *Abschied* (Farewell). Nevertheless, although *Scenes of childhood* is frequently performed complete, the three sets of pieces are much more often dismembered. *Aufschwung* (Soaring), *Warum* (Why) and *Grillen* (Whims), op. 12, nos. 2, 3, and 4 of *Fantasy pieces* are familiar to thousands who are possibly unaware of the existence of the sensuous, dreamlike *Des Abends* (In the evening), (no. 1), the passionate *In der Nacht* (In the night) (no. 5) and the vivid narratives *Fabel* (Fable) (no. 6) and *Traumes Wirren* (Restless dreams) (no. 7). Two pieces from *Scenes of childhood*, *Träumerei* (Revery) (no. 7) and *Am Kamin* (At the fireside) (no. 8), the victims of countless transcriptions, have achieved universal recognition. Their eleven less obviously melodic companions, which include the sensitively-wrought *Bittendes Kind* (Entreating child), (no. 4) and *Kind im Einschlummern* (Child falling asleep) (no. 12), are prized by the music-loving few. Among the nine movements of *Forest scenes*, which suggest a coherent story of woodland life, only one, or at most two, can be reckoned as indispensable items in every pianist's repertory: the eerie *Vogel als Prophet* (Bird prophesying) and *Verrufene Stelle* (Haunted spot), nos. 7 and 4. They are immeasurably more fantastic and poetic in expression than the other movements, but they lose much by being plucked from their native forest background.

The three later *Fantasy pieces*, op. 111 (1851) have no individual titles. In expressive mood they are not dissimilar to their earlier namesakes though they lack their intense conviction. Only the second in A flat major, the outer sections of which are pervaded by a wistful questioning phrase, is instinct with the magic of its predecessors in op. 12.

*   *   *   *

Liszt was even more dependent than was Schumann upon external stimuli for his compositions. His miniatures, no less than his large-scale works, bear names denoting their indebtedness to literary sources or to the inspiration of scenery, paintings or sculpture. The six *Consolations* (1849-50), the best known of all his shorter piano pieces, take their title from Sainte-Beuve's poems, *Les Consolations* (1830). With their cantabile melodies, the *Consolations* are essentially 'songs without words', though the words are not far to seek. Equally vocal in character are the six small-scale items of the ten *Harmonies poétiques et religieuses* (1845-52): '*Hymne de l'enfant à son réveil*', no. 6, named after a poem by Lamartine, 'Ave Maria', no. 2, and 'Pater noster', no. 5, the Latin words of which are printed above the melodic line. These three pieces are transcriptions of choral works by Liszt, as we have already noted in Chapter 8. In 'Miserere', no. 8, which also has the relevant Latin words printed in the score of the opening paragraph, the melodic outline is surrounded by a wealth of decorative broken chords. 'Andante lagrimoso', no. 9, headed by two verses of Lamartine's poem 'Une larme ou consolation,' and 'Cantique d'amour', no. 10, are both in the same luxuriant style as the *Liebesträume*.

The miniature travel-sketches in the First Book of the *Années de Pèlerinage* include three impressionistic portrayals of places visited by Liszt during his residence in Switzerland in 1835-6. The 'Chapelle de Guillaume Tell', no. 1, contains realistic echo-effects; 'Au Lac de Wallenstadt', no. 2, is based on a uniform figure of accompaniment that evokes the lapping of the waters, and 'Les Cloches de Genève', no. 9, is a nocturne in which the sounds of bells are both simulated and implied. The two last-named pieces are each preceded by quotations from Byron's *Childe Harold*. In other pieces in the First Book the scenic background is general rather than particular. 'Pastorale', no. 3, is a typical eclogue in its simplicity of style. 'Au bord d'une source' (Beside a spring), no. 4, prefaced by three lines from Schiller, is a masterpiece of delicate piano writing that evokes the 'murmuring stillness' of the spring to which the Schiller quotation alludes. 'Le mal du pays' (Homesickness), no. 8, gives realistic expression to the despairing and hopeful moods of the exile. It consists of a series of paragraphs alternating between sparse recitative and opulent melody. In the Second Book (Italy) are the quietly ecstatic 'Sposalizio', no. 1, inspired by Rafael's painting, 'The Wedding of the Virgin', and the solemn 'Il Pensieroso', no. 2, sub-titled 'Michelangelo's monument to Giuliano de' Medici'.

The pieces just mentioned date from comparatively early in Liszt's career: from the 1830s to the 1850s, when his piano writing embraced every possible sensuous and virtuosic keyboard effect. In later years he modified his exuberant style. Although he still continued to write piano music which displayed his unrivalled command of pianistic resource, for instance, the Third Book of the *Années de Pèlerinage* which contains the resplendent 'Jeux d'eau à la Villa d'Este', he also composed movements in which all extraneous decoration is shorn away and the music reduced to bare essentials. Compositions which exemplify less familiar aspects of Liszt's production have latterly been published for the first time in an English edition, in two volumes issued by the Liszt Society. To musicians whose acquaintance with the composer's piano music has been confined to the well-known concert-pieces and studies, the restrained style and experimental character of these miniatures and larger pieces may come as a revelation.

Two tiny pieces in F sharp major from *Vier Klavierstücke* (Four piano pieces) (1865-76) each comprise only four lines of music. They are of the utmost simplicity in their economical texture, but each has its magic moment. In no. 3, the tonality suddenly shifts into the comparatively cooler key of A major nine bars before the end and remains there until a deft touch restores it to the tonic for the final cadence. No. 4 culminates in a tenuous line of thirds that rise above a couple of light syncopated chords and then fall semi-staccato as the sustaining-pedal melts the single notes into a haze of sound. *En rêve: nocturne* (1885-6), too, contains startling harmonic effects. The quietude of the opening is shattered in the tenth bar when the smoothly-flowing melody leaps up a sixth to form an acute discord with the left-hand part two octaves beneath. At the very end, a series of enigmatic, inconclusive chordal progressions leaves the music suspended in mid air.

Even more daring harmonically, and tonally more mysterious, are four pieces with descriptive titles: *Nuages gris* (Grey clouds) (1881), *Sinistre* (Disaster), *La lugubre gondola* (The funeral gondola) (in two separate versions, 1882) and *Richard Wagner— Venezia*, which was composed after Wagner's death at Venice in 1883. All are heavy with a grief that strives for expression in fragments of melody running in severe plain octaves or desolate unison, weird hollow-sounding chords and ominous tremolandos deep in the bass. The musical atmosphere is tense with foreboding as the composer seems to grope his way towards a new and terrible realm of sound.

*   *   *   *

The interpretation of visual images and mental states in terms of the piano, the art in which Schumann and Liszt so greatly excelled, was practised with equal fervour if with less convincing musical results by their younger contemporaries and successors, Smetana, Mussorgsky, Tchaikovsky, and Dvořák, to name only those whose works in other branches of composition are of greater importance than their piano music.

Dvořák wrote three books of Poetic Pictures, op. 85 (1889) which, like the *Dreams* of his older compatriot Smetana, depict moods and scenes. The piano writing is far more elaborate than in the composer's Eclogues and Humoresques. Many of the passages are so awkwardly laid out for the hands that the pieces often make the effect of being transcriptions of orchestral works rather than original piano solos. Mussorgsky (1835-81) drew a fanciful sketch of *Children's games: Puss in the corner* (1859-60) and a portrait of *The Sempstress* (1871); he wrote an Intermezzo (1861) inspired by the sight of peasants crossing a snow-clad field, and two travel-sketches of the Crimea: *Gurzuf* and Capriccio (1880), each with a central section in oriental dance rhythms. His most notable and enduring contribution to the literature of the piano took the form of a programmatic suite, which we shall study, with other examples of the species by Liszt, Tchaikovsky, and Borodin, at the end of this chapter.

* * * *

Grieg, who wrote more consistently and more sympathetically for the piano than did any of the composers last named, included a number of descriptive movements in the ten books of *Lyric Pieces* which he composed between 1867 and 1901 and which he supplemented in 1905 with a final volume of seven pieces in the same style, entitled *Moods*. In this comprehensive collection of seventy-three pieces, all Grieg's styles of piano writing, familiar and unfamiliar, are represented. A few of the movements such as 'Arietta', op. 12, no. 1, 'Canon', op. 38, no. 8, the two 'Album Leaves', op. 12, no. 7 and op. 47, no. 2, 'Scherzo', op. 54, no. 5 and 'Melody', op. 47, no. 3 are abstract music, and several are dances, Norwegian and otherwise. The remainder bear descriptive titles which they fully substantiate. Only one book of the pieces is well known as a whole: the Third, op. 43, containing the vividly descriptive 'Butterfly', 'Lonely wanderer', and 'Little bird', and the romantic 'To the spring', 'In my native land', and 'Erotik'. Throughout the other nine books and the *Moods* there are many pieces which, although little known, are of equal, if not greater interest to the pianist. The whole collection well repays exploration, but only a few of the most original can be mentioned here.

The early 'Watchman's Song', op. 12, no. 3, composed after a performance of *Macbeth*, contains an interlude headed 'Spirits of the Night' in which Grieg summons up the distinctive timbres of the drums and horns with deep, pianissimo arpeggios and light common chords at a higher pitch. The 'Shepherd Boy', op. 54, no. 1, is built up from a little pipe-tune motive of descending notes that appears and re-appears in every part of a texture shot through with chromaticisms which intensify its native simplicity. 'Mountaineer's Song', no. 7 of *Moods*, is an impressionistic study throughout which short canonic imitations, transformed by the sustaining-pedal into prolonged waves of sound, evoke echoing fragments of song. Another nature-study, 'Evening in the Mountains', op. 68, no. 4, achieves an equally telling effect by different means. After the brief introduction in bare octaves has set the rugged scene, a long tune of pastoral character is 'piped' by the player's right hand without any accompaniment and is then restated above a foundation of chords that give meaning to all its latent harmonies. 'Bell-ringing', op. 54, no. 6, possibly the most original of all the *Lyric Pieces*, simulates the hum and the clangour of bells by means of a continuous succession of fifths, some of which are made more resonant by acciaccatura thirds. In its insistence upon the percussive quality of the piano and in its utter dependence upon the blurring effect of the sustaining pedal, this little impressionistic movement may be compared with Debussy's *La Cathédrale engloutie* (The submerged cathedral).

Fresh aspects of Grieg's art of musical landscape-painting are displayed in the plashing 'Brooklet', op. 62, no. 4, which, like the earlier 'Butterfly', is composed throughout in busy semi-quavers, but makes an entirely different effect by the more percussive style of the finger-work; and 'Summer Evening', op. 71, no. 2, in which the magic stillness depicted by the luminous harmonies is emphasized by periodic cascades of semiquavers in quivering broken fourths. Two other, more familiar aspects are manifested respectively in lively rhythmic pieces such as 'Norwegian Peasants' March', op. 54, no. 2, 'March of the Dwarfs', op. 54, no. 3, 'Wedding-day at Troldhaugen' (the composer's home), op. 65, no. 6 and 'Puck', op. 71, no. 3: and in

the leisurely, sensitively-harmonized melodies of 'At the cradle',
op. 68, no. 5, 'Students' Serenade' and 'Folk-tune', nos. 6 and 4
of *Moods*.

*   *   *   *

'Folk-tune', which is based on a genuine folk-song from the
Valdres district of Norway, exemplifies a type of composition to
which Grieg was greatly addicted: the transforming of folk-
songs or dances into piano solos.

Grieg based many of his now well-known original works upon
Norwegian folk-melodies: the Ballade, op. 24 for piano solo, the
Variations, op. 51 for two pianos, the Symphonic Dances for
piano duet and other compositions that we shall meet in succeeding chapters. In two sets of much less familiar pieces he
made the music of over forty Norwegian folk-songs and dances
available to musicians in the form of miniatures for piano solo.
Norwegian Dances and Songs, op. 17 (1870) contains twenty-
five little pieces of this kind, the tunes of which Grieg took from
a published collection of national music and harmonized in his
own distinctive manner.

The much later Norwegian Folk-tunes, op. 66 (1896) comprises nineteen tunes which he himself collected from peasant
singers and players. Among these pieces are cradle-songs, nos. 7,
15, 17 and 19; herdsman's calls, nos. 1 and 8, and songs from
many parts of Norway. Each is a little tone-poem in which the
given tune is incorporated in harmonic texture that forms its
ideal setting. In several of these 'songs without words' each
'verse' is treated in different pianistic styles so that the pieces
resemble miniature sets of variations. Two of the most remarkable are 'In Ola dale', no. 14, the tune of which has subsequently become well known through having been used by
Delius in *On hearing the first cuckoo in spring* (1912); and 'In
deepest thought I wander', an 'adagio religioso', no. 18, the
longest and pianistically the most elaborate of the entire group.
Its three verses are presented successively in four-part harmony
as if for choir, then as a tenor solo below a right-hand accompaniment in double notes, and lastly in heavy chords reinforced

by octaves spread upwards from the depth of the bass; a layout that suggests the effect of performance by full choir and organ.

*   *   *   *

Unlike Schumann, Grieg did not design any of his books of imaginative pieces in the form of suites in which the separate items were closely inter-related either in key or style, or by being the musical equivalent of a story or the expression of homogeneous or contrasting moods. Schumann's suite-like *Papillons*, *Carnaval*, *Davidsbündler*, *Kreisleriana* and *Forest Scenes*, which were written between 1832 and 1849, found a successor many years later in a programmatic suite of an entirely original kind: Mussorgsky's *Pictures from an Exhibition*.

Written in 1874, but not published until 1886, this set of ten pieces conveys the composer's impressions of pictures by the Russian painter Viktor Hartmann which were shown at a memorial exhibition in St. Petersburg that year. The pieces are linked together by an introduction and by interludes entitled 'Promenade' based on similar thematic material. They are intended to depict the spectator (Mussorgsky himself) as he wanders through the gallery looking at each exhibit in turn. Since the music is published with written descriptions of the pictures concerned: portraits, landscapes, *genre* pictures, and a design for a clock, musicians can form their own opinions as to how far the composer has succeeded in bringing the canvasses to life.

Mussorgsky's skill in musical characterization, which was highly developed by his experience as a composer of operas, was stronger than his feeling for pianistic style. As musical portraiture the work is vividly descriptive, especially in the movements depicting the dancing of the ungainly 'Gnome', no. 1, the lumbering 'Polish Ox-waggon', no. 4, the 'Two Polish Jews, rich and poor', no. 6, whose respective dominant traits, self-importance and servility, are realistically sketched in heavy octaves and wheedling single notes; and the 'Hut on Hen's Feet', no. 9, the home of the witch Baba Yaga, who rides in a fury of chromaticisms 'allegro con brio, feroce' through the longest of the ten movements. As piano music, the suite is less successful. It taxes the performer's skill without compensating him by beauty or ingenuity in the keyboard writing. The orchestral version made by Ravel in 1922 brings out all the variations in tone-colour that the original version lacks, and the work is now generally performed in this more effective form.

*   *   *   *

Liszt's *Christmas-tree* suite, also composed in 1874, is made up of twelve pieces descriptive of Christmas celebrations, religious and secular. It includes settings of well-known carols and hymns, nos. 1, 4 and 8; a presto 'Scherzoso', no. 5; a 'Berceuse', no. 7 and a characteristic piece, 'In former times', no. 10, both of which are composed in the flowing, richly-harmonized style of some of the 'Consolations'; a brilliant Hungarian March and a Polonaise, nos. 11 and 12; and two little tone-poems, 'Carillon', no. 6 and 'Evening Bells', no. 9 which evoke the timbres of chiming and pealing respectively. The movements are written in free narrative style. As some of them end indefinitely (nos. 2, 7, 8, 9, and 11) and lead with hardly a break into their successors, the suite as a whole is marked by a strong sense of unity. At the same time, it contains vigorous contrasts in pianistic style. For instance, between the gently-rocking accompaniment of 'The Shepherds at the Manger', no. 3, the light chords of the flickering 'Scherzoso', the fierce harmonies and strong rhythms of Hungarian March and the sensuous, resonant pedal-effects in 'Evening Bells'.

No such marked contrasts exist in Tchaikovsky's suite *The Seasons*, op. 37 (1876), which consists of twelve movements portraying subjects and activities typical of the twelve months from January to December. As characteristic pieces they create the musical atmosphere defined by their respective titles, but they are little differentiated in length and structure and the piano writing is uniform in style. They do not form a convincing whole work. Only the 'Hunting Song' (September) stands out noticeably from the others by virtue of its strident horn-calls and thick octave passages, and this piece is perhaps the least pianistic in character of all the movements. Although the suite is monotonous when performed complete, the movements are effective played singly. Some have become familiar apart from their context: 'Snowdrops' (April), 'Clear Nights' (May), 'At the fireside' (January) and 'Sleigh ride' (November). The 'Song of the lark' (March), 'andante espressivo' in G minor, claims special attention, not only on account of its intrinsic beauty but because it is conceived in a very different manner from the simpler, more spontaneous piece of the same title, Lentamente in G major, no. 22 of the composer's *Album for the Young*, op. 39 which we studied in the previous chapter.

*   *   *   *

Borodin's much slighter *Petite suite* (1885) consists of seven brief movements. Unlike the three suites just mentioned, it has no central imaginative idea to unify it, but it is musically homogeneous through being composed in a simple style tinged with the characteristics of Russian folk-music. Only the first piece has a programmatic title: 'At the convent', which it actualizes by conjuring up the sounds of bells and of processional chanting. The 'Serenade', no. 6, with a thrumming, guitar-like bass, is likewise graphically evocative of its subject. The other movements are less picturesque but each presents interesting features in the piano writing, and although all, except the tiny 'Rêverie' no. 5, are composed in sections, the musical material is developed organically. In the Intermezzo, no. 2, and the second of the two Mazurkas, no. 4, the melodic line of the outer sections grows in significance on being passed from one hand to the other. The first Mazurka, no. 3, makes a feature of pedal-point effects, both sustained and intermittent. In the Nocturne, no. 7, a feeling of dreamlike, soothing monotony is induced by the repetition of characteristic figures in both the melody and the accompaniment, and by the periodic interchanges between them. (The treble line of bars 5-10 becomes the tenor melody of the succeeding bars, and so on).

This is Borodin's only work for the piano. Pianists who know the Polovtsian Dances from his opera *Prince Igor* will recognize in the *Petite suite* turns of melody and rhythmic patterns which are reminiscent of the riotously brilliant orchestral pieces. They are easily discernible in the opening theme of the Intermezzo, the syncopations of the first Mazurka and the Serenade, the endings of all three sections of the second Mazurka, the melodic ornamentation in the 'Rêverie' and the repetition of short figures and phrases in every one of the seven movements.

Grieg's suite *From Holberg's time*, op. 40 (1884) belongs to another category. It is a sequence of five pieces composed in the early dance forms. In this sense it is a lineal descendant of the eighteenth-century suite, a type of music to which brief reference will be made in the next chapter on the music of the dance.

— 11 —

Dance Forms

Origin of dances as pieces of keyboard music; early forms and later survivals. The Waltz, Écossaise, Ländler, German Dance, and Polonaise before Chopin. Chopin: Waltzes, Mazurkas, Polonaises; Liszt: Polonaises, 'Mephisto' Waltzes; Schumann: Papillons, Carnaval; *Brahms:* Waltzes. *Nationalist dances: Smetana, Dvořák, Tchaikovsky, Grieg.*

WHEN the instrumental music which for centuries had served as the accompaniment to dancing and singing eventually broke away to develop as an independent art, it inevitably retained the rhythmic and formal characteristics of the two arts with which it had been so closely associated.

The earliest pieces of music for the keyboard were based on the tunes of songs and dances. It was the grouping together of two or more pieces of this kind for the purpose of securing contrasts in rhythm and expressive style that led to the foundation of the sixteenth-century suite. The dignified *pavan* in common time and the more robust *galliard* in triple time, a pair of dances of Italian origin, were among the first to be treated in this manner, and were sometimes each supplemented by a single variation and prefaced by a short prelude.

These two dances were presently superseded by another pair similarly contrasted in character, the *allemande* and the *courante*. When in the course of time the two last-named were united with the *sarabande* and the *gigue*, the four movements formed the nucleus of the seventeenth-century suite. Composers of a later period extended its scope by adding other kinds of dances. The French clavecinistes also modified its constitution by introducing descriptive pieces with imaginative titles and by increasing the number of movements. Some of the suites or *ordres* published by François Couperin between 1713 and 1730 comprise as many as ten or fifteen pieces; the longest contains twenty-three.

Bach and Handel, both of whom were influenced by the work of the clavecinistes, varied the construction and style of the eighteenth-century suite in several ways, the most notable being the addition by Bach of long preludial movements, and by Handel of stately fugues and variations. The suite continued to exist as an independent art-form until about the middle of the eighteenth-century, after which time it could no longer hold its own against the sonata.

Some of the individual dances have remained in being as formal types until the present day although they have undergone fundamental changes in speed, mood and expression. The *chaconne* and the *passacaglia*, which were originally Spanish or Italian dances with music built on a ground-bass, have developed into the most recondite of all compositions in variation form. The trochaic metre of the gigue persists in the light-hearted finales of many sonatas and symphonies. The *minuet*, a rustic French dance which found its way into the suite during the seventeenth century, was implanted in the symphony during the eighteenth century by Haydn, who quickened its pace and lightened its stately character. It was later transformed by Beethoven into the fast-moving *scherzo*, in which guise it became an integral movement in many of his sonatas and symphonies as well as in those of his contemporaries and successors. At the same time, its original tempo and precise style were preserved, first in the minuets for piano solo composed singly or in groups by Beethoven and Schubert, and then throughout the closing years of the nineteenth century in characteristic pieces in archaic style such as Grieg's *Grandmother's Minuet*, op. 68, no. 2 (1898) and Ravel's *Menuet antique* (1895).

The *polonaise*, a rare movement in the eighteenth-century suite, was an even more rare movement in the piano sonata. The *Polonaise en rondeau* in Mozart's Sonata in D major, K. 284 furnishes a well-known example. As an independent piano solo

R

or duet the dance underwent extremely diverse treatment at the hands successively of Wilhelm Friedemann Bach, Beethoven, Weber, Schubert, Schumann, and Wagner before it was re-created as a tone-poem by Chopin. The long-neglected pavan acquired a new expressive significance, first in Chausson's *Pavane* (*Quelques Danses*, 1896) and later in Ravel's rondo-form *Pavane pour une Infante défunte* (1899). The *forlane*, an Italian dance (from Friuli), which was also revived by Chausson in the set of dances just mentioned, was reborn in a maze of chromaticisms in Ravel's suite *Le Tombeau de Couperin* (1914-17). Debussy resuscitated the lively Breton dance, *passepied*, in his *Suite Bergamasque* (1890). Instances could be multiplied indefinitely.

*　　*　　*　　*

At the dawn of the nineteenth century the suite was virtually extinct. Its successors, the sets of short pieces with fanciful titles by Schumann, Liszt, and others, which we studied in the previous chapter, were derived from the French *ordres* rather than from the Bach suites. Grieg's suite *From Holberg's time: Prelude, Sarabande, Gavotte, Air and Rigaudon*, written in 1884 to celebrate the bi-centenary of the birth of Ludvig Holberg, the 'Molière of the North' and a contemporary of Bach's, was, however, a conscious imitation of the Bach suite, designed to recapture the musical spirit of the Baroque period. A few isolated pieces in the style of the early dance forms were written by well-known nineteenth-century composers. They include a gigue each by Schumann (op. 32, no. 2, 1838-9) and by Dvořák (op. 52, no. 3, 1880), and two pairs of sarabandes and gigues (1855) written by Brahms at the age of twenty-two as essays in the 'severe' style but not published until 1938. While Brahms himself did not consider these four little pieces worthy of print in their original version, he kept one of them in mind for close on thirty years; the haunting, modally-inflected Sarabande in A, which begins and ends in the major although it bears the key-signature of the minor. When he came to write his String Quintet in F major, op. 88 in 1882 he incorporated the material in the central movement. In the new context the two compact eight-bar phrases of the Sarabande, now transposed into C sharp, were detached and re-distributed. The first forms the basis of the thrice-recurrent main section; the second performs its original balancing function only once towards the end of this combined slow movement and scherzo.

*   *   *   *

Of the large quantity of dance music written by the principal composers of the nineteenth century, only a very small proportion was produced for use in the ballroom. The bulk of it was composed for purely artistic purposes. It comprises a multitude of pieces embodying the rhythms and evoking the distinctive atmosphere of specific dances, national and international. This kind of music includes many works by composers who cultivated the traditional melodies and rhythms peculiar to their respective homelands, and who sought to strengthen the nationalist aspirations of their fellow-countrymen by idealizing their native music.

*   *   *   *

The dance that awakened the greatest enthusiasm, both in the ballrooms of many countries and in the sphere of instrumental music, was the *waltz*. It had become popular before the turn of the century. Among its early composers were Haydn, Clementi, Mozart, and Beethoven, who wrote waltzes for performance at the masked balls held in the *Redoutensaal* in Vienna. Beethoven also wrote music for other kinds of dances: the *Ländler*, a more homely type of waltz native to Austria and Bavaria; the *Deutscher* or German Dance in slow waltz time, and the *Écossaise*, a species of *contredanse* in quick 2/4 time. Some of these pieces by Beethoven were composed for orchestra but were published for the piano, in which form they are still extant. As music for playing, they lack the grace and the tunefulness of Weber's dance movements: his Waltzes (1812), Six Écossaises (1802) and the Twelve Allemandes which are the equivalent of German dances, not of the older type of allemande familiar in the eighteenth-century suite. Weber's dances, charming as they are, stand far behind Schubert's in spontaneity and diversity, and most of all, in profusion.

Schubert composed an immense quantity of dance music, much of which he wrote for piano solo and for performance by himself at the small private dances given at the houses of his friends in and around Vienna. He was a born composer of dance music; his natural affinity with the rhythms of the dance is manifest in a large number of his compositions of all kinds. His compositions in dance forms, which are distinguished by irresistible rhythmic flow, singing melodies, and deeply expressive harmonies, exercised a powerful influence upon the waltzes written by those of his contemporaries and successors who specialized exclusively in the production of music as the accompaniment to dancing: Joseph Lanner, the Strauss family, and Joseph Gung'l. They also determined the style of Brahms's and Dvořák's Waltzes about forty and fifty years after his death, and were the inspiration of Ravel's *Valses nobles et sentimentales* composed in 1911.

*   *   *   *

The artistic dance music written during the early part of the century is for the most part slight in dimensions. The dances that engendered it were usually composed in two balancing sections of eight bars. Only by stringing together several of these sections could composers secure any musical continuity.

Both Beethoven and Schubert wrote sets of dances in which all the individual items are in the same key: an arrangement that inevitably accentuates the monotony of the uniform rhythmic scheme. Compositions which represent this type and show its limitations include Beethoven's Six Écossaises in E flat major and his two groups of Ländrische Tänze in D major consisting respectively of six and seven movements with a coda. Similar in planning are Schubert's Eight Ländler in B flat major and Five Écossaises in A flat major. The more satisfying musical effect produced by a wider range in tonality is exemplified in Beethoven's Six Minuets, which begin and end in C major and are interspersed with movements in the major keys of G, E flat, B flat and D; and in the great majority of Schubert's more than thirty sets of dances: Ländler, Écossaises, Waltzes, Minuets, Galops, and a Cotillion.

*   *   *   *

The series of keys in which Schubert arranged his dances varies with every set and follows no fixed plan. In a few sets, such as the Six German Dances, only flat keys are used. The Twelve German Dances and several other sets are entirely in sharp keys. Elsewhere, sharp and flat keys follow one another at random. A set that starts in a sharp key may end in a flat one (the Seventeen Ländler) and vice versa (Galop and Écossaises, op. 49). By placing dances in distantly-related keys side by side Schubert effected many stimulating contrasts in tonality. Unexpected successions of keys occur in the Twelve Ländler, op. 171: a dance in A flat minor is followed by one in B major; another in A flat major by one in E major. The musical interest of this complete set is also enhanced by many variations in the style of the piano writing as well as by chains of transient modulations and by the starting of several of the dances out of the basic key.

The set of Eight Écossaises in seven keys (1815) is unique in the manner in which it holds a balance between continuity and variety in tonality. The dances are arranged in four pairs, all except one in different keys. As the first dance of each pair is repeated after the second has been played, the set is extended to twelve movements which are distributed into four groups of three. The most striking contrasts in key occur between the outer sections of each group. The planning of this set in recurrent sections may possibly have suggested to Liszt the idea of arranging selected items from the Schubert dances into groups in the manner already described in Chapter 8 among transcriptions (the *Soirées de Vienne*).

The pianistic style of Schubert's dances accords perfectly with the simplicity of their expressive character, which is alternately light-hearted and wistful. Although the music is not technically difficult to play it includes a large number of different types of piano writing. Many of them will be recognized by pianists who are already familiar with the minuet-and-trio movements of Schubert's sonatas and with some of the *Moments musicaux*. Of numerous interesting features, only a few can be mentioned here. The dark colouring of the Écossaise (composed 21 February, 1815) which opens in D minor and closes in F major, and of nos. 3 and 4 of the Seventeen Ländler; the dream-like quality of nos. 5 and 8 of the same series; the sudden changes in pitch in the first Waltz of op. 127 and the ingenious cross-hand passages in the attached trio and in the ninth Waltz of op. 18; persistently syncopated accentuation in the sixth Waltz of the same opus and in no. 11 of the Twelve Ländler, and the extreme sparseness of the harmonic basis of some of the Twenty Waltzes, op. 127, particularly of no. 9 which, together with its trio, hardly goes beyond the confines of tonic and dominant. In a few of the dances the native Austrian style is expressed in imitations of yodelling: in nos. 18, 19 and 28 of the Original Dances, op. 9 and in several of the *Grätzer Waltzer*, op. 91. A thorough explora-tion of this whole body of compositions reveals a wealth of fascinating details.

*   *   *   *

The sectional construction which characterizes every one of the little pieces so far discussed also underlies a very large number of the dances composed during the nineteenth century; even pianistically decorative movements such as Chopin's and Dvořák's waltzes and mazurkas. Dance movements of a more expansive kind began to appear in the first two decades of the century. They developed side by side with the simpler types and eventually culminated in the highly-organized forms exemplified by Chopin's Polonaise-Fantasy and Liszt's 'Mephisto' Waltzes. Early examples are provided by Beethoven's and Weber's Polonaises.

Beethoven's Polonaise in C major, op. 89 (1814), his only medium-length piano solo in dance form, combines elements of both ternary and rondo forms. After an opening paragraph of rushing scales and arpeggios, the principal theme in polonaise

rhythm is announced. It subsequently makes three appearances
in the original key as well as one in A major after the longest of
the interludes, and it also supplies the material of the extensive
coda. This extremely high-spirited piece, which is still occasionally performed in public, shows an entirely different conception
of the polonaise from that of Beethoven's predecessor sixty years
earlier, Wilhelm Friedemann Bach. His twelve short Polonaises
in various tempi and in expressive styles ranging from the brisk
to the deeply meditative, are all composed in symmetrical
binary form.

Weber's large-scale Polonaises, which had been preceded by
the 'polacca' Finale of his Variations on 'Vien quà Dorina bella'
in 1807, are nearly similar to Beethoven's in dimensions and
construction but are more consistently florid in their pianistic
style. The *Grande Polonaise* in E flat, op. 21 (1808) is preluded by
a dramatic Largo in the minor mode in duple time based upon
a dactylic figure native to the polonaise (♪ ♪. ♪ ♪ ♪), after which
the 'alla polacca' opens in 3/4 time with a dashing theme in
dotted notes. The clear-cut form of the whole approximates to
older rondo, but the first episode consists largely of a development of the tune of the refrain. The coda, too, is founded on this
ever-resilient tune. Only the second episode in C major supplies
any strongly-marked contrast. The *Polacca brillante* in E major,
op. 72 (1819) is in modern rondo form. The bold principal
theme, like that of the *Grande Polonaise*, is in strongly dotted
rhythm, but the second subject flows in graceful curves of triplet
semiquavers. The interlude is placed unusually, after the first
statement of the refrain instead of in the centre of the movement.
It opens with a sustained cantabile air underlaid with the
dactylic figure on every beat in the middle voice. This distinctive paragraph is not heard again, but the succeeding energetic
and heavily-accented theme reappears to form the coda.

These two effective polonaises of Weber's are far surpassed in
interest and renown by his *Invitation to the dance*, op. 65 composed
in 1819. The work may be considered epoch-making, since it
was the first composition to embody the waltz in a full-length
piece of piano music and was the forerunner of Chopin's

waltzes. The programmatic connotations of the introduction and coda to this piece have already been referred to in the chapter on Romantic Music. Here, it remains to note the ingenious and effective interweaving of the seven or eight different thematic fragments into a kind of continuous rondo which is endowed with a rare unity of style by the predominating rhythm of the waltz. The shimmering tone-colours of the brilliant orchestral transcriptions made successively by Berlioz and Weingartner have unfortunately robbed the original version of its native charm.

*   *   *   *

The Chopin Waltzes, although they too have been transferred to the sphere of the orchestra to form the accompaniment to a ballet, have never lost their original attraction for pianists, either in public or in private. Their rhythmic verve, their wealth of melody, their power to evoke well-defined moods and to re-create the atmosphere of excitement, nostalgia, or languor have exercised an irresistible fascination upon generations of music-lovers.

Chopin began to write waltzes in his boyhood. Some that he composed in early manhood and later, but did not publish, were printed posthumously. Those that he himself published date from 1831, the year he settled in Paris, to 1847, two years before his death. They include his finest and best-known works in this genre: the Waltzes in E flat, op. 18 and in A flat, op. 42 and the three Waltzes each of opp. 34 and 64.

The formal outlines of the individual dances vary to a considerable extent. Several are composed in ternary form, but only a few include a conventional *da capo* repeat. In others, the opening section is heightened in interest on its reappearance, either by a rearrangement of the sections or by new developments in the material. For instance, in the Waltz in A flat, op. 64, no. 3, the music makes a sudden excursion into an unexpected key, and although it soon returns to the tonic it never resumes its normal course but runs without a break into a decorative coda. Others of the Waltzes proceed in a series of clear-cut sections, some of which recur periodically. In the Waltz in A minor, six different musical ideas alternate in irregular sequence. In the Waltz in A flat, op. 42, each of the well-defined paragraphs is separated from the next by a purely ornamental passage of sixteen bars which runs like a ritornello through the piece and forms a strong contrast to all the other thematic material, especially to the duple-rhythmed principal section. These two Waltzes, mutually so different, but equally convincing in expression, display the same ingenious rondo design as Weber's *Invitation to the dance*.

Far less subtle in build and less vivid in character are the Waltz in A flat, op. 69, no. 1, which is in older rondo form, and the F minor, op. 70, no. 2, which comprises two statements of the same stretch of material, each identical in every respect except that the second omits the repeat of the opening twenty bars. The Waltz in C sharp minor is an unusual amalgam of rondo and ternary forms. It contains a central interlude in the major, but the second section of the outer panels, which is made of quicksilvery passage-work, both precedes and follows the interlude as well as taking its rightful place in the reprise. Despite the different tempi and contrasted pianistic styles of the three component sections, this waltz does not increase in intensity of expression as do some of the longer waltzes. They work up to a climax and are rounded off with a coda in accelerated tempo which emphasizes salient features of the musical material and sums up the whole movement. Of this type are the Waltz in E flat, the two in A flat, op. 34, no. 1 and op. 42, the F major, and the E minor, all of which are prefaced with introductory sections varying in length and in forcefulness of expression.

*   *   *   *

The composition of dances other than those inspired by the music of his native Poland did not call forth Chopin's highest creative powers. The Waltzes, with few exceptions, notably the plaintive A minor, display only the more facile side of his genius. The Bolero in C major, op. 19 (1834) with its overlapping phrases in irregular bar-lengths is interesting from the aspect of rhythm. The swirling presto Tarantella in A flat, op. 43 (1841) is cumulatively brilliant in effect, but neither of these pieces represents the composer at his most typical. The short Écossaises that he wrote at the age of sixteen are exquisitely light in texture, though in harmonic interest they do not compare with Schubert's. On the other hand, the Mazurka in A minor, op. 17, no. 4, which Chopin first sketched when he was only fifteen, and the *Rondo à la Mazur* composed a year later, both show that the melodies and rhythms of Polish national music fired his imagination and exerted a decisive influence upon his whole musical style.

Chopin did not use actual folk-tunes in his compositions except upon the rarest occasions. (We came across an instance in the first Scherzo in B minor). He assimilated the distinctive features of the folk-idiom and transmuted them into a kind of music which is profoundly personal, and at the same time both national in style and international in appeal. He composed about sixty mazurkas, fifty-one of which are printed in practical performing editions. They include movements in the lively, moderate and slow tempi which are distinctive of three different kinds of mazurka: the *oberek* (*obertas*), the *mazur*, and the *kujawiak*.

The mazurkas range in dimensions and design from short pieces in simple ternary form, such as no. 4 in E flat minor which flashes past in the twinkling of an eye, to movements in extended form. In these, either the several sections are arranged in irregular succession, with the principal section recurring from time to time, or the thematic units are welded into a highly organized structure. Movements of the latter type are characterized by the re-introduction in fresh keys of portions of the musical material, or by the development of themes in symphonic manner. Among numerous examples, nos. 17 in F minor, 26 in C sharp minor, 38 in F sharp minor and 39 in B major are representative. Intermediate in size and pattern are many mazurkas in different types of rondo or ternary form. No. 15 resembles a scherzo with two trios; nos. 27 and 28 are in 'arch' form, strict, or free, respectively.

In studying Chopin's *Rondo à la Mazur* in Chapter 7 we found that this early piece was tinged with the characteristics of Polish folk-music. Among other melodic idiosyncrasies in the mazurkas which may be regarded as deriving from the same source are the hovering of a tune around one note, the repetition of short figures and phrases and the introduction of triplets at significant points. In the seventh Mazurka in F minor, op. 7, no. 3, every one of these features may be observed. In addition, the movement contains examples of a characteristic type of accompaniment: the drone bass; and of two rhythmic traits inseparable from the mazurka: the accenting of either the second or the third beat of the bar and the ending of a phrase on the second beat.

*   *   *   *

The Chopin mazurkas owe their unique expressive quality to the perceptive integration of primitive material and highly-developed musical art. The blending of the modally-flavoured themes, polychromatic harmonies, and tireless rhythms into a contrapuntally vital texture makes these pieces a highlight, not only in Chopin's own production, but in the dance music of the whole nineteenth century. The prevailing moods of the individual mazurkas are reflected in many different styles of piano writing. The exuberant gaiety of no. 23 in D major manifests itself in endless repetitions of an eight-bar tune with a sturdy accompaniment. The melancholy inherent in no. 27 in E minor finds expression in quiet chordal progressions that become passionate in their intensity. In no. 34 in C major, robust peasant humour is portrayed first by the tying of a repetitive melody to heavy tonic chords, and then by a series of artless scale-passages that chase one another up and down in canon at the octave.

The piano writing itself is more restrained in style than in the waltzes. Brilliant passage-work finds no place in it, and the music seldom ventures to the higher octaves, although it penetrates to the depths of the keyboard, often with telling effect. In some of the light-hearted movements the melodies are clearly

distinguished from their accompaniments. The well-known
Mazurka in B flat, no. 5 affords a typical example. More often
however, they form an integral part of a texture in which they
appear alternately in the upper, middle or lower voices, varying
in expressive character according to their importance in the
musical argument. In some of the longer mazurkas the many
changes in mood involve as many changes in the figuration.
The pensive no. 25 in B minor, (mesto), the modally-flavoured
nos. 26 and 32 in C sharp minor and nos. 33 in B major and 35
in C minor which are distinguished by many changes in tonality,
contain some of the most effective, as well as some of the most
closely-wrought contrapuntal writing in the whole collection.

The melodic significance of the left-hand parts is one of the
salient points of the pianistic layout. Another is the great variety
of colour-effects which are produced by simple means. They
include the plentiful use of ornaments (acciaccature and trills),
the spreading of light or heavy chords by the left hand, the
separating of the two hands by wide differences in pitch, the
insertion of a series of purely decorative chords over a pedal-
bass or of colour-washes of frictionless quavers between paragraphs of more solid texture, and the interpolation of recitative-
like passages in single melodic lines or plain octaves.

*   *   *   *

The mazurkas as a whole are distinguished among all
Chopin's collections of works by the comparatively few technical
difficulties they offer in performance. They contain almost no
wide stretches or intricate passages, neither do they require to
be played at excessive speed. They afford the pianist of average
attainments unrivalled opportunities of acquiring familiarity
with the composer's most intimate style.

The Polonaises reveal another aspect of Chopin's musical art.
The processional, ceremonial character of the traditional dance
inspired him to compose music in a more majestic style than did
the light steps of the mazurka. The typical metrical figure
(♪ ♫ ♩) lent itself to a kind of treatment that added a martial
tinge to the compositions. But it was Chopin's own conception

of the polonaise, as a tone-poem which should portray the departed glories, the despair, and the hopes of his native country, that determined the large dimensions and the heroic manner of the splendid, colourful works of his maturity.

Chopin wrote his first Polonaise in G minor at the age of seven. It was published at the time (1817), but neither this immature piece nor the other polonaises that he wrote up to his seventeenth year are printed in current practical editions. The earliest examples now in general circulation are the three dating from 1827 to 1830. They were published posthumously as op. 71 and are seldom played in public. Between this group of relatively unimportant examples of the species and the series of six Polonaises and the Polonaise-Fantasy which Chopin composed between 1834 and 1846 and which are universally known and loved, came the *Grande Polonaise brillante* in E flat, op. 22 (1830). It is a virtuoso piece for piano and orchestra that can also be played as a solo. Compared with its magnificent successors it is lacking in depth, but the assured style of the piano writing and some daring harmonic clashes compel admiration. An acutely dissonant passage which occurs just before the first tutti is particularly noteworthy.

The *Andante spianato* in the style of a nocturne, which forms the long introduction to the Polonaise was composed about four years later and is musically unrelated to it.

The three Polonaises of op. 71, although they are of no great intrinsic interest, repay study as forerunners of the important works that followed. The first in D minor (1827), which is contemporary with the glittering 'alla polacca' of the 'Là ci darem' Variations, contains a similar preponderance of decorative figuration. The second in B flat major (1828) and the third in F minor (1829) are progressively more melodic in style and rhythmically more diversified. In every one of the three, the principal phrases and paragraphs end in characteristic polonaise fashion on the third beat of the bar. All are in clear-cut ternary form with a central interlude in a closely-related key and a *da capo* repeat. Their prevailing formal angularity is emphasized by the tripartite division of each of the main sections, but the sharp outlines of the third are softened. The purposeful opening theme relapses into a spacious eight-bar phrase above a dominant pedal, and later, a short ornamental passage links the section of energetic figuration to the returning principal theme.

The style of the cantabile theme of this Polonaise in F minor and the melodic line in dotted notes at the very end of the interlude in A flat faintly anticipate features of the succeeding Polonaise in C sharp minor, op. 26, the first of the 'idealized' polonaises which Chopin began to compose in 1834. Throughout this picturesque movement the rhythm of the dance is immanent, but it is not strongly in evidence in the musical substance which, after the first explosive phrases, consists chiefly of impassioned melodies accompanied by heavily-beating chords. The Polonaise in C minor, op. 40, no. 2 (1838-9) is equally serious in expressive character though it occasionally breaks impatiently into passages of rebellious semiquavers. As in the C sharp minor Polonaise, the melodic substance is divided between the two hands, but the accompanying chords beat more firmly and the whole movement is resolute rather than resigned in feeling.

The Polonaises in E flat minor, op. 26, no. 2 (1834-5) and in A major, op. 40, no. 1 (1838) are alike in their insistence on the element of rhythm but are utterly dissimilar in expression. The former smoulders with pent-up emotion and sometimes bursts into flames; the latter is perpetually martial, unconquerable, exultant. With their rich chordal texture and the extensive use they make of the heights and the depths of the keyboard, these two pieces convey an impression of greater weight than do the

Polonaises in C sharp minor and C minor. The structural plan
of the four movements just mentioned is almost identical, but
the Polonaise in E flat minor is longer than the others and is
rounded off with a brief but dramatic coda. The *da capo* repeat
in the C minor Polonaise is shorn of two-thirds of its length, but
opens the more expressively by retaining in the treble part of
the first four bars a melodic figure from the last bar of the
preceding interlude.

*　　*　　*　　*

With the Polonaise in F sharp minor, op. 44 (1840-1), Chopin
created a new, highly-developed type of form in which the many
and varied thematic units are brought into close mutual relationship. The work opens with a prelude based on a four-note
figure that later acquires fresh significance. The eighteen-bar
principal section in F sharp minor is presented three times, the
third time varied. Its eight-bar pendant in B flat minor appears
twice in its own key, as well as once in C sharp minor in the
centre of the turbulent passage-work that leads up to the core of
the movement, a 'tempo di mazurka, doppio movimento'. The
gentle mazurka, whose lilting rhythm forms an effective contrast
to the martial tread of the polonaise, is composed of two themes
that alternate with one another in a succession of keys and at
different pitches. They die away eventually in fragments as the
four-note figure of the prelude steals in pianissimo in longer
notes in the bass. Thereafter, the movement re-opens with the
prelude in its original form, and after having recapitulated the
salient musical material, fades out in a coda. In the last few
bars, the scale-figure of the principal section re-affirms its
inspiriting message deep in the bass.

The Polonaise in A flat, op. 53 (1842) is shorter and far less
highly-organized than its predecessor but is no less convincing
in expressive power. It tells a tale of victory, with only passing
reference to captivity and oppression. The movement is dominated by the exhilarating theme in A flat which is announced
after an introductory paragraph and is repeated, complete, no
fewer than four times during the course of the piece. The inter-

lude in E major, which is equally stimulating in character, derives its cumulative force from the hundredfold repetition of a short figure of accompaniment in staccato octaves in the left hand; a figure that recurs momentarily in the coda to escort the theme in A flat to its sforzando close. The musical material lacks any striking constrast in mood such as is created in the Polonaise in F sharp minor by the incorporation of the graceful mazurka within its more robust framework. An antithesis in expressive styles is perceptible between the untramelled freedom of the two themes in A flat and E major and the feeling of hopelessness conveyed by the long passages following the interlude, during which the semiquavers try in vain to escape from the narrow confines of upper and lower pedal-points.

*   *   *   *

The Polonaise-Fantasy, op. 61 (1845-6) forms the climax of Chopin's production of music inspired by the dance. In this long, picturesque and brilliant work, one of the most mature of all his compositions, he blended the narrative style of the Ballades with the plasticity of form which he had already achieved in the Polonaise in F sharp minor and in the great Fantasy in F minor composed at the same period. He no longer relied on the repetition of whole sections as one of the chief means of building up the musical structure. Instead, he concentrated all his skill upon thematic development. Whereas the Polonaises of opp. 26 and 40 make an immediate effect with their successive panels of strongly-contrasted subject-matter, the large-scale works create a deeper and more lasting impression by the continuing tension maintained between their many constituent parts.

The Polonaise-Fantasy is endowed with a symphonic character that differentiates it from all the other compositions in this group. The peremptory opening chords, the dreaming arpeggios, and the ever-shifting tonality of the opening paragraph immediately establish the poetic atmosphere that surrounds this alternately meditative and rhapsodic movement. The song-like principal theme in A flat, already foreshadowed in the introduction, spreads its flowing lines across the first few pages together with its more lively attendant theme and they both undergo extensive development. The interlude, which begins in B major with a melody of narrow span over a rocking accompaniment, opens out into a more expansive paragraph that culminates in a pianistic effect unparalleled in Chopin's compositions. A long trill above a dominant pedal grows naturally out of the preceding melodic curve and gains in intensity of expression as it increases from an alternation of single notes, pianissimo, to an almost overwhelmingly vibrant chordal tremolo. After this shattering outburst the fateful opening chords and single-line arpeggios return to prelude the final section. During the closing pages, the curving theme in A flat and the tranquil melody from the interlude, now transposed into A flat, are carried along in triumph by a train of pulsating chords that completely transforms their original expressive qualities. The wide extent of the tonality, the many different types of figuration, and the fastidious workmanship throughout this noble movement display Chopin's harmonic mastery and his art of writing for the piano at their very finest.

*   *   *   *

The unique quality of Chopin's polonaises is realized more keenly if these works are compared with the two composed by Liszt in 1851. Chopin's, which give passionate expression to an exile's burning love for his country, plumb the depths of musical feeling. Liszt's, the virtuoso productions of a cosmopolitan who cultivated the dance-forms of several nationalities with indiscriminate fervour, hardly penetrate its surface. While they preserve the rhythmic features of the polonaise they take no account of its dignified ceremonial character. With their brilliant piano writing, their elaborate variation of the thematic material, and their showy cadenzas they come within the category of the concert-study.

In point of formal construction each polonaise consists of a series of episodes which are arranged in markedly different order in the two pieces. In the first in C minor, the contrasting

s

interlude in the relative major that follows the opening section is later recapitulated in the tonic major and is succeeded by a long section of new material. The corresponding interlude in the second Polonaise in E major is not referred to again until the coda, and then only briefly. The cadenza in each piece, too, serves a different purpose. In the E major Polonaise it is a purely decorative interpolation, whereas in the C minor, it takes the form of a longish episode, 'lento, quasi cadenza, improvisata' comprising a meditation on the preceding material. The manner of varying the subject-matter, which in the last-named work consists in passing the melody from one hand to the other in the centre of a four-part texture, changes in the E major Polonaise to the stretching of the melodic thread to the utmost limit of its flexibility.

*   *   *   *

Liszt's polonaises are shallow rather than stirring in effect. His *Csárdás macabre* and the Third and Fourth 'Mephisto' Waltzes strike an altogether different note. In these three longish pieces composed in his old age, Liszt did not exploit the more brilliant qualities of the piano as was his wont in earlier years, but by an unusual economy of means he produced novel effects in tone-colour which vividly conjure up the dance-scenes indicated by the titles. The gruesome atmosphere of the dance of death which surrounds the *Csárdás macabre* is evoked by crude chords in bare fifths, by countless repetitions of grim, expressionless phrases, by eerie passages in single-line staccato notes and by a final descent in double octaves that touch the very lowest note of the keyboard.

The Third 'Mephisto' Waltz (1881) and the Fourth (1885) are by contrast sensuous pieces of music which seem at the outset to promise untold harmonic luxuriance. As they proceed, they tantalize the listener by their frequent restatement and elaboration of alluring phrases which, for all their many changes of key, never bring the musical argument to a decisive climax. By virtue of the elusive tonal basis and subtle rhythm the music is realistically Mephistophelean in character. In this sense it is a logical continuation of the First 'Mephisto' Waltz, a transcription for piano made by Liszt twenty years earlier of his own orchestral piece *The scene in the village inn,* one of two episodes from Lenau's *Faust.* The Third 'Mephisto' Waltz begins and ends harping on an unforgettable chord made up of a major third and two per-fect fourths spread out in single or double notes and shaped into ascending and descending curves which are merged into a cloud of evanescent sound by the sustaining-pedal. It is an astound-ingly modern colour-effect, as is also the long succession of hollow-sounding doubled fifths proceeding by semitone at the opening of the *Csárdás macabre.* The Fourth 'Mephisto' Waltz, which is less than half the length of the Third, evades the issue of established tonality even more persistently by hovering between the major and minor modes and between keys a semi-tone apart. It finally dies away in a phrase of plain octaves that owes no allegiance to a definite key-centre and leaves the listener in suspense.

These three sinister dance-poems, (the Third and Fourth 'Mephisto' Waltzes and the *Csárdás macabre*), differ from the majority of Liszt's longer piano pieces by their relative freedom from severe technical difficulties in performance. Like the miniatures of his later years which we studied in the previous chapter, they show how drastically he simplified his style of piano writing as he grew older.

*   *   *   *

Schumann's contribution to the literature of dance music for piano solo is specialized and extremely individual in character. While Beethoven and Schubert wrote sets of short dances that could be used for either practical or artistic purposes and Chopin poetized the rhythms of national dances in movements of longer span, Schumann enshrined the spirit of the dance in two sets of romantic miniatures, *Papillons* and *Carnaval.*

The twelve little movements of *Papillons* bear no titles, but their character as dance music is unmistakable, for the prevailing rhythms are those of the waltz and the polonaise. The culmina-tion of the series in the *Grossvatertanz,* a seventeenth-century tune which symbolizes the conclusion of the ball, and the striking of the clock as the dancers disperse, are graphic touches that round off a composition that is pervaded through and through with the spirit of revelry. In *Carnaval*, every item of which has a title, the portrait-sketches outnumber the dance movements, but the whole is enveloped in the atmosphere of the masquerade. The work is both artistically and musically an indivisible whole.

Spontaneous though both these compositions sound in performance, they came into being in laborious fashion. Schumann's manuscript sketches reveal that *Carnaval* was originally conceived as a set of variations on Schubert's *Sehnsuchtswalzer* (Le désir), only one variation of which survived to become the opening section of the *Préambule*. The ultimate development of *Carnaval* as a sequence of free variations upon a four-note motto theme was referred to in Chapter 6. *Papillons* was designed first as a group of waltzes, then as a set of variations, and every single item of the work as it now stands underwent revision or fundamental alteration before reaching its final state. In composing nos. 5 and 11, Schumann borrowed phrases, and even complete paragraphs from the Eight Polonaises for piano duet which he had written a few years previously. These Polonaises, the earliest of his piano compositions now readily available in print, will be referred to in the next chapter with other music for four hands.

Among Schumann's few detached dance movements for piano solo, one is well known as the third of the *Five Album Leaves* in *Bunte Blätter*, op. 99. This graceful Waltz in A flat, together with another in the same key and one in A minor, nos. 15 and 4 of the *Albumblätter*, op. 124, were all rejected from *Carnaval*, but they breathe the poetic spirit of that work. Of the three remaining dances, a Waltz in E flat, op. 124, no. 10 is curiously heavy by comparison, and a Ländler in D major, op. 124, no. 7, a charming piece of piano writing, is robbed of its native lilt by a series of wayward syncopations. The Fantasy Dance, presto in E minor, no. 5 of the same opus, despite its extreme brevity, is passionately expressive after the manner of the composer's Romance in D minor, op. 32, no. 3.

*   *   *   *

The Brahms Waltzes, op. 39, which date from 1865, were

written originally for piano duet, but they are much better known and more frequently performed in public in the version for piano solo made by the composer. Brahms, who was Viennese by residence, paid no heed to the example set by Chopin in composing longish pieces of music that recapture the atmosphere of the ballroom although they are not intended as the accompaniment to waltzing. Taking Schubert as his model he produced a series of short movements whose intimate style recalls that of the Ländler and German dances by his Viennese-born predecessor.

The sixteen Brahms Waltzes are more diversified in structure than are Schubert's. A few are made up conventionally of three eight-bar phrases, but the majority avoid rhythmic squareness by means of expansions and contractions in the phrase-lengths. In some of the waltzes the opening phrase returns to conclude the movement; in others, it never recurs note-for-note. Instead, the material is imitated or developed in other keys from the first double-bar onwards.

The last two waltzes differ in character from all the others. The well-known no. 15 in A flat major is a miniature rondo with three repetitions of the refrain, the third being varied. No. 16 in C sharp minor makes a feature of double counterpoint; the upper and middle voices of the first eight bars exchange their functions during the succeeding phrase, without, however, disturbing the natural flow of the music.

The waltzes as a group exhibit a considerable range of musical and expressive styles. The Brahms of the meditative Intermezzos may be perceived in the grazioso no. 5 in E major; in no. 7 in C sharp minor, 'poco più andante'; in the sparse no. 9 in D minor and the deep-pitched no. 12 in E major. The sprightly no. 6, vivace in C sharp major has affinities with the Capriccio in B minor, op. 76, no. 2; the dashing, vigorous nos. 11 in B minor, 13 in B major and 14 in G sharp minor emanate from the same musical climate as the composer's Hungarian Dances. Of the others, nos. 2 in E major, 3 in G sharp minor and 15 in A flat major display most clearly one of the principal harmonic characteristics of the waltz as it is most generally known: the basing of the three beats of each bar upon notes of the same chord.

*   *   *   *

By virtue of their derivation from the Austrian ländler, the Brahms waltzes stand on the borderline of nationalist music. Smetana's *Polkas* and *Czech Dances*, which incorporate native folk-tunes, come more definitely within that category, although the wealth of pianistic decoration that surrounds the tunes almost destroys their artless character.

Dvořák's eight Waltzes, op. 54 (1880) hold a midway position. Their melodies and rhythmic patterns show the influence of Czech folk-music, but the waltzes are expansive pieces of music in which the style of the piano writing and the thematic content claim equal consideration. They resemble those by Chopin in being made up of several longish recurrent sections in different keys, and in sometimes being preluded, interpolated, and concluded by a purely ornamental passage, as are nos. 2, 3, and 7. The fifth Waltz in G minor recalls Chopin's in A flat major, op. 42 in its metric pattern of combined 3/4 and 6/8 time (♩♪♪♩♪♪).

The piano writing, which is constantly varied and is interesting to the player, includes picturesque colour-effects, especially towards the endings of the movements. The coda of the sixth Waltz in F major, a series of tonic and sub-dominant harmonies, is poetized by chromatic alterations and by the dwelling upon a yearning discord:

The final cadence of the fourth in D flat major is fascinatingly delayed by the frequent repetition of the falling leading-note above a long-held tonic pedal:

Tchaikovsky's several waltzes, mazurkas, and polkas are almost entirely lacking in national colouring, but his Russian dances, such as the Andantino in A minor, op. 40, no. 10, and no. 13 in G major in the *Album for the Young*, preserve the primitive and exotic elements of Russian folk-music. Grieg's finest Norwegian dances, which are deeply permeated by the idiom of his native folk-music, are nationalist music in the truest sense.

*   *   *   *

The writing of dance music interested Grieg from early till late in his career and his compositions in this category exemplify many aspects of his musical and pianistic styles. Between the little Mazurka, op. 1, no. 3, which he composed as a nineteen-year old student in Leipzig, and the collection of seventeen *Slåtter*, op. 72 written five years before his death, he produced a long succession of dances: miniature waltzes, the movements of the 'Holberg' Suite, characteristic pieces based on dance rhythms, and Norwegian dances conceived both as original compositions and as transcriptions. In addition, he inserted sections in dance rhythms into a number of his other piano works: the 'alla menuetto' movement of the Sonata in E minor, op. 7, the 'alla burla' variation in the Ballade, op. 24 and the 'tempo di menuetto' and 'tempo di valse' variations in the Romance for two pianos, op. 51. He also introduced paragraphs of this type into the central interludes of the third and fourth *Album Leaves*, op. 28, and into some of the *Lyric Pieces* such as 'Vanished days' and 'Homesickness', op. 57, nos. 1 and 6, 'From early years', op. 65, no. 1 and 'Once upon a time', op. 71, no. 1.

Of these many compositions, those that show little or no trace of the influence of Norwegian folk-music are in the minority.

They include the 'Holberg' Suite, an intentional pastiche; the facile Waltzes in A minor, op. 12, no. 2, and in E minor op. 38, no. 7, and the characteristic pieces *She dances*, op. 57, no. 5 and *Valse mélancolique*, op. 68, no. 6.

Midway in style between this artificial type of salon music and the dances in distinctively Norwegian style comes the *Valse Impromptu*, op. 47, no. 1. The melody, which contains intervals typical of folk-music, and the simple accompaniment of twanging chords which is frequently at variance with it in mode and tonality, combine to produce an effect of harmonic crudity that looks backwards to primitive music and forwards to modern bi-tonality. The discreet piano writing in the intervening passages reconciles the two opposing styles.

*   *   *   *

The series of Grieg's Norwegian dances begins with those included in two collections of transcriptions: six in the twenty-five Norwegian Dances and Songs, op. 17 (nos. 1, 3, 5, 7, 18, and 20), and nos. 1, 3, and 5 of the Six Mountain Melodies (without opus number). It continues with several examples of his own conception of the *Halling* and the *Springdans*, in the Second, Fourth and Ninth Books of the *Lyric Pieces* (opp. 38, 47 and 71), and culminates in the *Slåtter*, op. 72, in which Grieg's art of transcription appears at its most daring.

*   *   *   *

In his treatment of folk-songs Grieg sometimes drew heavily upon the resources of chromatic harmony. When composing or transcribing dances, he tended to employ a more diatonic type of chordal progression. The occurrence of the sharpened fourth degree of the scale in the melody, a characteristic trait of Norwegian as well as of Polish folk-music, was responsible for the introduction of chromatic discords which add a distinctive flavour to those movements that are otherwise simply harmonized.

Grieg was ideally qualified to re-interpret the native dance tunes in his own musical language. He spent much time in remote parts of Norway where he had unrivalled opportunities of becoming familiar with the peasant dances that still survived in their natural setting and of hearing music played on native instruments. All his life he cultivated friendships and maintained close contacts with notable performers on the traditional Hardanger fiddle. From them he acquired inside knowledge of the technique of their instrument. When he adapted their music to the keyboard he knew instinctively how to evoke the timbre of the strident chords and florid ornamentation, and how to indicate the subtle vagaries in rhythm by which it is characterized.

*   *   *   *

Three kinds of dances claimed Grieg's attention almost exclusively: the *springdans* (leaping dance), which runs smoothly in triple time; the *halling*, an energetic dance in brisk 2/4 time and the *gangar*, which moves at a more stately pace in 6/8 time. The last-named is marked by the alternation of compound duple with simple triple time, which Grieg sometimes re-interpreted by using both concurrently. The halling, too, when it is written in 6/8 time, as it is occasionally in the *Slatter*, exhibits the same rhythmic irregularity, which greatly enhances its already invigorating character.

Most of Grieg's national dances consist of one or more variations upon either a single melody, or upon two or sometimes three alternating melodies within the framework of a short introduction and a longer coda. The uniformity in design is largely offset, both by the ever-changing figuration which displays the material in a series of increasingly effective settings, and by strong emphasis upon its rhythmic peculiarities. The piano writing maintains a high level of interest and is endlessly fascinating to the player. Even at its very simplest it rarely consists only of a melody with conventional accompaniment. More usually it comprises a texture made up of several strands which lead an independent existence, either rhythmically or melodically. At its most complicated, it offers the performer a number of problems in negotiating wide skips, sudden changes in pitch and cross-hand passages requiring extreme agility, and in sustaining a steady rhythm despite these many technical distractions. Among particularly noticeable features that recur again and again in the dances are the lavish use of every kind of ornament, and of pedal-basses which often persist for long periods at a time; once for a whole dance: the Halling in D major, *Lyric Pieces*, op. 47, no. 4.

*   *   *   *

The *Slåtter*, op. 72 (1902) occupy a unique position in Grieg's production. (*Slåt* is the name given to dance tunes played on any kind of native Norwegian instrument). The set of seventeen pieces was the outcome of a request made to him by a renowned Hardanger fiddler to save this particular kind of traditional music from extinction. Grieg arranged for the Norwegian violinist Johan Halvorsen to take down the dance tunes as exactly as possible in notation for the ordinary violin. He then proceeded to transform them into adventurous individual piano music which even today astonishes by the audacity of its harmonic and pianistic styles. The entire collection of pieces is as notable for fidelity to the given material as it is for imaginative realism in the transferring to the piano of music written for the two-centuries-old stringed instrument. A comparison of the versions by Halvorsen and by Grieg shows with what great understanding Grieg interpreted this very unusual kind of string music in terms of the keyboard.

The whole work furnishes a parallel to Schumann's transcription for piano of Paganini's *Caprices* for violin, but Grieg's task was the more difficult as it was undertaken in the interests of folk-culture as well as of instrumental music.

The *Slåtter* include a few Bridal Marches, for playing at weddings was, and still is, one of the most important activities of the Hardanger fiddlers. The piano writing in the Marches recalls that of Grieg's well-known 'The Bridal Procession passes by' from *Scenes from Folk Life*, op. 19 which he had composed thirty years before. The style of this piece of descriptive music goes to prove how deeply Grieg had already penetrated the spirit of his country's folk-music so many years earlier.

Duets

Origins and early history. Duets for four hands on one piano by Beethoven, Weber, and Schubert. Duets for two pianos: Chopin, Schumann, Brahms, Grieg. Duets for four hands on one piano by Mendelssohn, Schumann, Bizet, Brahms, Tchaikovsky, Dvořák, Grieg.

THE literature of the piano duet, which attained vast dimensions during the nineteenth century, first came into existence during the latter part of the eighteenth century.

Music written for two players at one or two keyboard instruments is known to date back to the sixteenth century, some of the earliest compositions in this medium being a piece by Nicholas Carlton for organ or virginal, *A Fancy* by Thomas Tomkins and Giles Farnaby's *Alman* for two virginals. Later compositions for two harpsichords include a Sonata in two movements by the Italian composer Bernardo Pasquini (1637–1710) and an Allemande, a few musettes, and pieces with fanciful titles included by François Couperin in his *Livres de Clavecin* between 1713 and 1730.

Among the earliest examples of printed music for two performers at one *piano* are some sonatas by J. S. Bach's sons, Johann Christoff Friedrich and Johann Christian, and by Dr. Charles Burney. These compositions are of interest principally to historians. For practical musicians, the piano duet starts with Mozart, whose principal works in this category were written between 1772 and 1791. His sonatas, variations and fugues, and the two Fantasies originally composed for a mechanical organ, are the only works of this period that hold a permanent place in the duettist's repertory. Clementi's and Dussek's piano duets which, as music, cannot be compared with

Mozart's although they are not without pianistic interest, have fallen into oblivion. Haydn's only composition for duet, a set of variations for 'master and pupil' published in 1781, comprises a series of echo-effects between the two players. It is now known only to specialists, but if it were more easily available it would probably be greatly enjoyed by practising duettists.

The duets that were written in varying numbers by almost every one of the principal nineteenth-century composers of piano music extend far beyond the few types cultivated during the previous century. Indeed, they include examples of all the many kinds of composition we have studied in these pages, with the one exception of the concert-study which, as it had been designed first and foremost to demonstrate the individual player's command of the keyboard, did not lend itself to division between two performers.

The great number of original compositions for two pianists at either one or two keyboards was increased beyond all reckoning throughout the century. In the first place, by transcriptions of orchestral, chamber, and other music made for the purpose of study; a type of duet that does not come within the scope of the present survey. In the second place, by the alternative versions which composers made of their own works. For instance, Brahms's transformations of his *Liebeslieder* and *Neue Liebeslieder* for vocal quartet with piano duet accompaniment into pieces for piano duet alone; Liszt's four-hand arrangement of his organ Fantasy and Fugue, *Ad nos, ad salutarem undam*; Grieg's transcriptions for orchestra of his Symphonic Dances for piano duet, and in general, many other works of this kind that enjoy equal status with their respective alternative versions.

With the exception of the very few compositions written originally for performance on two pianos, which will be discussed in two consecutive paragraphs, all the compositions now to be referred to are piano duets in the commonly accepted sense: for four hands on one piano.

* * * *

The history of the nineteenth-century piano duet, like that of piano solo music, begins just before the turn of the century with a set of variations and a sonata by Beethoven. His eight Variations on a Theme by Count Waldstein (1792) are nearly contemporary with the solo set on Dittersdorf's 'Es war einmal ein alter Mann', but are less elaborate in pianistic style. They contain typically Beethovenian touches in the precipitate scales in contrary motion in the second variation, the antiphonal explosions in the fourth and the alternations of recitative and passage-work in the long Finale. The six Variations in D on the song 'Ich denke dein' (1800) are pianistically uneventful but melodically more gracious. Some of the individual variations resemble the simplest and most tuneful of the Bagatelles. The Sonata in D major, op. 6, which Beethoven composed in the same year as the solo Sonata in E flat, op. 7 (1796), is altogether slighter in calibre than that romantically-coloured work. It consists of two short movements: an Allegro in exiguous sonata form and a simple rondo which displays not a vestige of the subtlety and elegance that distinguish the 'poco allegretto e grazioso' Finale of the Sonata in E flat. The three Marches, op. 45, composed in 1802 show Beethoven in a more characteristic mood. All are rhythmically inspiriting, especially the second and third, in which the style of the piano writing vividly suggests drum-rolls and trumpet fanfares.

After 1802 Beethoven wrote no more duets. His entire production of only four small works does not betoken any great enthusiasm on his part for the duet as a medium of expression. The pieces themselves are of relatively little importance, either among his own compositions or in duet literature as a whole.

*   *   *   *

Weber's three compositions for piano duet are of another kind, both musically and in their relationship to the composer's other works. They comprise two sets of short pieces which in construction and style display attributes of both the sonata and the suite, and a third collection of longer pieces which are less closely inter-related.

The first of these compositions, *Six petites pièces faciles*, op. 3

(1801), and the second, *Six pièces*, op. 10 (1809), open and close in the same key and are composed of items so slight in dimensions that they can hardly be performed as single units. Each set begins with a movement in miniature sonata form and ends with a rondo; the intervening pieces, which differ in type and arrangement in the two sets, include dances, variations, slow movements in ternary form and a march. The eight pieces of op. 60 (1818–19) are longer, more substantial and better adapted for performance individually.

As Weber wrote no miniatures for piano solo other than a few waltzes, écossaises and German dances, this whole series of duets occupies a special position among his piano works. Within its limited range it embodies prominent features of his art. Glowing melodies, ebullient rhythms, brilliant and delicate figuration such as distinguish his most important compositions for piano solo are all manifest in these short works, but scaled down in accordance with their slender proportions. For musicians who are unfamiliar with Weber's principal works for piano solo, the duets form an admirable introduction to his musical style. In addition, they possess an intrinsic fascination in being diminutive replicas of the composer's full-scale sonata-movements, variations, and dances. The Menuetto in B flat, op. 3, no 3, presto like those of the sonatas, is equally vivacious and light on the wing. The alternately leisurely and impassioned Adagio in A flat, op. 10, no 5 recalls the Adagio in F of the First Sonata. The Rondo in B flat, op. 60, no. 8, concise as it is, displays the same mosaic-like construction, the long anticipatory links and the cross-bar rhythm of the 'moto perpetuo', and the dance movements resemble those in the 'Schöne Minka' and 'Castor and Pollux' Variations.

As duets, the compositions are almost equally pleasurable to both partners. *Secondo* is allotted attractive figures of accompaniment, and in many instances, a large share of the musical interest. In the 'andante con variazioni', op. 3, no. 4 he plays the theme in the centre of the keyboard during the first variation; in the second he performs as soloist in twelve bars out of sixteen. He opens the Mazurka, op. 10, no. 4, with an eight-bar solo, and in the picturesque Allegro in A minor, op. 60, no 4, he and *primo* exchange functions as soloist and accompanist during successive paragraphs. They meet on equal terms in the sparsely-textured third variation of op. 10, no. 3. In the *Tema variato*, op. 60, no. 6, they both play interesting independent parts which together make up a rich tissue of sounds.

In recent times three of the Weber duets have been promoted to a higher musical rank. The Allegro (originally 'alla zingara'), op. 60, no. 4, the Andantino, op. 10, no. 2, and the March, op. 60, no. 7, were selected by Hindemith as the basis of three of his four *Symphonic Metamorphoses on Themes by Weber* (1943), in which context they shine in all the variegated splendour of modern orchestral colouring.

*   *   *   *

Before Weber had completed the writing of his last book of duets in 1819 Schubert had already embarked upon the composition of the great body of works that forms the largest and most important single contribution to the whole literature of the duet. As a boy of thirteen in 1810 he composed the first of three long, rambling fantasies which are now of interest only as specimens of his youthful production. A few years later he began to write the overtures, variations, sonatas, rondos, dances, marches and pieces of other kinds which add up to a total of some thirty works, several of them divided into groups of two, three, or six items.

Among the duets are many that have no counterpart in Schubert's works for piano solo: the overtures, the polonaises, the divertissements and the fugue. Most important of all is the Grand Duo which, although it is structurally a sonata, is symphonic in proportions and style and is unparalleled either in Schubert's own production or in the duets of any other composer. The duet sonatas are few compared with those for piano solo: three, as against twenty-one. The dances, too, comprise a relatively small group. The marches, which count only one representative among the solos, are seventeen in number and form the largest and most varied class of all.

In some aspects of style and expression the duets differ considerably from the solos. A large number are orchestral in feeling, both in their intricate texture and in the employment of colour-effects that need the distinctive timbres of orchestral instruments to bring them to life. It is not impossible that the duets of this type were conceived for orchestra, and that they were written for four hands only because no opportunities occurred for their performance as originally intended. They are not altogether easy to perform, but the piano writing in most of the others presents few difficulties.

Musically, the whole collection affords the players endless interest and enjoyment. Some of the duets, such as the overtures, the polonaises, the rondos and the shorter marches, which include the well-known *Marches militaires*, are much lighter in character than the majority of the solos. They show the influence of Rossini and are easy-going, tuneful pieces, ideally suited for musical recreation. Others are deeply serious in mood and expression, most particularly the Grand Duo and the Fantasy in F minor. Tragic and dramatic elements predominate in the *Grande marche funèbre* and the *Grande marche héroïque*; the lyrical element is supreme in the *Grand Rondeau* and in the Variations in A flat, one of which is pervaded by an indefinable, other-worldly beauty. Opposite extremes in Schubert's style, the picturesque and the severe, are illustrated respectively in the long *Divertissement à la hongroise* and in the little Fugue in E minor which was originally written for the organ and was first played in this form by Schubert and his friend the composer and conductor, Franz Lachner at the Cistercian Abbey of Heiligenkreuz the day after it was composed in June, 1828.

The large number of the duets makes detailed examination of their individual qualities impossible here. Discussion must be limited to a few which are either of special interest musically, or which represent aspects of Schubert's pianistic art that are not exemplified in his solo compositions.

*   *   *   *

The Grand Duo in C major, op. 140, composed in 1824 is

T

surrounded by an aura of mystery. Its status as a duet has been questioned by historians, who think it may be a transcription by Schubert of one of his orchestral works which is now lost. It has several times been orchestrated (in the first place by Joseph Joachim), and it is periodically performed as a symphony, but there is no documentary evidence of its having been intended as anything other than a sonata for piano duet. Duettists are not unjustified in regarding it as an original work of unprecedented importance.

This large-scale sonata in C major, throughout which the thematic substance is more fairly divided between the players than in any other of the composer's duets, is in four movements. The opening 'allegro moderato' begins, as do several of Schubert's solo sonatas, with a phrase in plain octaves. The second subject, first announced by *secondo* in the unusual key of A flat major and recapitulated in the tonic *minor*, is rhythmically similar to the principal subject. Melodically it is so little differentiated that the movement makes the impression of being monothematic. The tonal range is extensive, but less so than in the Finale. This movement opens in a foreign key and hovers during the coda between C sharp minor and D flat major before it swings back to the tonic for the closing section.

In the concise thematic material and the symphonic style of development, these two outer movements present a contrast to some of Schubert's sonatas for piano solo, in many of which, as we noticed in Chapter 4, the copious subject-matter is leisurely and expansive in character and does not lend itself to development.

The abrupt staccato theme in the bass of the Scherzo of the Grand Duo is little typical of the composer, but the sweeping melodic curve of the Trio recalls the Schubert of the Impromptus. The weirdly syncopated accompaniment is unique in his piano music of any kind. The slow movement, an Andante in A flat major in 3/8 time, is of the same serenely lyrical type as the slow movements of the 'Fantasy or Sonata' in G major, op. 76, and the 'unfinished' Sonata in C major ('Reliquie'). Contrapuntally it is richer. The musical content is not only supremely tuneful on the surface, but each of the three accompanying voices is itself melodically significant. The movement is compact of beautifully flowing contrapuntal harmony which is enhanced in effectiveness by periodic interchanges of melodic fragments between the two players. As music for piano duet, it is profoundly satisfying.

Schubert's two other, less important duet sonatas are different in style and build, both from each other and from the Grand Duo. One, a *Grande sonate* in B flat, op. 30, composed in 1818, consists of three shortish movements; two in sonata form flanking a central 'andante con moto' in D minor. The other, written *c*. 1825, is made up of three longer pieces that were originally published under two separate opus-numbers and are not even now printed in practical editions as a complete work. This sonata is made up of the *Divertissement en forme d'une marche brillante et raisonnée* in E minor, op. 63, the *Andantino varié* in B minor, op. 84, no 1, and the *Rondo brillant* in E minor on French themes, op. 84, no. 2, as the Finale. In musical and pianistic interest the three pieces stand far behind the others in their respective categories: the *Divertissement à la hongroise*, op. 54, the Variations in E minor, op. 10, and in a A flat major, op. 35, the *Rondeau*, op. 138, and the *Grand Rondeau*, op. 107.

* * * *

The *Divertissement à la hongroise* dates from 1824, in which year Schubert spent the summer at Zseliz in Hungary with the Esterházy family. It is composed in three sections, the first and last of which are of considerable length and are sub-divided into self-contained paragraphs in various keys. The work opens in G minor, andante, with a Hungarian folk-tune; a long haunting theme in five-bar phrases which Schubert heard sung at Zseliz and which he made the basis of the whole first section. The second, a short March in C minor with a Trio in A flat major, is followed by an Allegretto in G minor. Schubert wrote this last section originally for piano *solo* on the 22nd of September 1824, but it was not published in this form until over a hundred years later.

The musical style of the *Divertissement* is vivid and picturesque. The dotted rhythms of Hungarian dances play a prominent part in the musical material. The piano writing is enlivened by passages in which the colour-effects of the Hungarian cimbalom are reproduced by tremolandos, repeated notes and ornaments divided evenly between the players, and by swirling cadenzas of scales in demisemiquavers for performance by *primo*. Different as it is in structure from the Impromptu in F minor, op. 142, no. 4, it resembles that rhapsodic solo in point both of its Hungarian style and colouring and of its extreme effectiveness as piano music.

*   *   *   *

The sets of Variations in E minor and A flat major, each con-sisting of eight variations, are mutually contrasted in scope and style. The former, which is based on an old French song, 'Reposez vous, bon chevalier', was composed in 1818 and was dedicated to Beethoven who played it with his nephew Karl. Although it starts in simple fashion with diatonic harmonies, it soon expands in tonality. At the third variation the key-signa-ture changes to C major and the music makes an excursion into E flat major. The sixth variation is in C sharp minor, the fifth and the eighth are in E major, and during the last-named, fragments of the theme are introduced in A flat major and minor. The work is cumulative in expression. The first four variations follow the theme exactly, the fifth is a double varia-tion and the seventh is extended to include an anticipatory link to the eighth. In this long 'tempo di marcia' the original outline and shape of the theme are lost in a riot of decorative passage-work.

The Variations on an original Theme in A flat (1824) make an entirely opposite effect. First, because by being composed on a theme twice as long as that of the set in E minor, the varia-tions are double the length, and owing to their elaborate pianis-tic style they attain the status of whole independent pieces. Secondly, because the basic tonality persists with little inter-mission throughout the entire work. The fifth variation, pianissimo and mysteriously dark in colouring, is in the minor mode. The seventh, the expressive climax of the work and an unforgettable piece of music, bears the signature of four flats and opens ostensibly in F minor, yet it is perpetually elusive in tonality. From the very first bar the music proceeds in a series of transient modulations. Although it periodically finds sanctuary in a cadence, it sets forth again in quest of new harmonic adventures, never reaching a definite ending, and eventually merging without a break into the Finale. The piercingly beautiful harmonies vibrate in the player's memory long after they are silent.

* * * *

The two rondos are discursive, placid compositions. Throughout their whole length the duettists carry on a conversation in a type of music which though symmetrical and well-balanced seems to have neither beginning nor end but to exist in a space-time continuum. The *Rondeau* in D major, op. 138, sub-titled 'Notre amitié est invariable' (1818), composed in older rondo form, closes with the theme divided between the two players in octaves in the heights of the treble. This type of layout, which was seldom used by Schubert, necessitates the crossing of *secondo*'s right hand over *primo*'s left, which is engaged in playing figures of accompaniment in the centre of the keyboard. The longer *Grand Rondeau* in A major, op. 107 (1828) in modern rondo form is lyrical in character. More than any other of the duets it recalls the style of the Schubert songs such as 'Wohin' (Whither), 'Liebesbotschaft' (Love's messenger), 'Gretchen am Spinnrade' (Gretchen at the spinning-wheel), 'Frühlingsglaube' (Faith in spring) and others whose accompaniments flow in patterns of quickly-moving notes. It is an exquisitely quiet piece of music, seldom rising to a forte, and marked to be played pianissimo for long stretches at a time.

* * * *

The *Grande marche funèbre d'Alexandre I*, op. 55 (1825), stands apart from the composer's many marches, not only by virtue of its inevitably solemn expressive character, but because the Trio constitutes a piece of tone-painting such as does not exist in any other of the duets. It is a graphic representation of the unceasing sounds of muffled drums, interpreted in *secondo*'s part by uniform figuration in tremolandos and quickly-repeated notes:

Primo's chordal progressions are characterized by the dotted metrical pattern native to the funeral march. The *Grande marche héroïque* (1826), a coronation march for the Czar Nicholas I, symbolizes the pomp and the variegated splendour of the occasion in a long piece distinguished by a multiplicity of rhythmical designs within the signature of common time. It is divided into sections in different keys and modes and has two trios as well as an extensive coda which forms an anthology of the principal themes. In the vigorous style of the piano writing the march is as heroic as its title.

In striking contrast is the Children's March in G major that Schubert composed in 1827 for an eight-year-old child, Faust Pachler. In sending the duet to the boy's mother, who had asked for the composition so that she might play it with him on her husband's name-day, Schubert wrote that he did not feel he was 'exactly made for this kind of composition'. And indeed, the playing of six quavers in a bar by *primo* against four by *secondo* throughout the whole of the trio section cannot have been altogether easy for the young performer.

*   *   *   *

The Fantasy in F minor, completed in April 1828, seven months before Schubert's death, bears comparison with the 'Wanderer' Fantasy for piano solo in being composed in four well-defined sections, the last of which is fugal in character. Unlike the 'Wanderer', however, it is not dominated by a single motto theme. Yet it is to some extent unified by the periodic restatement of the initial phrase in F minor and by the reappearance in the fugue of another theme in F minor first heard in the bass in the opening section (beginning at bar 48). The latter theme is presented in longer notes in the major mode at the end of the opening Allegro, where it preludes the sudden wrenching of the tonality from F major pianissimo to F sharp minor fortissimo for the Largo movement, without a single intervening chord to soften the abrupt transition. Again, at the end of the flowing, rondo-like central movement in triple time, the tonality undergoes another fundamental change: from F sharp minor to F minor, but this time by means of an enharmonic modulation.

The Fantasy sums up many of the expressive and pianistic qualities of the most important of Schubert's duets: the broad melodic outlines, the variety of figuration, the sharp contrasts in mood and in key, the rhythmic independence of the two parts, and the give and take between the players.

*   *   *   *

In the Schubert duets the classical elements predominate over the romantic. The majority of the works are composed in established forms. Others show leanings towards the freer musical structures favoured by the romantic composers, and others still are nationalist in character. After Schubert's death the piano duet entered upon a new phase. Works with a classical basis were still composed, principally sets of variations; but the greater number of duets took the form of programme music or of dances, chiefly dances with national colouring.

*   *   *   *

Among the works with a classical basis are a few for two pianos by Chopin, Schumann, Brahms, and Grieg. Chopin's Rondo in C major, written in 1828 (originally for piano solo) and published posthumously as op. 73, is a decorative composition with hardly a trace of the composer's well-known pianistic style. Schumann's Andante and Variations in B flat, op. 46

(1843) shows few evidences of the subtle art of variation which is exemplified in the variations for piano solo composed during his earlier years: the Impromptus, the slow movement of the Sonata in F minor and the *Études symphoniques*. The variations of the Andante embellish the theme with great effect but they shed very little new light upon it. The work was written in the first place as a piece of chamber music with the accompaniment of two cellos and a horn, but, even before it was first performed by Clara Schumann and Mendelssohn, Schumann had rewritten it more practically for the two pianos alone. Without the distinctive timbres of the string and wind instruments to lend it colour, however, the Andante lacks an ingredient essential to its effectiveness in performance. The original was not published until many years after Schumann's death, although it was played in this more attractive version during his lifetime, and is still occasionally heard in public.

Of Brahms's works for two pianos, the set of Variations on a Theme by Haydn is an alternative version of the orchestral work, and the Sonata in F minor an earlier version of the Piano Quintet, op. 34. Although they are not the exclusive property of duettists they are greatly prized by them and are not infrequently performed in public. Grieg's *Old Norwegian melody with Variations*, op. 51 (1891), however, is an original composition for two pianos, even though it also exists in an orchestral arrangement made by the composer nearly ten years later. Like the Ballade, op. 24 for piano solo, it is based on a Norwegian folk-song, but the piano writing is more florid and far less intimate in expression than that of its poetic forerunner written sixteen years earlier.

*   *   *   *

The contributions of the romantic composers to the literature of original works for four hands on one piano vary greatly in number and style. Chopin's is the smallest of all, for his only composition in this medium, a set of Variations in F major which he wrote in 1826 as a boy of sixteen, was never published. That he composed no piano duets in his maturity may perhaps be ascribed to the fact that his supreme gifts as a solo performer disinclined him to divide the pianistic texture of his compositions between two players.

Liszt's two pieces, neither of them easily available, are of little value to practical duettists: a *Festpolonaise* composed in 1876 on the occasion of a royal wedding, and a single variation on the 'Chopsticks' theme (1880) written for inclusion in a set of pieces on this theme by four Russian composers. César Franck's Duo on 'God save the Queen' (1841), composed in his early youth, is equally unserviceable; Wagner's Polonaise in D (1831) is no longer in circulation, and Mussorgsky's Allegro and Scherzo of a Sonata in C major have hardly crossed the frontier of his country.

Mendelssohn's contribution, small as it is, possesses genuine interest for players, both musically and pianistically. The Andante and Variations, op. 83a, is not simply an arrangement of his Variations in B flat, op. 83 for piano solo which we studied in Chapter 6. It is an enlarged and much enhanced variant. The theme is the same, but it is extended by four bars and the variations are increased in number from five to eight. Only two are closely related to those of the solo version. The first is nearly identical in both sets and the second is moved forward to become the seventh. The fourth finds an echo in the sixth, and the fifth is preserved in part of the Andante preceding the long Finale, allegro, which remains practically the same.

The alterations in the piano writing are as drastic as those in the structure. Two of the new variations are composed entirely in fluent demisemiquaver figuration: in no. 3, *secondo* adds a scudding accompaniment to *primo*'s tuneful outline, and in no. 4, *primo* superimposes delicate overtones upon *secondo*'s melodic and harmonic foundation. In the fifth variation, the parts for both players are laid out in scintillating rhythmic patterns of eight semiquavers to the bar in the left hand and eight demisemiquavers on the off-beats in the right, the whole variation being marked staccato and vivace. The eighth, the only one in either set which is written in the minor mode, abounds in fragmentary canonic imitations between the two players.

Mendelssohn's one other duet, *Allegro brillante,* in A major, op. 92 (1841), a movement in irregular sonata form, exemplifies two familiar aspects of his musical style. The main subject is a fleet-footed scherzando melody which, together with its accompaniment in broken chords, has many affinities among the individual pieces of the *Songs without Words.* The brilliant piano writing in this composition and in some of the variations of op. 83a, calls for quicker and more precise finger-work than does that in the majority of the piano duets written at this period. The two pieces well repay study.

*   *   *   *

Schumann started his career as a composer for the piano with a set of Eight Polonaises which he composed for, and dedicated to, his brothers in 1828 when he was eighteen. He did not publish them, but when he started to compose *Papillons* the following year he drew heavily upon the duets for thematic material. The Polonaises remained unpublished for over a hundred years. When they eventually saw the light of print in 1933 they provided duettists with a set of pieces that are refreshing and enjoyable to play. In addition, they gave musicians in general a new opportunity of gaining insight into Schumann's early style and his methods of composing.

Schumann greatly admired Schubert, whose Six Polonaises, op. 61 and Four Polonaises, op. 75 written *c.* 1825 undoubtedly stimulated the writing of his own Eight Polonaises. A comparison of the two composers' works in this class reveals many similarities in the metrical figures and the irregular phrase-lengths, as well as in the rhythmic vigour of the Polonaises and the lyrical character of the Trio sections. Typical features of Schumann's well-known later style are already discernible in these early pieces. For instance, his tendencies to present the musical ideas in two-bar or four-bar units; to put strong accents on weak beats and to make extensive use of syncopation; to combine two or more rhythmic patterns simultaneously and to devise canonic imitations in the part-writing. Representative examples of his more contrapuntal pianistic style occur in the

Trios; expressive little movements to which Schumann gave imaginative titles in French, such as *La douleur*, *L'aimable*, etc. Perhaps the most interesting point in connexion with the Eight Polonaises is their relationship to *Papillons*. Musicians familiar with the latter will recognize in the third and fourth Polonaises the sources of no. 11 of *Papillons*, the long piece in D major which precedes the Finale; and in the Trio of the seventh Polonaise, the forerunner of no. 5, the restful movement in B flat with a particularly expressive left-hand part.

The Polonaises had no successors for twenty years. In 1848 Schumann wrote the first of four sets of short compositions which are of a different type from their predecessors. The *Bilder aus Osten* (Oriental pictures), op. 66, sub-titled Six Impromptus, owes its inspiration to Schumann's reading of Rückert's German translation from the Arabic of Harari's *Makamen*. He did not claim to have written music descriptive of actual scenes from this work, but to have given musical expression to the underlying thought and to have re-created the oriental atmosphere. The music is in the narrative style of the Novellettes but lacks their rhythmic vitality, and the whole set makes an impression of monotony which is emphasized by the fact that every movement is written in duple or quadruple time. As duets, they offer few attractions to performers. Only in nos. 2 and 4, the shortest and most intimate in expression, is there any give and take of significant musical ideas between the players. Elsewhere, *secondo* has either to keep in step with *primo*, or to act merely as his accompanist. In Schumann's next composition for piano duet, a set of twelve little pieces, *secondo* comes into his own.

The *Twelve Duets for children, young and old*, op. 85, the most spontaneous of Schumann's later four-hand compositions, were written in 1849 in response to his publisher's request for a group of pieces similar in scope to the *Album for the Young* which he had produced that year. The twelve items, which vary in length and which all bear descriptive titles, are characteristic pieces in Schumann's happiest vein. Throughout the whole opus the musical material is divided between the players in more inter-

esting fashion than in any other of the composer's collections
of duets. Five of the items are particularly notable for the extreme independence of the two parts. In 'Bear dance', no. 2,
the most graphic and imaginative of all, *secondo* (the senior bear)
is chained growling to a barrier of tonic chords while *primo* (the
cub) executes a frisky *pas seul* in semiquavers. In 'Croatian
march', no. 5, *primo*'s part comprises all the instruments of the
military band except the percussion, which is allotted to
secondo. Throughout 'Grief', no. 6 and in parts of 'Ghost story',
no. 11, *primo*'s melody, chiefly in quavers and crotchets, is
counterpointed by *secondo*'s scurrying semiquavers. In the final
'Evening-song', *secondo* supplies the entire chordal foundation
below the tenuous melodic line played by *primo*'s right hand
alone. In the other pieces the style of the parts for the two
players is little differentiated except in the central interlude of
no. 9, *At the fountain*, which is pianistically the highlight of the
whole series. In the outer sections of this aqueous sketch in 3/8
time, marked to be played 'as quickly as possible', the layout
for both partners is composed of six semiquavers in each hand,
a demisemiquaver apart in time: a pattern that effectively
conveys the lulling sound of cascading waters.

By comparison with this vivid and entertaining series of
miniatures, Schumann's two later sets of duets are secondary in
interest. *Ballscenen* (Ball scenes), Nine Characteristic Pieces,
op. 109 (1851), is made up of seven dance movements placed
between a 'Préambule' and a 'Promenade'. The ground-plan
recalls *Carnaval*, but *Ballscenen* lacks the romance and the sparkle
of its inimitable forerunner, even though it possesses attractions
of its own in the varied rhythms and contrasted styles of piano
writing in the several movements. As in the *Oriental pictures*, the
parts for the duettists are on a level, except in the brisk 'Hungarian Dance', no. 4, in which each player retains his own
identity in no uncertain fashion.

In *Kinderball* (Children's Ball); Six Easy Dance Movements,
op. 130 (1853), *primo*'s and *secondo*'s parts are consistently differentiated in style, most of all in *Écossaise*, no. 4. In this piece
primo's coruscating finger-work is supported by *secondo*'s hum-

drum bass and the players unite in striking the pairs of heavy chords that punctuate the movement. In 'Round dance', no. 6, however, *secondo's* busy accompaniment is placed so low on the keyboard that it completely overweights *primo's* solo.

As music that is designed either for performance by young people, or simply for their entertainment, *Kinderball* is far surpassed in charm by a work in the same vein but pianistically more fanciful written about twenty years later: Bizet's *Jeux d'enfants* (Children's games), op. 22. It is a sequence of twelve pieces descriptive of traditional nursery pastimes; a witty, softfooted, picturesque composition which possesses attractions for players of any age and which is easily available both in print and on gramophone records.

*　　*　　*　　*

Brahms's contribution to the piano duet represents two extremes in style; the classical and the popular. His first work in this category was a set of ten Variations on a Theme by Schumann; the long theme in E flat major in 2/4 time that had formed the basis of Schumann's own very last, unfinished composition for piano solo, to which reference was made in Chapter 6.

These 'Schumann' Variations, op. 23, were written in the same year as the 'Handel' Variations (1861), but in point of technique and expression they diverge considerably from the monumental solo. The great difference in the character of the theme, alone, sets the two works apart. The 'Schumann' Variations contain many kinds of effective, colourful piano writing and the composition as a whole gathers strength as it proceeds. Opening 'andante molto moderato' with three decorative variations in the tonic major and one in sparse harmonies in the minor mode, it begins to quicken in pace in the fifth variation, a quiet, lilting movement in the relatively bright key of B major which forms a contrast to all the preceding and succeeding variations by being written in compound triple time. The basic key and duple time of the theme are restored for the sixth and seventh variations, 'allegro non troppo', and the work mounts by way of the eighth in G minor, 'poco più vivo' to a tremendous climax in the ninth variation in C minor in common time. It ends solemnly with an 'alla marcia' in the tempo and style of a funeral march and is rounded off by a condensed statement of the theme above *secondo*'s accompaniment of muffled drums which continue to roll or to beat ominously until the very last bar.

Completely antithetic in style to this deeply-felt, serious work are Brahms's duets in dance forms: the Waltzes, op. 39, which, because they are more generally performed as solos, we studied in the previous chapter; and the four sets of Hungarian Dances, twenty-one in all, composed between *c.* 1858 and 1880.

Unlike the Waltzes, the Hungarian Dances are not original compositions, but are arrangements of melodies by known, popular native composers. Their racy tunefulness and rhythmic verve exercised a great fascination over Brahms from his early years onwards and even influenced the style of some of his instrumental compositions. The piano writing of the Hungarian Dances, as also that of the 'Schumann' Variations, is full of interest for the players. Brahms's own mastery as an executant declares itself in the effective distribution of the musical material over the whole keyboard. Each performer takes an active but not unduly arduous part in presenting it in an unending variety of harmonic and rhythmic guises and in creating an exotic atmosphere by means of vivid colour-effects. Brahms arranged ten of the dances for piano solo and five (nos. 17–21) were orchestrated by Dvořák. But perhaps none of these transcriptions gives so much satisfaction to the players as do the original versions so sympathetically devised for the duettists.

*   *   *   *

Tchaikovsky's Fifty Russian Folk-songs (1868–9) are likewise transcriptions of national tunes, many of which the composer used in his original works. We have already met no. 24 of Peters Edition as 'Russian Song' in the *Album for the Young*.

Dvořák's Slavonic Dances are entirely original compositions. They belong almost equally to the literatures of the piano duet

and the orchestra, for Dvořák composed both versions con-
temporaneously. The first set of eight Slavonic Dances, op. 46,
appeared in 1878 and was succeeded in 1886 by the eight New
Slavonic Dances, op. 72. The first dance in the second collection, a 'molto vivace' in B major and minor, is a reworking of
the last of the Four Eclogues mentioned in Chapter 10; a graceful Allegretto in E major and minor which gives no hint of the
violent change in expressive character that it was later to
undergo.

The Slavonic Dances as a whole group are much more varied
than Brahms's Hungarian Dances. They comprise examples of
the dances of several nationalities, Polish, Serbian, Ukrainian,
Bohemian, and Slovakian. Moreover, they are written in different time-signatures, whereas every one of the Hungarian
Dances is in 2/4 time. In type, they range from the graceful
Bohemian *sousedská* in slow waltz time (nos. 3, 4 and 16) to the
impetuous Serbian *kolo* (chain-dance) in presto 2/4 (no. 15).

The harmonic style touches extremes of diatonicism in nos. 7
and 8, and of chromaticism in no. 12. The latter, tonally volatile
movement, which bears the signature of D flat major and ends
in that key, begins hesitantly in E flat minor, continues in A flat
major and minor and contains a section that hovers between
C sharp minor, E major and other keys. After being wrenched
back to D flat major at the last possible moment, it is finally
clinched by a superlatively chromatic plagal cadence. In most
of the other dances the tonality is comparatively equable,
though it is never lacking in unexpected fluctuations. Even the
few dances which are written in one key-signature throughout
are animated by chains of shimmering transient modulations.

An essential musical characteristic of the dances, which is
reflected in the style of the piano writing, is the great abundance
of counter-melodies. They form a vitally interesting pianistic
texture and constitute a never-failing source of enjoyment to
the players, both jointly and severally.

Dvořák also wrote a set of Scottish Dances, op. 41 (1877)
which is unknown to practical duettists. His two remaining
four-hand compositions, *Legends*, op. 59 (1881), and *From the*

Bohemian Forest, op. 68 (1884), are generally familiar but they have never achieved the popularity of the Slavonic Dances.

The ten Legends are clear-cut pieces of varying length, in the majority of which the rhythms of marches and dances, quick or graceful, are immanent. Others composed in the narrative style are more interesting in point of the piano writing which is, in the main, less exuberant than in the Slavonic Dances. The sixth Legend in C sharp minor contains the greatest variety of figuration, the most independent part for *secondo* and a series of electrifying harmonic clashes which seem to have no justification musically but which add pungency to the dark-hued subject-matter. No. 8 in F major, an expansively melodic 'allegretto quasi andantino', is distinguished from all the others by its lilting 6/8 rhythm. No. 9 in D major is unique among the Legends in its extreme conciseness and monothematic style.

In the six pieces of *From the Bohemian Forest*, the rhythms of the dance are little in evidence but the rhythmic element is strong in the first, 'In the spinning room', throughout which the piano writing simulates the whirring of the spinning-wheel, and again in the third, 'Witches' Sabbath' and the sixth, 'In troublous times'. To both the latter, paragraphs of dotted beats or galloping triplet quavers impart a march-like rhythm. More romantically expressive are 'On the dark lake', no. 2, and 'Silent woods', no. 5, and the disjointed 'On the watch', no. 4 —so restlessly watchful that it only reluctantly admits a tune towards the end. All the six movements are programme music. 'In the spinning room' even contains a written indication that the repeated octave D in *secondo*'s part on the last page represents the striking of twelve o'clock.

* * * *

Grieg's piano duets differ as a whole collection from those by all the other nineteenth-century composers. Every one of them exists in an alternative version made by the composer himself either for orchestra or for piano solo. The earliest, Two Symphonic Pieces, op. 14, comprises the slow movement and Scherzo of a Symphony in C minor which Grieg wrote at the age of twenty-one on the suggestion of the Danish composer Niels W. Gade in 1864 but which he never published in its original orchestral form. The next duet composition, *In Autumn*, op. 11, was written as a concert-overture for orchestra in 1866. It was, however, first published as a Fantasy for four hands in 1867 and did not take its final orchestral shape until twenty years later. It is based on the solo song 'Autumn storm', op. 18, no. 4, which Grieg had composed the previous year, but it is prefaced by a new, separate introduction embodying a theme that recurs later in the piece and has an entirely different ending. The work shows few traces of the composer's typically Norwegian style, which was then only gradually evolving but which by the time he came to write the Norwegian Dances in 1881 had grown to maturity.

The four Norwegian Dances, op. 35, which Grieg also published for piano solo, and the much later four Symphonic Dances, op. 64 (1898) which he arranged for orchestra either before or after writing them for piano duet, are based principally upon Norwegian folk-tunes. They are transcriptions in the same sense as are his two sets of folk-tunes for piano solo (opp. 17 and 66), but they are of larger dimensions and are more highly developed in musical style. The fourth Symphonic Dance, which is composed of the two melodies that Grieg had already transcribed with extreme simplicity as nos. 23 and 24 of op. 17, demonstrate his manner of employing folk-tunes as material for symphonic development.

The individual dances which, with one exception are of the 'halling' type in 2/4 time, are all in ternary form. Each contains a contrasting interlude in the opposite mode and usually in a different tempo and expressive style. The material of this central section is sometimes derived from that of the outer panels. In the fourth Norwegian Dance in D major, the episode in the minor is founded entirely upon the theme of the introduction; and in the third Symphonic Dance, which is also in D major, a 'springdans' and the only one in triple time, the same pair of melodies is used in the major and the minor and in different rhythmic patterns throughout every section of the movement.

U

The opening theme of the third Norwegian Dance in G major, 'allegro moderato alla marcia', is later presented tranquillo in augmentation (doubled note-values) in the minor, its melodic outline gaining in significance by being placed above changing chromatic harmonies. Again, in the first Symphonic Dance, likewise in G major, the vigorous principal phrase is transformed rhythmically as well as in mode and tempo in the 'più lento' interlude. At the climax, a four-note figure is reiterated seven times, as if to emphasize the extremity of the chromatic fate that has befallen it. The episode of the second Norwegian Dance draws its substance from a phrase in the opening section in A major which is translated into the relative minor, is accelerated in pace and tossed up and down the keyboard in reckless fashion.

*   *   *   *

Throughout these two sets of dances Grieg employed every technical device known to him for enhancing the musical and expressive qualities of the native songs and dance tunes that formed their basis. In his only other work written originally for four hands, the two *Valses-caprices*, op. 37 (1883), which he also arranged as piano solos, he worked with a very different kind of material and treated it in more conventional fashion. Nevertheless, a bracing northern blast blows through these polished salon pieces. Elements of folk-music may be recognized in the frequent flattening of the leading-note as well as its downward progression by leap in the presto episode of the first Valse-caprice in C sharp minor, and in the dark-coloured outer sections of the second in E minor.

In the trio (in E major) of the latter, another feature derived from Norwegian folk-melody, the hovering of a tune around two notes, inspired Grieg to write a page of music which, for harmonic originality and sensuous beauty, is unequalled in any of his other works for piano, solo or duet.

With the utmost economy of means he created a kaleidoscopic musical effect. Throughout nine successive phrases, each consisting of two contrasted units at different pitches, the melody

in every phrase except the last comprises only two notes, a
semitone apart. The chordal foundation shifts with every phrase,
sometimes with every bar or beat, touching many points of the
harmonic compass. Yet despite the many chromatic deviations,
the music never loses its shapely contour or its sense of direction.
The rhythmic uniformity of the component phrases assures it of
a homogeneity in character which the harmonic vagaries are
qualified to enhance but have no power to destroy. The passage
must be heard to be believed. It is one of the most striking in
the whole literature of the later nineteenth-century piano duet.

EPILOGUE

Summing-up and a
Glance Forwards

DURING the course of this survey of nineteenth-century music we have spent much time in studying the works of a composer who was born thirty years before 1800, but we have paid no attention to the works of one who was born many years before 1900. It is a curious anomaly of musical history that Beethoven, who lived more of his life in the eighteenth than in the nineteenth century, should nevertheless have become one of the dominating personalities in the music of the later century; and that Debussy, who lived thirty-eight years in the nineteenth century and only eighteen in the twentieth, should be considered a twentieth-century composer *par excellence*.

The turbulent, romantic character of some of the first ten of Beethoven's sonatas, which include the 'Pathétique', makes it difficult to realize that these epoch-making compositions were written only a few years after Mozart's death and while Haydn was still living. Similarly, the advanced style of Debussy's later piano pieces, *Estampes* (1903), the two sets of *Images* (1905 and 1907), the two books of *Préludes* (1910 and 1913) and the twelve *Études* (1915), all of which are landmarks in twentieth-century piano music, makes it equally difficult to realize that the composer was born as long ago as 1862, the year in which Brahms was composing the 'Paganini' Variations.

When a survey of the piano music of the whole twentieth century eventually comes to be written, historians will need to turn back to the later years of the nineteenth century to study the first beginnings of the careers of at least three composers of piano music, besides Debussy, who were born long before 1900, yet who are by general consent regarded as belonging to the twentieth century: Sibelius (1865), Scriabin (1872), and Ravel (1875).

Consideration of the early works by all these composers has had to be omitted from the present volume because their main production falls outside the period under survey, but we may at least remind ourselves that several well-known compositions of theirs were written before 1900. Debussy's *Deux Arabesques* (1888), *Suite Bergamasque* (1890), the *Sarabande* (1896) later included in the suite *Pour le Piano* (1902), and the *Petite Suite* for piano duet (1888); Sibelius's Six Impromptus and Sonata in F, both in 1893; many of Scriabin's sets of Preludes and the first three of his sonatas during the 1890s; Ravel's *Menuet antique* (1895) and *Pavane pour une Infante défunte* (1899).

The piano music of the present age is commonly held to be fundamentally different in character and expression from that of the classico-romantic nineteenth century, just as is the latter from the harpsichord music of the preceding period. Yet the changes in the nature of the keyboard music of the successive centuries did not take place rapidly. Early nineteenth-century composers accepted established musical forms without question. They only gradually remoulded them in accordance with new modes of thought while at the same time cultivating new expressive styles. As the century advanced, some of the composers of romantic piano music occasionally looked backwards for inspiration: Mendelssohn and Schumann to Bach; Brahms to Beethoven and Schubert. Others habitually looked towards the future: Chopin, Liszt, Dvořák, and Grieg. It was they who began to lay the foundations of twentieth-century music.

Chopin's advanced chromaticism and his imaginative use of the sustaining-pedal for evoking poetic tone-colouring influenced Liszt in the direction of polytonality and impressionism. Liszt in his turn widened Dvořák's and Grieg's harmonic outlook and lent them artistic support in their explorations into new spheres of tonality. All these composers played their part in determining the pianistic styles of their successors. Each of them, most especially Chopin and Grieg, also made a valuable contribution towards the truer appreciation of the folk-music of his respective native land; an achievement that has not been without effect upon succeeding generations of composers.

As a formative influence upon the piano music of the present era, nineteenth-century piano music is not even yet a spent force. As music for playing, it still remains an inexhaustible treasury.

BIBLIOGRAPHY

Abraham, Gerald: *Design in Music*, Oxford University Press, 1949.
A Hundred Years of Music (second edition), Duckworth, 1949.
Chopin's Musical Style, Oxford University Press, 1939.
Blom, Eric: *The Romance of the Piano*, Foulis, 1928.
Everyman's Dictionary of Music, Dent, 1947.
Calvocoressi, M. D.: *Mussorgsky*, Dent, 1946.
Chissell, Joan: *Schumann*, Dent, 1948.
Colles, H. C.: *The Growth of Music*, Oxford University Press, 1912–16.
(Ed.) *Grove's Dictionary of Music and Musicians* (fourth edition), Macmillan, 1940.
Dale, Kathleen: Essays on the piano music of *Grieg, Schubert, Schumann* in the respective volumes of the *Symposium* series, ed. Gerald Abraham, Oxford University Press, 1948–52.
The Three C's (Clementi, Czerny, Cramer): *Pioneers of pianoforte playing*, in *Music Review*, Vol. VI, no. 3, 1945.
Dessauer, Heinrich: *John Field, sein Leben und seine Werke*, Langensalza, 1912.
Deutsch, O. E.: *Schubert: a Documentary Biography*, Dent, 1946.
Dickinson, A. E. F.: *Tchaikovsky: the piano music* (in *Tchaikovsky: a Symposium*), Oxford University Press, 1945.
Fuller-Maitland, J. A.: *Schumann's Pianoforte Works* (Musical Pilgrim Series), Oxford University Press, 1927.
Harding, Rosamond E. H.: *The Piano-forte. Its history traced to the Great Exhibition of 1851*, Cambridge University Press, 1927.
Hedley, Arthur: *Chopin*, Dent, 1947.
Hipkins, A. J.: *Description and History of the Pianoforte*, Novello, 1896.
Hipkins, E. J.: *How Chopin Played*, Dent, 1937.
Latham, Peter: *Brahms*, Dent, 1948.
Macpherson, Stewart: *Form in Music*, Joseph Williams, 1930.

May, Florence: *Life of Brahms* (second edition), William Reeves, 1948.

Morris, R. O.: *The Structure of Music*, Oxford University Press, 1935.

Robertson, Alec: *Dvořák*, Dent, 1945.

Saunders, William: *Weber*, Dent, 1940.

Scholes, Percy: *The Oxford Companion to Music* (ninth edition), Oxford University Press, 1954.

Scott, Marion M.: *Beethoven*, Dent, 1934.

Schumann, Robert: *Gesammelte Schriften über Musik und Musiker*, 4 vols., Leipzig, 1854; English translation, 2 vols., London, 1877; New translation, selection in 1 vol., London, 1947.

Tovey, Donald F.: *Essays in Musical Analysis*, 6 vols., Oxford University Press, 1935–9.

　Essays in Musical Analysis: Chamber Music, Oxford University Press, 1944.

　Beethoven, Oxford University Press, 1944.

　Musical Articles from the Encyclopedia Britannica, Oxford University Press, 1944.

　Essays and Lectures on Music, Oxford University Press, 1949.

Walker, Frank: *Salvator Rosa and Music* in *Monthly Musical Record*, October, 1949.

APPENDIX I

Particulars of Recently Published or Unfamiliar Works

PIANO SOLOS

Balakirev: *Islamey: Oriental Fantasy*, Richard Schauer, London, W.C.2.

Borodin: *Petite Suite*, Augener.

Brahms: *Sarabandes and Gigues*, Hinrichsen, 1938.

Cramer: *The Cramer-Beethoven Studies* (Shedlock), Augener.

Dvořák: *Four Eclogues, Impromptus, etc.*, Prague, Hudební Matice, 1949; London, Bernard Wilson, Hampstead.

Franck: *Short Piano Pieces*, Peters, 1942.

Grieg: *Six Mountain Melodies* (Sex norske fjeldmelodier), Copenhagen, W. Hansen; London, Augener.

Liszt: *Late miniatures, Csárdás macabre, Third Mephisto Waltz, Trauermarsch*, Vol. I, Liszt Society's Publications, Schott, 1951.
Fourth Mephisto Waltz, Vol. 2, Liszt Society's Publications, Schott, 1952.

Schubert: *Sonata in E minor*, British & Continental Music Agencies, 1948.

Schumann: *Variations on an Original Theme* (Schumann's last composition, first published in 1939), Hinrichsen.

Smetana: *Album Leaf*, published in *Contemporaries of Schumann*, Hinrichsen, 1938.

Tchaikovsky: *Variations in F major*, op. 19, no. 6, Hinrichsen, 1950.

Tomašek: *Ten Eclogues*, Augener.

PIANO DUETS

Bizet: *Jeux d'Enfants*, Paris, Durand et Cie (1950); London, United Music Publishers.

Mendelssohn: *Original compositions*, New York, Schirmer; London, Chappell.

Schumann: *Eight Polonaises*, Universal Edition, 24 Great Pulteney Street, W.1, 1933.

Tchaikovsky: *Russian Folksongs*, Peters, 1940.

APPENDIX II

Table of the Numbering of Schumann's and Liszt's 'Paganini' Studies

SCHUMANN	PAGANINI
Studies after Caprices by Paganini, op. 3	*Caprices*, op. 1
No. 1	No. 5
2	9
3	11
4	13
5	19
6	16

Études de concert d'après des Caprices de Paganini, op. 10	
No. 1	No. 12
2	6
3	10
4	4
5	2
6	3

LISZT	
Grandes Études de Paganini	
No. 1 Preludio ⎫ Étude ⎭	No. 5 6
2	17
4	1
5	9
6	24

APPENDIX III

Table of Composers' Dates

Bach, Carl Philipp Emanuel	1714–1788
Bach, Johann Christian	1735–1782
Bach, Johann Christoph Friedrich	1732–1795
Bach, Johann Sebastian	1685–1750
Balakirev, Mily Alexeivitch	1837–1910
Bartók Béla,	1881–1945
Bax, Arnold	1883–1953
Beethoven, Ludwig van	1770–1827
Bennett, William Sterndale	1816–1875
Bizet, Georges	1838–1875
Bononcini, Giovanni Battisto	1672–?1755
Borodin, Alexander	1833–1887
Brahms, Johannes	1833–1897
Bull, John	1563–1628
Burney, Charles	1726–1814
Byrd, William	1543–1623
Carlton, Nicholas	early sixteenth century
Chausson, Ernest	1855–1899
Cherubini, Luigi	1760–1842
Chopin, Frédéric	1810–1849
Clementi, Muzio	1752–1832
Couperin, François	1668–1733
Cramer, Johann Baptist	1771–1858
Czerny, Karl	1791–1857
Daquin, Louis Claude	1694–1772
Debussy, Claude	1862–1918
Delius, Frederick	1862–1934
Dittersdorf, Karl Ditters von	1739–1799
Dowland, John	1563–1626
Dressler, Ernst Christoph	1734–1779
Dussek, Jan Ladislav	1760–1812
Dvořák, Antonin	1841–1904

Farnaby, Giles	*c.* 1560–*c.* 1600
Field, John	1782–1837
Franck, César	1822–1890
Gade, Niels W.	1817–1890
Grieg, Edvard	1843–1907
Gung'l, Joseph	1810–1889
Handel, Georg Frideric	1685–1759
Haydn, Joseph	1732–1809
Hindemith, Paul	b. 1895
Hüttenbrenner, Anselm	1794–1868
Kodály, Zoltán	b. 1882
Kuhnau, Johann	1660–1722
Lanner, Joseph	1801–1843
Liszt, Franz	1811–1886
Loewe, Karl	1796–1869
Méhul, Étienne	1763–1817
Mendelssohn, Felix	1809–1847
Meyerbeer, Giacomo	1791–1864
Moscheles, Ignaz	1794–1870
Mozart, Wolfgang Amadeus	1756–1791
Mussorgsky, Modest	1839–1881
Paganini, Niccolò	1782–1840
Pasquini, Bernardo	1637–1710
Poglietti, Alessandro	? –1683
Prokofiev, Sergei	1891–1953
Purcell, Henry	1659–1695
Rachmaninov, Sergei	1873–1943
Rameau, Jean Philippe	1683–1764
Ravel, Maurice	1875–1937
Reubke, Julius	1834–1858
Righini, Vincenzo	1756–1812
Rosa, Salvator	1615–1673
Rossini, Gioacchino	1792–1868
Scarlatti, Alessandro	1660–1725
Scarlatti, Domenico	1685–1757
Schubert, Franz	1797–1828
Schumann, Robert	1810–1856

Index of Musical Illustrations

Index of Composers and Works

(Where works are discussed in detail the page references are italicized)

General Index